The Black Book
of Johnathan Knotbristle

a Devil's Parable and Guide for Witches

The Black Book
of Johnathan Knotbristle

a Devil's Parable and Guide for Witches

Chris Allaun

Chicago, Illinois

Special Limited Edition, 2023
Paperback ISBN: 978-1-959883-06-7
Library of Congress Control Number: 2023930646

Cover design by Wycke Malliway.
Typesetting by Gianna Rini.
Edited by Becca Fleming.

Published by:
Crossed Crow Books, LLC
6934 N Glenwood Ave, Suite C
Chicago, IL 60626
www.crossedcrowbooks.com

Printed in the United States of America.

Contents

FOREWORD...XI

JOHNATHAN KNOTBRISTLE...1

1. How it Happened....................................4

2. Old Henry....................................14

3. The Pitchfork....................................24

4. The Well....................................34

5. The Full Moon....................................46

6. The Ghost Road....................................63

7. Mother Goose....................................84

8. The Ghost and the Gate....................................103

9. A Hunt on Chirstmas....................................121

10. The Spirit Doctor....................................138

11. The Witch's Bottle....................................152

12. The Faeries in the Woods....................................169

13. The Spirit Box....................................187

14. The Witch's Tree....................................198

15. The Crooked Path....................................216

THE SPELLS OF
JOHNATHAN KNOTBRISTLE THE CHARMER...219

List of Spells

To Obtain the Powers of the Witch..............220

To Create the Pitchfork or Stang...................221

To Create the Vessel for the Devil

The Witch's Trance...............................223

The Witch's Rocking Chair

The Power of the Stars and the Land

The Witch's Connection to the Powers...........225

To Obtain a Spirit Familiar.....................226

The Magick of the Cauldron
(Momma's Cooking Pot)........................227

To Fly in Spirit, Using the Witch's Broom.....228

To Speak in Spirit Tongues.....................229

To Summon a Ghost.............................230

Invoking Spirits, Ancestors, or Gods.............232

The Spells of Mother Goose.....................233

The Devil's Feast...............................234

To Summon a Ghost for a Seance...................236

To Protect Against Spirits......................237

To Summon the Devil
and the Dame for Magic...238

Perchta's Thread:
To See the Fate of Another................................239

To Heal with the Power of the Spirits,
Ancestors, or Gods...240

    To Banish the Spirit of Disease

The Witch's Bottle...242

Shapeshifting into an Animal...............................243

Faery Magic..244

    To Slip into the Faery World
    and Find a Faery Teacher

    Faery Healing

The Spirit Box...246

A Witch's Doll of Love.......................................248

Night Battles and the Harvest..........................250

Foreword

I've been aware of spirits of land and place, the dead, and divine beings of various sizes, shapes, and demeanors since I was a child. I'm now in my 60s and have been a witch for three-quarters of my life. I first became acquainted with Chris Allaun through his book *A Guide of Spirits*. Working with the otherworlds and spirits is at the core of most witchcraft, and I found his book useful. Eventually, I read *Underworld: Shamanism, Myth, and Magick, Deeper into the Underworld: Death, Ancestors, and Magical Rites*, and *Upperworld: Shamanism and Magick of the Celestial Realms*. We later became friends, and I came to appreciate not only his approach to the work but his good nature as a person. I was thrilled when I was contacted to read an advance copy of this book.

I was really intrigued when I read the premise for *The Black Book of Johnathan Knotbristle the Charmer*. There is a long tradition of occultists writing fiction as a way to offer teachings in a different mode and format. Certainly, Dion Fortune had as broad, if not broader, an impact on modern witches through her novels such as *The Sea*

Priestess and *Moon Magic* as she did with her nonfiction. I think this is because stories can carry and convey the essence of magic in ways that are more difficult to do in nonfiction. Even if you can read a musical score or choreography, it is not the same as hearing and seeing the song and dance. We are touched in different and sometimes deeper ways by stories, and that is certainly true for *The Black Book of Johnathan Knotbristle the Charmer.*

The book's focus is Traditional Witchcraft, sometimes referred to as Folkloric Witchcraft. It is not the witchcraft of the Atlantic isles of Ireland and Britain, nor that of Europe. It is the home-grown ways that sprouted in the United States from the seeds of many cultures. The location for the story is somewhere in the American South in the late 1800s with a strong sense of Texas in the background. Interest in this type of witchcraft has been on the rise in the last several years, and this book offers methods and perspectives that differ from and complement the books and blogs that focus heavily on the work coming from the other side of the Atlantic. It also centers more on craft and practice than on any particular set of beliefs of theology.

I found that I got the most out of the book by deciding to take it in as if it were a guided visualization or as a pathworking. Read each chapter slowly, hearing the words in your mind, and see the story play out on the inner projection screen of your mind. It may take some time to adjust to the dialect and perspectives of the time period. As you progress through the book, everything said and described will become more vivid and feel more real. By doing so, you will absorb the lore and the methods as if they were lived experiences.

This book is not a historical account but has the ring of truth. Chris Allaun is from Texas and has listened and learned from old-timers, which is evident in the stories. His work as a witch, a psychopomp, and a healer makes itself known in the way that he makes choices about the order and appearance of the different events in Jonathan's journey. It is a story, and as such, is told organically, but it is also a structured introduction to ideas and practices arranged so that they build upon each other. The book also stirs your emotions, and you become more invested in Jonathan's story. Emotions help anchor memories which will increase the effect of *The Black Book* as a series of lessons masquerading as a novel.

Chris does include the spells, rituals, and practices used in the chapters at the end of the book in step-by-step descriptions. This is a very useful addition to the book, and you may be tempted to start using them before you have finished reading all the chapters. I strongly suggest you read the entire book before attempting to use any of these workings. A good amount of these workings' powers comes from being immersed in the atmosphere, culture, and feel of the times and places that gave birth to these practices. Witchcraft arises from more than just the conscious mind. Experiencing the narrative of the stories plants the seeds of context in the soil of your imagination where they take root and bring hidden powers to fruition.

The Black Book of Johnathan Knotbristle the Charmer takes a very different approach to the teaching of Traditional Witchcraft; one that I found to be very effective. I encourage you to commit to traveling through the world of this book rather than merely reading it. If you do, you may return home from this quest with much more than you were expecting.

Ivo Dominguez Jr,
author of *Spirit Speak: Knowing and Understanding Spirit Guides, Ancestors, Ghosts, Angels, and the Divine*

Johnathan Knotbristle

***

JOHNATHAN KNOTBRISTLE was born in 1855 in the American South. He had little to no formal education like most people during that time in the Southern United States. His mother taught him to read by reading the Bible, but that is most likely the extent of his education. He was born and raised on a small farm outside of his small town. Most people during this time sustained themselves by having a small farm where they could grow produce, and most of it was jarred so they would have food throughout the winter months. Most of his days were spent working on his family's little farm.

Johnathan was a witch. By the 19th century, there were no more witch trials or witch hunters, but that didn't mean that local people didn't sometimes take laws into their own hands. Hanging witches in the 19th century was rare, but the American Christian communities still condemned people for practicing witchcraft by ostracizing them from the community. It's important to understand that most people who practice what we currently call "witchcraft" did not call themselves a witch, at least not publicly. Also, witchcraft was not a religion. In fact, most people during that time who practiced magic or witchcraft, considered themselves to be Christians and went to church on Sunday like everybody else. This may be a shock to modern witches, but it's true. My mother, who is extremely psychic, still says her dreams and intuitions come from Jesus. Maybe they do. Who am I to say how one practices their gifts?

If you have ever read any of the old witch trial transcripts, you will see many examples of people who became a witch because of necessity. Often when tragedy strikes, there is the real possibility of not surviving because of a lack of money, food, and resources. In the 19th century, there were no organizations set up to help the poor, especially in the Southern United States. When someone became a witch, it was because they were desperate. They needed the powers of the witch to survive. We also need to remember that not everyone was a "God-fearing Christian" back then. Some people, when presented with the opportunity to become a witch and use magic, took the it without fearing the punishment of hell.

Johnathan was a witch who became popular because of his skill in his craft. He doesn't think of himself as special. In fact, he finds himself to be ordinary. I believe that is why Johnathan Knotbristle was so successful in his magic; because he was able to relate to the pain and sorrow of others because he himself had suffered. He lived a modest life on a small farm and made enough money to buy the things he needed to survive. He never called himself a witch in public, and both he and his clients kept up appearances of normality, not because he didn't want to be discovered to be a witch, but because he truly believed he was no more special than anyone else in his small town.

This is Johnathan's story. It is told in the first person because this is *his* story. Johnathan has almost no education and is from the South, so you will find him speaking to you in a Southern dialect. Because he didn't have much of an education, you will notice that his grammar is poor. Being from the South myself, I found that many people in rural areas still speak in this same dialect and use the same grammar that Johnathan does. Hearing this dialect reminds me of growing up in the deep Texas country and listening to the old-timers tell their stories.

Each chapter is written as a story, just as Johnathan told it. A first-person narrative. I also chose not to correct his grammar because I wanted it to be authentic in the way he told his story. This is not just a book of stories on witchcraft; each chapter contains actual witchcraft and magical techniques that are woven into the story. I would venture to call these "teaching stories." Each story is told in such a way that enriches the reader's experience of these magical techniques. It might help the student on witchcraft to write down each of these techniques in a way that helps them understand them. For me, I learn better with numbers and bullet points, so I will write down each technique that says "Step 1, Step 2, Step 3, etc." However, if you learn better by simply reading the story, then all the better.

Some readers are not familiar with Traditional Witchcraft or *Old Craft*, and may be unfamiliar with how witches often referred to the Horned One as "the Devil." If one researches some of the old witch trial manuscripts, you will see that witches often use the term "Devil." This is not the same as the Christian "Satan." The Devil in Old Craft was the "Witch Father," "The Old One," or "The Horned One." Many country folk often heard the preachers talk about how *"The Devil had horns and hooves and witches followed him into the dark forests."* This seemed like the same spiritual being that witches honored, so they would often call the God of the Witches "The Devil."

I hope you enjoy the stories of Johnathan Knotbristle the Charmer. So, pour yourself a glass of whiskey or good strong tea. Sit back in your rocking chair. Light some candles and listen to this old country charmer tell you his story.

Before we start, Johnathan needs to light his old smoking pipe. Can you hand him his glass of whiskey? Thank you. He likes a good pipe and a glass of whiskey while he's telling you his story.

Johnathan, shall we begin?

1

How it Happened

I LIVED IN A SMALL TOWN. It was like many small towns, I 'spose. It had a church, a general store, a bank, a tavern, and all the things that small towns have. Most of the folks was Protestant and went ta'church ever-Sund'y. Most of the folks 'round here are farmers. Most of the farms are small and was just the right size ta'feed a family. There's a couple'a big farms on the outside of town. Those farmers sold most of their crops to the general stores here and in the surround'n towns. Those was the rich ones. But most folks was common folk. We all tried ta'mind our business, but with any small town, if someth'n happened, then we all heard 'bout it. Ever-body knows me 'round here, hell, I've helped a lot of 'em with my magic. Folks be need'n magic from time ta'time with all sorts of things. Love, money, heal'n. All sorts. Some folks call me a healer, other folks call me a charmer, and under their breath, some might even call me a witch.

Ever-one has their work that God intended 'em ta'do. Some folks was farmers while others had a trade ta'sell. The kinda work I do is heal'n work. Well, the kinda heal'n work I do, no doctor can do. Doctors cut and bandage and give you powders ta'drink. The kinda doctor'n I do goes deeper than those bones you have. I go as deep as the soul, and maybe even deeper'n that. That's what heal'n rightly is. I don't just bandage you up and send you on your way. I go into the parts of your heart that most folks don't like ta'be look'n at. That's the part that I wanna see. That's where the real magic is. Most folks hide their prayers in their heart, but if you look under where them prayers are, you see the shit them folks don't want you ta'see. That's where their pain and all kinds'a shit is. That's the part you gotta heal. That's the part you gotta fix. If you don't heal the blackness in their heart, they just gonna get sick and do bad again. Or maybe even die from it.

I kinda like the word "charmer." It sounds kinda mysterious. Like it means someth'n. The word "witch" seems ta'scare some of the good folks and keep 'em away from me and that's a'right by me. I never need none'a them's comp'ny anyhow. I like be'n alone sometimes. Just me and the spirits. Well, and the chickens and goats, too. Can't be forget'n 'bout them. Them town folk come 'round when they need me. When they need me ta'get the devil outta 'em. Or when they need their husbands ta'come home or when things get real bad and they need a change in their luck. You know, a change in how their money is. A while ago, one'a the town ladies and her husband brought their boy ta'me, ask'n for me ta'make him better. I did what I do and he got better. They was all thankful at the time, but they barely say hello ta'me at church. That's a'right. I understand. It don't hurt me none when folks be think'n in their ways.

I wasn't always like this. I wasn't always...a witch. I was born like most folk on a farm and lived with my Momma and Daddy and I had two brothers named Timothy and Joseph. Joseph was older'n me by a couple years and Timothy was younger. I did chores like most boys and got into a little trouble with my Daddy from time ta'time. Nuth'n too important, just little kid stuff. When I got caught do'n someth'n bad, Daddy'd take a belt ta'me and that'd be the end of it. Whatever me and my brothers did, we never did it again 'cause when Daddy gave you that whoop'n, boy, you ain't never did it again.

When I was 15 years old, my brother Timothy got real sick. The kinda sick your Momma prays over you for. The kinda sick the town doctor can't seem ta'figure out. My Momma prayed real hard and made my Daddy pray with her, too. He wasn't a godly man or nuth'n, but he wasn't tak'n no chances with his son. Nor with the wrath of my Momma for not pray'n. Timothy never got better, and he died a little while after get'n sick. Then my Momma and Daddy both got sick too. Ain't nobody came over and prayed, 'cause they figured whatever they had it was contagious, see'n that Momma and Daddy got it from my brother. Momma told me and my older brother Joseph ta'go in town ta'church and pray, but the Pastor Howard said it was best ta'pray outside 'cause the town folk was think'n we might bring in whatever was mak'n Momma and Daddy sick. Like I said, Daddy wasn't s'much a God-fear'n man like Momma, so folks started say'n stuff and whisper'n things. Joseph got wind of what they was say'n up in town and he surely was pissed. They was say'n that Daddy let the Devil come into our house. They said the Devil had a holt on our house s'bad that Momma's prayers wasn't do'n noth'n.

Now, I gotta say, s'far as I can tell, Daddy din't let no Devil into our house. Folks get sick and that's just how life goes. Folks are born, they live, and sometimes they get sick and they die. Folks believe what they want ta'believe, and you can't talk no kinda sense into 'em. You ask me, it's that kinda stubborn think'n is what lets the sickness in. And when 'em same folk get sick with their stubbornness, they pray. But pray'n don't do nuth'n 'cause they don't believe in what they're say'n. They pray ta'scare the Devil away, not 'cause they believe in what they're say'n. Hell, I don't even think they believe that they are talk'n to God sometimes.

Well, anyhow, Momma and Daddy died and me and ma'brother Joseph buried 'em next ta'my little brother out back. We put a couple'a stones over the grave. We din't want ta'use wood 'cause that ain't gonna last too long and we wanted someth'n that'd last. Joseph was always the angry type, but after Momma and Daddy died, he was straight mad as hell. Not the kinda mad where folks are hoot'n and holler'n 'bout someth'n, but the kinda mad that's way down in your soul. 'Member me say'n that some sickness gets back, deep in your heart behind your prayers? Well, that's the kinda mad he had. He never spoke 'bout Momma and Daddy again.

Joseph got ta'drink'n here and there. Then "here and there" seemed like all the time. He'd come home mad 'bout someth'n. Most of the time noth'n had happened or noth'n I thought was worth all the commotion, but he was mad just the same. He'd come home with bruises and scuffs on his face and hands. Sometimes I couldn't tell if he hit a man or the wall. I never asked him noth'n 'cause I din't want him gett'n mad at me for noth'n. So, I kept my mouth shut and let things be.

One night, I heard a knock on the door. I knew someth'n wasn't right, 'cause my brother wasn't home, and ain't nobody never came knock'n on our door. I opened up the door and there stood the Pastor Howard. This was someth'n odd, 'cause pastor Howard never came ta'our house for noth'n. Even when Momma and Daddy was sick he never came. I was think'n that's 'cause he wasn't no real kinda preacher. Not the kind who's not 'fraid ta'stand up to the Devil and give him what's what. He's the kinda preacher that did what he was 'spected ta'do and nuth'n more. He's the kind that kept ever-thing nice and never went outta his way ta'help nobody. Well, at least nobody like us anyhow. Pastor Howard stood in front of my house with his head down and his hat off, hold'n it at his waist. "Your brother's gone," he said. "Got into a big fight with a bunch of men and one'a them pulled out a gun and fired. I'm sorry. You can come see him if you want to. Then we'll have some of the boys bring him back here if you want to bury him with your Momma and Daddy."

I stood there not know'n what ta'do or say. I went with Pastor Howard ta'see my brother's body and then some of the men loaded him up in their wagon and they brought him back home. The whole time I din't say noth'n. What was there ta'say? My brother proved them town folk right. He might not'a had the Devil in him, but he did what the Devil does and started trouble. One'a the men helped me bury my brother next ta'my Momma, Daddy, and little brother. He din't say a word the whole time. Din't look at me or noth'n. After the last pile of dirt was put on my brother's grave, the man got in his wagon and went home.

There I was. 15 years old and my family gone. Momma told us that when you die, you go up ta'heaven ta'live in the house of the Lord. I think that was true for 'em. Even for Joseph. I don't think drink'n and rustl'n 'round keeps you outta heaven. It wasn't all his fault. He was mad and had that dark spot behind his heart. I don't think he could'a helped it even if he tried. I think God welcomed him home. There ain't nuth'n in heaven ta'be mad at, so I can't see my brother caus'n no problems.

I wasn't used to be'n this alone. I dunno if I could'a run that farm alone. The farm was small, but there was lots ta'do and we always had my entire family ta'help. We had chickens and a couple'a cows and a small piece of land that my Daddy'd grow differ'nt kinds of vege'ables on. Noth'n big, but it was 'nuff ta'feed us and have some extra ta'sell up in town from time ta'time. I wasn't sure what I was gonna do. I could sell the land and maybe go to the city, but that seemed like a world away. I was old 'nuff ta'get married I guess, but I don't think no kinda God-fear'n girl wanted ta'be wound up with someone the likes of me.

So, what'd I do? I din't do noth'n. I think I started ta'get some of that dark behind my heart, too. Not the kinda dark my brother had that makes you mad, but the kinda dark that won't let you feel noth'n. Noth'n at all.

I spent many days alone. I din't leave the house. Days was silent and the darkness behind my heart was the only thing I could see. The feel'n behind my heart was my only companion. It was my friend 'cause it became the blanket that kept me from know'n my pain. I don't 'member feel'n noth'n. I don't 'member much 'bout 'em days. Just hours and hours of not feel'n noth'n. I do 'member see'n the sunlight come'n through the winda' of the house. The house's dark dur'n the day 'cept that sunbeam that shined through the winda'. I thought it was funny that this little beam of light was the only thing that kept me comp'ny. Was that God? Or what is some little angel that was keep'n watch over me while I drownt in my own solitude? Either way, the sunbeam was my companion. He ain't offered no words of wisdom or no advice none. He's simply there, keep'n me comp'ny.

Nighttime was 'specially dark. It was late summer, and the nights became colder each pass'n day. The wind'd pick up at sundown and the branches of the trees was shake'n s'hard they kept hitt'n the windas.

I din't sleep much those days, and the only light came from a single candle that I lit ta'keep me comp'ny. It was too warm in the house ta'light the hearth fire. I din't feel much like light'n the fire anyhow. The candle's all I needed. Ever-night, I'd watch the candle flame stay steady in the dark of the house. Momma kept candles in a box in her room. I ain't never went into Momma and Daddy's room. No reason to. 'Cept for those candles. I'd stare at that flame and wonder...when you die, is your soul like this here candle flame? Alone in the darkness? The only light in the dark of heaven.

One'a them nights, there was a knock on the door. Who inna hell was come'n ta'see me? No one never came knock'n on the door. 'Specially at night. What inna hell did they want? When I opened the door, there was a plate with pork and some bread on it. I wondered who'd done that. "Hello?" I called out into that dark night, but no one answered. I wasn't 'specially hungry, so I took that plate inside and put it on the table. Still no appetite. No feel'n in my heart or my stomach.

I woke up the next day and found that I was sleep'n on that table all night long. I guess I'd fallen asleep on the table right in front'a that plate of food. It was untouched. I din't want no stranger's pity. They wasn't there for my family. I don't have a mind for 'em now. I took that plate of food outside and threw it to the chickens. Chickens'll eat anything. I woulda given the meat to a dog, but unlike most folks, we din't have no dog. Them chickens gobbled ever-last piece of that pork. That day, I did some small chores 'round the farm. Chickens and cows was fed, so then I was need'n ta'feed the rest of the animals. There was other stuff that needed ta'be done, but I din't have the heart nor the strength ta'do none'a it.

That night, again I sat and watched that candle burn. Feel'n sorry for ma'self. Well, maybe not even for ma'self. I guess I was feel'n sorry for Momma, Daddy, and my brothers. Maybe they was in heaven. Or maybe nuth'n. Storms was come'n in again. Not s'much the rain, but the winds. Tree branches bang'n 'gainst the windas. Fall was come'n. I was sit'n in Momma's rock'n chair when there come a knock'n on the door, just like the night b'fore. This time I walked over and opened the door, and sure 'nuff, there was another plate of food on the ground with some bread. Looked like the bread had butter on it this time, too. I looked out toward the barn, and I saw a man dressed all in black with a brimmed black hat. I couldn't make out his face or noth'n, but it was someone. What inna hell did that man want? "Hey there!" I called out. "I see you. Might as well come on out!"

The man walked back into the night like he was step'n into noth'n. I walked over ta'that spot where he was at and looked 'round. It was dark, but not s'dark you couldn't see a man run'n away. There was noth'n there. I wondered if that was the Devil hisself come ta'take me away. I went back to the front porch and took that food; I was gonna give it to 'em chickens again. Or maybe the goats'd eat it. I din't know if it was the Devil or not, but there ain't no sense in eat'n food that the Devil give you. When I got to the barn, I couldn't hear noth'n. Even at night you can hear the animals mov'n 'round. But they was still as could be. I thought maybe that man came up in the barn and killed all those animals, but when I looked, they was a'right. They was just real quiet. Like they din't want ta'breathe in case the man in black heard 'em.

The third night I was wait'n for that man ta'knock on the door again. I sat in Momma's rock'n chair, wait'n for him. Sure 'nuff, the man knocked on the door again. "I ain't open'n up that door for no Devil!" I shouted through the door.

Again, a knock on the door. I was real mad, so I ran to the door and said "What inna hell d'you..."

"I come with gifts", the man in black said. There was noth'n in his hand, but he gestured ta'look behind me, and when I turnt, there was a plate of food on the table with pork, bread, butter, and cheese.

I heard the pastor talk'n once in town, and he said that when the Devil come, he gives you stuff ta'trick you. Ta'trick you into do'n some bad stuff. He gives you presents ta'get you ta'do what he says. No way. That ain't happen'n ta'me. I ain't stupid 'nuff ta'fall for this shit. "I ain't tak'n your food, Devil." In that moment, I was s'pissed off. Devil come up in here when my family dies and tries ta'get me. "Get gone Devil! You wait 'til I'm hurt'n real bad 'bout my family and you come up here with food, try'n ta'prey on my pain! Get gone!'

Now this man dressed in black was not phased one bit 'bout what I said. He looked at me with the blackest eyes, but I din't see the eyes of the Devil that the pastor was talk'n 'bout. I saw eyes that looked into my soul and saw me. He said, "I do not come to take advantage of your pain. I come to relieve you of your pain, child. I come not out of malice, but of salvation."

"I don't want anyth'n from the Devil," I said.

"Look into my eyes and tell me what you see," he says ta'me. His voice seemed calm like and steady, but that don't mean noth'n.

I wasn't scared of him, no way. I looked right into his eyes, and I dunno what I was 'specting. Maybe darkness. Maybe evil. That's not what I saw though. I saw someone who saw me back. Someone who wasn't talk'n 'bout me and my family like we was nuth'n. Someone who was connect'n ta'my soul.

"You can see me for who I am and I, you," he says ta'me. "I can deliver you from this nothingness. I can give you a talent that will feed your belly and bring you redemption to these town folk. They will see you for your worth. You will have the ability to do things they cannot. Meet me in the churchyard tomorrow at the dead of night. Walk backwards around the church three times. Each round, call to me. Call to me in fear and love, and I will come and create you anew." And with that, he stepped back into the night and was gone.

That night was a full moon. Small towns like mine are quiet dur'n a full moon. They says they don't believe in the spirits that walk the night on a full moon, but they ain't never come outta their houses, just in case. The good church go'n folk is 'fraid of the Devil, and even if they don't believe in ghosts, they be believe'n in him. And it was the Devil hisself I was gonna see. The church was dark and quiet. There I was in the churchyard, 'bout ta'call the Devil and the only thing I kept think'n was that I had nuth'n else ta'lose. The church build'n wasn't real big, so it din't take much ta'walk 'round it backward three times. When I came to the third pass I said, "Devil, I call you." And he appeared right there in front of me.

I saw the Devil more clearly now. I could see his face. He looked like no kinda ordin'ry man, but he was dressed in black. But the church pastor also dressed in black, so that din't bother me much. "Renounce your baptism. Become free of the chains of the righteous. The chains that bind the soul to be free and to work your will upon earth."

I was think'n of all the things that'd happened. My family was gone. I had no way ta'take care of ma'self 'cept for the little farm that could barely feed me. I ain't got no money and din't know what I was gonna do when the winter came this year. So, right then and there, I looked in the eyes of that there Devil and renounced my baptism. I gave back the baptism that the pastor'd done giv'n me as a child. And then...I was free. An enormous weight was lifted off my soul, like I was carry'n a big rock on ma'back and din't even know it.

The Devil whispered into my ear. I got real close like, and I could feel his breath on my neck. "Place one hand on your head and the other on your foot and pledge all that lies in between to me."

So I did, right then and there, what he said. I put one hand on my head and the other on my foot and pledged ever-thing b'tween ta'him. He din't say anyth'n for a while and looked at me like we was friends and maybe even relatives. I felt a deep kindred feel'n with him in that moment. Then he said, "Prepare to receive my power." He placed his hands on both my shoulders. His grip was tight, and for a moment I wondered what was gonna happen. His arms was strong and even if I wanted ta'get gone, I don't think I could. Then he leaned into me and gave me a kiss. Maybe it was all in ma'mind, but his tongue went clear down ta'my stomach. But I wasn't think'n 'bout that. What I was think'n 'bout was the power come'n from him and in ta'me. I was dazed for a minute but came ta'my senses. The Devil handed me a cup of wine, say'n, "Drink this wine. This is the alchemy of the stars and of the blood of the ancestors long dead." He handed me a piece of bread and said, "This comes from the seed of the land. The land that I have walked for many eons, redeeming man. This is the bread of the faery folks. Your powers are bound to me and to them."

He put his hands over my eyes and I din't know if what came next was real or a dream. Hell, it all felt like a dream. I followed him inside of the church. Church doors is always unlocked. I guess nobody ever did try ta'steal stuff from the inside of a church. I followed the Devil to the altar without a word. On that altar was a big black book. The book looked old as hell, and it was real thick, too. He opened the book. There was folks's names in it, but they was real blurry. Couldn't make 'em out. Under their names was space for more. He took my hand and used him his sharp fingernail ta'poke my finger. It bled a little and he said, "Write your name in this book." And so I did.

You woulda thought I'd have some hesitation 'bout the whole thing, but I din't. You see, folks be wonder'n why I gave up my baptism and why inna hell I'd be sign'n my name in the Devil's book. Let me tell you how it is, though. Folks think that ever-body was God-fear'n Christians and we prayed all the time, but that weren't how it was at all. Some folks believed in Jesus and the Bible and the angels, and some folks din't. Pastors was always talk'n their shit, try'n ta'scare folks, and most of us knew it's just 'em preachers tryn ta'do what they do. Maybe it's real and maybe it's horseshit, but the pastors'll try ta'make folks feel bad for be'n normal ever-day folk. We know that many folks died in the name of Christ, and most of us is know'n that they all died for no goddamn reason, but pastors be say'n what they say'n. Another thing is that the pastors be say'n the Devil is the king of evil, and when you see the Devil, you know he's a liar. That's not what I saw. I saw a be'n who made sure I was a'right and give me ever-thing I needed. He made sure I was fed and that I could help ma'self. No God or no Jesus never did that for me. The town folk never did that for me. It was the Devil who made sure I was a'right. So I'm think'n the pastors either be lie'n themselfs or they don't know. They certainly never met no Devil.

So, that's how it all happened. That's how I met the Devil and became ma'self a witch. Sometimes folks don't understand what the word "witch" means, so oftentimes I don't say "witch." I say "charmer." We all charm folks from time ta'time. We charm our wives and husbands. We charm folks ta'get what we want. We all do it. The only differ'nce is when I charm someone, I do it in the Devil's name.

2

Old Henry

LET ME TELL YOU 'BOUT OLD HENRY. Henry is what we call a spirit familiar. He does stuff for me and helps me when I need. He teaches me stuff too, sometimes. Sometimes if Old Henry doesn't know someth'n, he'll take me ta'someone who does. I can't 'magine my life without Old Henry. Henry is prob'ly my best friend. I dunno what I would do without Henry.

After the Devil made me a witch, I went back home, wonder'n what inna hell happened ta'me. Now, 'member, I wasn't feel'n bad or nuth'n. In fact, I was feel'n pretty good. The best I've ever felt my whole life. I was happy but I was also a little sad. Not 'cause anyth'n the Devil did, but 'cause after I became a witch, I started know'n stuff. On my walk home dur'n that full moon, I was feel'n things in my heart. I could feel the joy and sorrow of them trees and I could feel the souls of them birds in them. When I looked up at the moon, I could feel her power, but I was also feel'n her sadness in her solitude. Night after night, she traveled the sky, look'n down on us folks, hope'n someone'd talk ta'her. You know folks are 'fraid of the moon, too. These folks is 'fraid of ever-thing. Anyth'n that jumps or crawls or has an opinion, they're 'fraid of. Why, I don't pay no mind ta'no folks anyhow. But anyhow, folks is 'fraid of the moon. That's where we get the word "lunacy." Folks think sometimes if you go out on a full moon, it'll make you crazy. I'll tell you what, the only thing that makes you crazy is listen'n ta'folks who don't know what they talk'n 'bout. It's better ta'talk ta'that there moon than it is listen'n ta'most folks' gibberish.

Not much happened after I became ma'self a witch. I din't 'spect noth'n much ta'happen, so I went on with things like I normally do. Work'n on the little farm, do'n chores here and there. It was 'bout ta'be fall soon, and the weather'd get rainy and cooler. Down South here, it don't get all that cold and snowy like up North. That's why I don't live up there. Too much damn snow and too much damn cold. Don't get me wrong, when winter really hits in Janu'ry we might get a couple inches of snow here and there, but it ain't much. It usually warms up soon after, and any ice or snow melts away, leav'n mud and slush.

One day, I was feed'n them animals and wonder'n which ones'd be dinner through the winter and which ones I'd keep 'round ta'feed. I had this overwhelm'n feel'n of sorrow and despair. This'd be my first winter alone and I had no idea what I was ta'be do'n. Momma and Daddy took care of ever-thing. A'course, me and my brothers'd take care of stuff and we had our chores, but Daddy took care of us in the way he could. We never had much, but we always had someth'n. I din't want ta'ask none'a the neighbors for help or advice. They prob'ly wouldn't help me anyhow. A thought hit my head: *what if they know I'm a witch?* Did anybody see me in the churchyard talk'n to the Devil? Or did I lose my mind and it was all a dream? Either way, I can't 'magine nobody help'n the likes of me.

It was 'bout midday on a day that was 'specially hot for late summer. I was sweat'n up a storm when I looked down on the road that led ta'my house and I saw a man walk'n up that road. He was dressed in normal britches and a shirt and wore a hat. He pretty much looked like any other man. At first, I was wonder'n what folks was do'n come'n up ta'my house. No one never came up here unless they wanted someth'n from Daddy, and he's dead now, so that can't be it. I stood there watch'n the man come up the road and said noth'n. He finally got up ta'me and said, "Hello, my name is Henry. How do you do?"

I went ta'shake his hand and I said ta'him, "I'm Johnathan Knotbristle."

"It's nice to meet you, Johnathan Knotbristle," Henry said.

Henry seemed nice 'nuff, but I was ponder'n what he wanted and what he was do'n out here. I din't trust nobody and I wasn't sure I could trust Henry. I looked him square in the eye and said, "What're you need'n, Henry? You know, most folks don't come up to the house. They usually stay away."

Henry smiled and his eyes seemed all kind and friendly like. It was almost like I knew him from somewhere. Like a cousin or someth'n I met once, and I forgot 'bout, 'cause I hadn't seen him in years and years. "Many people fear and judge things they do not know."

Daddy never liked nobody come'n to the house unannounced. He always had a 'spicion 'bout folks. Daddy used ta'say, "Careful how you let'n folks come into your life. They may seem nice, but most times they either want someth'n or is try'n ta'find out what kinda person you is. Folks is 'fraid of folks they don't know and things they don't know." I din't see no harm in Henry. Just like I could feel them trees, I could feel that Henry was a good kinda person. "Come on up to the house and I'll get you some water. It's hot 'nuff outside today."

"Thank you," Henry said and followed me to the house. He walked into my house and looked 'round. He looked a little disappointed like he was 'spect'n someth'n. I wasn't sure if he thought it'd be nicer inside or I dunno what he thought.

"Not much ta'look at," I said. "We never had much. Just the bare 'sentials."

Henry extended his hand ta'me and said, "Allow me to explain. I was sent here to you by the Devil himself."

I was confused 'bout what he was talk'n 'bout, "What d'you mean?"

"I am what is called a *familiar spirit*," Henry said. "Each witch has one that is sent to them by the Devil. Think of me as your teacher and best friend."

I 'membered hear'n things from the pastor and some'a them 'ole ladies from town say'n that witches had demon familiars that looked like cats, frogs, ferrets, mice, and many other things. Mostly they seemed like anyth'n that roamed 'round at night. "If you're a familiar, shouldn't you be a demon animal? Like a black cat or someth'n?'

"I am, that I am," Henry 'splained. "Christians think everything is either demon or angel. I, good sir, am neither of those things. I am a servant of the Devil, and I am here to help you when you need."

"Wouldn't the Devil just teach me the things I need ta'know?" I asked.

"The Devil does things how he does things. He is the great mystery, you know," Henry 'splained. "You see, there are things he shows you and then there are things I show you. You'll see as we go along."

I sat down on a chair and listened ta'what Henry had ta'say. He seemed ta'be the interest'n sort. If he was from the Devil, well, I guess I needed ta'be listen'n ta'what he had ta'say.

"First things first," Old Henry said. "I need you to obtain an animal skull."

"For what?" I asked.

"For my home, of course." Henry acted like this is someth'n someone just knows. Maybe when the Devil gives you the power, you are just 'sposed ta'be know'n things. Maybe I do know things and just don't know what I know.

"One'a the cats died a while back," I said. "I can dig it up and get the skull. Should be just bones by now."

"That will do just fine," Henry said. "You can use any kind of skull from any animal. Or, if you don't have a skull, you could make one from clay or a similar material."

Later that day, I took the shovel and dug up that 'ole cat that'd just up and died one day. We had that cat a long time. Daddy liked keep'n a cat out in the barn. He keeps the rats away, he'd say. He told us not ta'feed it too much 'cause then it wouldn't chase no rats if he weren't hungry. Momma would let that cat inside when it was too cold out. I'd feed it sometimes when she did. Never told Daddy that, but I'm sure he knew. I dug up that 'ole cat and it still had dried skin and fur on it. So, I figured it'd be best ta'throw it in Momma's 'ole cook'n pot and boil it. That's what you did if you was keep'n bones for some kinda reason. I took me a sharp knife and took off any skin that was still there, then I threw it in the pot of boil'n water. It din't take as long as I thought it would.

That night, I took that cat skull and placed it on the table right next to the candle. *What am I 'sposed ta'do with this now?* I thought to ma'self. Ever-day since my family was gone, I'd light that candle and just sink right into loneliness, but this time was differ'nt. Instead of feel'n my sadness, I started kinda day dream'n. I wasn't think'n 'bout nuth'n in pa'ticular. Just look'n at that candle. My breath started come'n slow and steady. Like me and that candle was breathe'n at the same time. That candle looked like the whole world ta'me. Ever-thing that was life was in that candle flame. Then I started think'n 'bout the Devil. I started think'n that I had some power that he'd been givi'n me. Someth'n real special. I dunno how long I was star'n at that candle, but I'd lost ma'self. Or maybe I done forgot what I was think'n 'bout 'cause I was start'n ta'stare straight through that candle flame.

All a sudden I started daydream'n 'bout that cat skull. I started dream'n that I put down two candles, one on both sides of the skull. Then I done cut my finger with my knife and put three drops of blood on the skull. After that, I took some of Daddy's leftover tobacca and lit his pipe. I blew that pipe smoke over the skull and I said, "Old Henry, Old Henry, come ta'me this night. Old Henry, Old Henry, from the Devil's flight. Old Henry, Old Henry, my familiar 'tis thee. Old Henry, Old Henry my familiar you'll be."

Then I snapped right outta my daydream.

So, I guess that's what I'm 'sposed ta'do. I did ever-thing that I seen in my daydream. I lit the two candles, put three drops of blood on the skull, and then said me that little rhyme. After I said the rhyme, well, noth'n happened. *Hmmm...must not have done it right.* I said it again. Still noth'n. *Well, hell,* I thought. *I'm gonna try this one more time.* After the third time, I was feel'n someth'n mighty strange. The cat skull kinda pulsed. Like it was alive. "Old Henry, are you there?"

"I'm here," Old Henry said from behind me. I turnt 'round ta'see Henry stand'n there with a wry look on his face. See'n him this time was differ'nt from the last time I'd saw him. This time, I felt like I'd known him my whole life. Like he'd been with me since the day I been born. Maybe he was, maybe he wasn't. Maybe he's been wait'n for this very day ta'start do'n the great work of witchery. Maybe he'd been watch'n me my whole life. A guardian angel, like. Din't matter much. Me and Old Henry had work ta'do. But I din't know yet what that work was gonna be.

I put the cat skull on the top closet shelf. I placed it in a small box. If I had stuff for Old Henry ta'do, then I ought be keep'n the box open. If I wanted Henry ta'let stuff be, then I oughta close the box. I dunno how I knew that, but I did. Maybe I was just mak'n it all up as I went along. Din't matter much. It was true. It worked. Ever know someth'n and you don't know how you know, but you just know? It's kinda like that. A thought that just jumps in my head and I can't tell if it's my think'n or come'n from somewhere else. Like a spirit or maybe the Devil. I figure it was Old Henry tell'n me how ta'do stuff.

That's one thing you gotta know 'bout spirits. Folks think they always appear like a white ghost. Like a specter in the darkest of nights, howl'n and holler'n, woe is me, and all that shit. That don't really happen like that. Now'd I think 'bout it, most witchcraft don't happen like folks suspect it happen. It happen how it happen, and sometimes we best not be ask'n all these questions 'lest we get ourselfs confused. Sometimes the spirits just put a thought or someth'n in your mind. That's how they talk ta'you. You get this idea or you get a hanker'n ta'do someth'n and it seems real important. Like at that moment it's the most important thing ta'do. That's the spirits. That's how they talk ta'ya sometimes. Don't get me wrong. They do sometimes just say it and you can hear their voice as clear as day. But whenever you get a thought that don't seem like it's yours, you better believe that it's a spirit say'n stuff ta'you. You best be listen'n, too.

Spirits tend ta'see things we can't see. They don't have no body or noth'n like that, so they can sit in a little stone or take up your entire house. They don't have no eyes the way we think 'bout eyes and they don't have no thoughts the way we're think'n 'bout thoughts. So they be see'n stuff we don't see and they be know'n stuff we don't know. So we best be listen'n. The only thing is that sometimes not all spirits who try ta'talk ta'us is want'n what's good for us. Just like folks. Sometimes spirits want what they want and don't have a care much 'bout you and what you want. You gotta be careful with those spirits.

I know what you're think'n right now. How do I know what spirits ta'listen to and which ones not ta'listen to? Well, that's a little harder ta'understand. You see, it's a feel'n you get. A lot of times, I get this feel'n in my heart or belly that says, *"Oh, this must be Old Henry talk'n ta'me."* You only get to know'n this when you get to know'n your spirits. Kinda like your family and friends. You know things they'd most likely say and things they sure wouldn't say. If you get this thought in your head that tells you ta'do someth'n stupid or someth'n you think you better not be do'n, then don't do it! Spirits are know'n things, but they dunno ever-thing. If you are just learn'n 'bout spirits, then best be listen'n ta'what is right and wrong. Listen ta'what your Momma and Daddy taught you and don't be doin' noth'n stupid and blam'n it on no spirit. Spirits can be say'n whatever the hell they want, but you ain't gotta be listen'n to 'em if they're get'n you into some kinda trouble. You can get into trouble and them spirits can go on their merry way.

Let me tell you more 'bout Old Henry. As the days passed, I was run'n outta food. You have ta'remember that our little farm was 'nuff ta'put food on the table for all of us, but it also took all of us ta'make it work. My family was gone and it was just me. Not much one person could do all by themself, but I did some and had a little food. It wouldn't last through the winter none. I had my Daddy's rifle and I could go hunt'n with that. Some birds, maybe a deer here and there, and that was 'bout it. There was still stuff I needed that I couldn't make ma'self. I needed oil for the oil lamps, feed for the chickens, cows, goats, and other stuff. So I went into town to the market ta'see if I could get some credit and maybe a job somewhere. Someth'n.

When I got into town, the folks'd all but forgot who I was. They din't pay much mind ta'me. Which was fine by me, 'cause I was wonder'n if they was still talk'n 'bout the Devil be'n in my house and kill'n my family. Boy, it's funny ta'think that folks was think'n that the Devil caused all my problems, when in truth, it was the Devil who done saved me. It was the Devil who done helped me. Not Jesus or these town folks, just the Devil. It's funny if you think 'bout it like that.

I went to the market ta'ask for some credit and that I would pay 'em back soon as I could. The man who owned that store was an old man named Mr. Picklesworth. He'd been own'n that store for a long time. Ever since I can 'member. He had him a small family. A wife and two daughters. That old man in the market looked at me like I was the craziest thing he ever seen. He looked at me even crazier when I asked for a job or if he know someone who could get me a job. The answer was a big no. I wasn't sure if it was 'cause of what folks was think'n of me or if there really wasn't no jobs 'round. Either way, I wasn't sure what I was gonna do. Live'n in the dark, eatin' venison I 'spose.

I had an idea. I went back home, and I took that 'ole cat skull off the shelf. I put my both hands on that skull, and I said, "Old Henry, Old Henry, I call to thee, Old Henry, Old Henry I summon thee. Go to the market and get for me the things I desire, get 'em for me." And then...nuth'n.

I 'spected ta'see Old Henry appear right in front of me. ready ta'do what I was say'n but he wasn't there. I repeated the spell three times and still nuth'n. Maybe it din't work or maybe I din't know what I was do'n. I'm guess'n I din't know what I was do'n. After a while, I done gave up and went 'bout my business for the day.

The next day when I woke up I could'a swore up and down I heard Old Henry's voice say'n, "Go back to the market and ask again." I figured I best be listen'n to Old Henry, so I went back down to the market and asked Mr. Picklesworth ta'give me credit once more. "I'm not gonna give you credit," he said, "but I am gonna give you a loan that you're gonna pay off by work'n in my store." Hmmmm, not really what I was hop'n for, but then again, it was a job. Someth'n ta'keep me busy and maybe a little bit of money ta'save. Mr. Picklesworth gave me the stuff I needed: some food ta'take home, feed for the animals, oil for the lamp, and I picked me up a new axe for chop'n wood. Daddy's axe's old and the wood handle was fall'n 'part and the metal was worn down s'much that sharpn'n wouldn't do it no good.

Ever-day I worked in that market. I swept floors, stocked shelves, cleaned stuff, and did ever-thing Mr. Picklesworth wanted me ta'do. He was get'n real old an' couldn't do most of the chores need'n be done 'round that store. I think I was help'n him just as much as he was help'n me, but he'd never admit ta'that. We kinda had a mutual understand'n that we was help'n each other out, but we wasn't 'sposed ta'talk 'bout it.

I knew it was Old Henry who got me that job and saved me from starv'n through the winter. He din't make what I needed just appear outta thin air but made it happen natural like. Like it was 'sposed ta'happen but with a little push from Old Henry. I guess Old Henry went and whispered in Mr. Picklesworth's ear, or maybe he went into his dreams. I'm not sure how it happened 'zactly, but you know spirits be do'n what spirits do without us folks know'n 'bout it.

I ask Old Henry for help in all kinds of stuff. Whenever I be need'n someth'n, I just light them candles and tap on that 'ole cat skull and tell Old Henry what I need him ta'do. I never ask him how he does stuff, he just does it. Often times, when I need ta'be know'n someth'n from someone, I'll send Old Henry down the road there and he'll come back tell'n me what's all go'n on. Sometimes he tell me straight forward, just like I'm talk'n ta'you, and other times I see things in my head. Either way, I get what I'm need'n ta'know. He does other stuff too for me, but we'll talk 'bout that later.

Old Henry wants me ta'tell you that familiar spirits come to the witch in differ'nt ways. Sometimes the Devil sends 'em. Sometimes they appear when the witch needs 'em the most. Some folks be think'n that the familiar and the Devil is one in the same. That ain't true at all. They're differ'nt. I'm guess'n the Devil don't have no time ta'be do'n ever-little thing the witch be need'n, so he sends a familiar ta'do magic and spells for 'em. Oh yes, Old Henry helps me with spells all the time, but we'll talk more 'bout that later. Old Henry wants me ta'tell you how ta'get your own familiar if the Devil ain't yet given one for you. I dunno why the Devil does what he do, so I'm gonna tell you what Old Henry's tell'n me here.

The first thing you need ta'do is get you a pitchfork or stang and set it up how it's 'sposed to. Make sure you put that candle b'tween the forked branches at the top and light it. They say that's for sure how you know the Devil be come'n outta that stang. It's his light. His presence. Be make'n sure you put out a little bowl of water as an offer'n and burn some herbs on a small piece of ember from the fireplace. The scent from the plants'll put your mind in a place ta'be open to the spirits and for call'n to the Devil. Make sure you have someth'n for the familiar spirit ta'live in. It can be a bone of someth'n, a box, vase, or anyth'n you are think'n you'd like for a spirit house. Call to the Devil in your own words. Have him come and be in the stang. When you feel the Devil in that stang, you can ask for a familiar spirit. Then you'll place two candles on either side of that vessel and use your own worlds ta'ask the Devil ta'send you a spirit. You oughta use a few drops of your blood on the vessel ta'anchor the spirit to the vessel and ta'you. Sometimes you can feel the spirit come'n to the vessel. It makes sense ta'me that when you're feel'n the power of the spirit, try ta'imagine what you think it looks like. It don't matter much if it's right or wrong. What matters is if it works. Once you got your spirit in the vessel, you can tell it ta'do things for you. Don't forget ta'feed it from time ta'time. You can give it milk, beer, alcohol, water, tobacca, or whatever it likes. Just be sure not ta'give it noth'n you don't want ta'give. I'm not giv'n it no animal blood. Just 'cause that's not someth'n I do.

3

The Pitchfork

⁂

I WORKED AN AWFUL LOT dur'n the last days of the summer at the market. I paid back Mr. Picklesworth soon as I could and then I started sav'n me money here and there. Mr. Picklesworth never said a kind word, but I could tell that he was happy ta'have me there. I think he needed the comp'ny. I din't know much 'bout Mrs. Picklesworth. She rarely came to the store and I just minded my own business. From time ta'time, someone would come into the store and ask 'bout her, and Mr. Picklesworth always said she was just fine. I got ta'wonder'n why I never saw her 'round, but I let ly'n dogs lie and never asked 'bout it. He was a private man and din't like folks, 'specially me, ask'n 'bout his come'ns and go'ns. I never paid much mind ta'nobody anyhow. I did what I did and worked in the store and that was 'nuff for him.

It was weeks since the Devil made me a witch, and with things look'n up as they was, I was mighty grateful. B'fore the Devil came, I wasn't know'n what I'd be do'n. Maybe'd be a'right or maybe'd be dead. Who knows. All I know is that the Devil wasn't as bad as the pastor be say'n he was. Or maybe the Devil was bad, but the Devil never did noth'n ta'me, so I guess we was get'n along. It's funny how folks are talk'n 'bout things that scares 'em. Turns out when they don't know someth'n, they make up stories ta'scare themselfs. Maybe they do that ta'keep themselfs safe. I learnt over time that there ain't no such thing as safe. You can be just fine one day and dead the next. No one's know'n what's happen'n 'til it happens. That's kinda how I feel 'bout the Devil right now. You never know what's gonna happen, but for now, I'm a'right and that's 'cause the Devil gave me stuff ta'make it a'right. God and Jesus never gave me noth'n. So there's that.

One day, just b'fore sunset, I was work'n 'round in the barn. I was feed'n them animals and straight'n up a little. With the money I had, I was able ta'buy some hay, and Mr. Picklesworth helped me get it home on his wagon. I was gonna find a way, or maybe pay someone ta'help me get home, but he offered ta'help. I guess that's his way of say'n that we was friends. I have me a wagon out behind the barn. An 'ole wagon that needed a new wheel. I'm not know'n how ta'make one or fix it ma'self, so for the time be'n, I don't right need no wagon. Town ain't far away. I walk there all the time. The walk is nice. But when it gets cold I'd be wish'n I had a wagon.

Anyhow, I was put'n some of that hay in the barn for 'em goats and chickens and I worked ma'self up a sweat. I was us'n that pitchfork ta'spread it out on the ground in the barn. Also clean'n up all kinds of animal shit here and there. It was collect'n, so I figured b'fore I put the hay down, I needed ta'clean up the barn. Plus, I needed ta'clean the chicken coop and make sure that the chickens had them some hay in there, too. Clean'n the chicken coop was a certain kinda hell. Chickens sure taste good for cook'n, but alive they're the nastiest creatures on earth. They shit ever-where and if you drop and crack one'a their eggs, they run over and eat it all up like some nasty cann'bal. Well, they's just stupid chickens, I spose. Have no purpose but ta'be dinner.

I was work'n ma'self a good sweat, so I put the pitchfork 'gainst the wall and I was dizzy too. It was a 'specially hot day at this time of year, and I was breathe'n all heavy like and sweat'n someth'n awful. I was pitch'n that hay and scatter'n it all 'round and clean'n shit. I guess I worked ma'self up in a sorta trance. I sat the pitchfork on the side of the barn wall for a minute with them tines pointed up, just so I could rest. I was still breathe'n heavy and sweat'n. I started day dream'n and look'n at that pitchfork. The barn door was open, and the sun was sett'n. The sun rays from that sett'n sun shone into the barn and hit them tines of that pitchfork and they's look'n like they was glow'n with fire. With magical fire, I guess. I have the kinda pitchfork that has two tines. Daddy got this here pitchfork from the blacksmith up in town. Matter fact, I don't 'member Daddy pay'n no money for this two-tined pitchfork. Maybe the blacksmith owed Daddy someth'n or maybe there was some kinda secret b'tween Daddy and the blacksmith I din't know.

The sunlight was shine'n right through the two tines of the pitchfork. I started think'n that was a beautiful sight. The golden tines of the pitchfork was glow'n. I guess I forgot ma'self, 'cause all a sudden, I started think'n of the Devil. I was think'n that folks said he had horns and hooves, and that's not what I saw when I saw the Devil. The Devil looked like an ordin'ry man. He looked like any ordin'ry man, but when you saw him, you saw that there was someth'n special 'bout him. He's attractive like any other man I 'sposed, but he had a charm 'bout him. When you saw him, he wasn't frighten'n or strange or nothin', but he did have him an otherworldly presence. You could tell that he wasn't from this place. It's funny, folks believe'n any 'ole thing that the pastor man be tell'n 'em. The pastor'll make up stories 'bout the Devil and they ain't never seen no Devil. All they saw was the pastor preach'n his nonsense in church. It seems that create'n fear and panic was more important to the pastor than tell'n the truth.

I know you won't be believe'n it, but I read the Bible. Momma made sure all of us could read by take'n out that Bible of hers and make'n sure we read it. She made us learn the letters and the sounds and she'd read the stories ta'us. Then, when she thought we was ready, she had us read the Bible ourselfs. She'd help us sound out each letter and each word 'til we got it right. Momma was always real patient with us. She joked that Daddy would never be able ta'sit with us and have the patience ta'teach us like she did. Momma used ta'say that when you looked real hard, there was magic and heal'n in that Bible. I never knew what she meant by that 'til much later.

When it come to the Devil and the Bible, it don't speak much 'bout him, 'cept a few times here and there. Did you know what else? Not once in the Bible does it say the Devil has him horns and hooves. It says he was an angel. I'm not sure I see him as an angel neither. But then again, I never saw no angel neither, s'maybe they look like ever-body else, the same as the Devil does.

Anyhow, I was look'n at the golden sunlight shine'n on those tines of the pitchfork, and it looked like magic ta'me. Like God hisself was try'n ta'show me someth'n on it. Someth'n I ain't seen b'fore. I must have been go'n into a trance or someth'n, 'cause I was stare'n and stare'n at that pitchfork. My breathe'n got deep and slow. Like someth'n was take'n control of my senses. I started think'n more 'bout the Devil and how some folks said he looked like the horned hoofed creature that scared folks. As the sun fell behind the horizon over yonder, I started feel'n the power of the land. I started smell'n the dark mud below my feet and then I was think'n 'bout the birds sing'n in that tree by the house. I kept stare'n and stare'n at that pitchfork 'til the golden light of the sun wasn't there no more. But, still, I thought I could see the golden light on those tines. And d'you know what? As sure as shit I saw the image of the Devil stand'n right over that pitchfork. This time though he looked a little differ'nt. He looked like a man just like b'fore but he *did* have horns like a deer or someth'n. I couldn't right see his feet, s'maybe he had hooves, maybe he din't. But his shape was like a specter stand'n over the pitchfork. "Is that you, Devil?" I asked. I wasn't 'fraid or anyth'n. Afterall, the Devil was good ta'me the first time, so I reckon there ain't no cause ta'be scared of him now.

"I am he who is the firstborn among angels," the Devil said. "I am father to witches. I am he who prosecutes humanity. I am known by the names Lucifer, Samael, Ha-Satan, Tubal Cain, and many others. To the common people, I am known as Devil."

I sat there listen'n to the Devil talk and I was transfixed on his presence. I couldn't look away. I din't want ta'look away. You see, the

Devil be have'n these eyes that fix on you. They look at your soul. But not in a way you'd be think'n he's gonna snatch up your spirit. He look in your soul like he know you. Like no one on earth or in heaven know you better. At that moment, he be know'n me better than Momma and Daddy ever did. It felt warm and nice. Like be'n wrapped in a warm blanket. And I'll tell you someth'n else; when he fixed his eyes on you, in that moment, you knew him as well. You be know'n his pain, his sorrow, and his love for all liv'n things. Make no mistake though, he's not one ta'be trifled with. He'll make sure he got him your back, but he will also come get'n you if you make him your enemy.

"This pitchfork is my sacred vessel," the Devil said. "Known to all of my witches. You may use this to call upon my name and work your secret rites."

When the Devil told me this, all a sudden I started daydream'n again. I saw witches stand'n in a circle 'round a pitchfork. They put a candle in the center. When they lit that candle, the Devil came to 'em, sure as hell. The witches started say'n stuff in a language that was real differ'nt ta'me. I ain't never heard no language like that b'fore. Maybe it was from Europe or someth'n. I'd heard Spanish and French b'fore, but I ain't heard no language like this. The witches chanted their language and danced 'round the pitchfork. After a while, you din't see the pitchfork no more, and where that pitchfork had been, the Devil was stand'n right there. The witches was happy and laugh'n and the Devil was laugh'n too. It looked like great fun. With the fun though, I could feel the power of them witches run'n through my veins. Then I heard 'em say someth'n clear as day:

"I summon, I stir, I conjure ye forth!"

Then they said it again, "I summon, I stir, I conjure ye forth!"

Then they said it one more time, "I summon, I stir, I conjure ye forth!"

That's when they came. The specters, the ghosts, and what looked like faeries, all came out from yonder and joined them witches in the circle. Then the daydream faded, and I was back in that 'ole barn, look'n at the Devil, stand'n where the pitchfork used ta'be. It'd dis'ppeared.

Not forever. The pitchfork dis'ppears from your sight when you call the Devil good and strong; when you focus on his presence and let his power surround your work'n area. You don't see that pitchfork no more; you see the Devil.

Now, one'a the things you need ta'be know'n 'bout the Devil, well hell, I guess you can say this 'bout all the spirits, is that they be teach'n you stuff you can't be learn'n in no books. I got some books from the mail order catalog that talks 'bout charms and things of that nature, but that's for them common folk. Hell, almost all the farmers 'round here got a Farmer's Almanac. This book talks 'bout the phases of the moon, when ta'plant, when ta'harvest, and even be talk'n 'bout astrology and the zodiac. Ever-one knows 'bout this book. As I said, the common folk always be know'n from those books. The real teachers of magic are them spirits. They'll teach you stuff that only the witches be know'n. Things that if you told anybody else, they wouldn't believe you anyhow.

The daydream of the witches' circle ended, and I was right back in that barn, stare'n at that pitchfork. Well, right then it wasn't the pitchfork, it was the Devil. He put his hand on my shoulder and said, "Look not with your eyes, but with your heart."

I was understand'n this ta'mean that when you look at things with your eyes, you see the world as the common folk see the world. You see all of God's green earth, but you don't right see. You don't right see all that is. There's many things that are real that common folk don't see. Hell, I think they could if they tried, but most folks don't try. They're happy keep'n them heads down and their heart closed ta'things they ain't ready ta'see. The world is made up of ghosts, spirits, faeries, and powers that if you really want ta'see 'em then you will. You see, your heart is where you are feel'n things. You can feel the whole world if you're want'n to. That's how you really "see" the spirits. You let your heart feel the powers and then you let your daydream put a pitchur to it.

I think energy and emotions are sim'lar. I think emotions is a kinda energy. So, ta'see energies and spirits you have ta'see with your emotions. Then you let your mind paint a pitchur of what you think that energy looks like. I don't mind much if your pitchur of the Devil and my pitchur of the Devil look differ'nt. He's still the Devil and he still does what the Devil does!

That's the other thing, too! You gotta let yourself go into a daydream ta'be see'n the spirits. Ta'be see'n the visions. You know how ta'daydream don't ya? I see you do it all the time. When you're bored at your job, and you be wish'n you was someplace else. Or you're wish'n you was someplace nice. I also see you play that conversation in your head when you and someone be argue'n 'bout someth'n. Sometimes folks just can't let someth'n go, so we gotta play it over and over in our minds. All these things is daydreams. The daydreams is where we get our visions.

After a while, the daydream ended, and the Devil went away. This pitchfork, some folks call a stang, was the vessel of the Devil and it is a sacred object. You know how Jesus be hang'n on the cross up in the church? Folks be look'n at that cross with Jesus and they get filled with the Holy Spirit. They feel his presence there. That's how it is with the pitchfork. This is the place where the Devil come, and we can use it in our magical rites. Don't worry if you ain't got a pitchfork. Us country folk always got a pitchfork lay'n 'round somewhere. But if you ain't got one, you can use a tree branch. Just go out yonder to the woods and find you a nice branch that look like a two-tined pitchfork and bring it home. Make sure the tines are at least up ta'your shoulder. I seen bigger ones and I seen smaller. But shoulder height is a good height. When you get it home, sand down the bark and you can put on an oil stain if you want it. Keeps it nice for a long time.

Don't forget 'bout the candle in b'tween the two tines. The flame of that candle is the fire of magic of the Devil. It's also mean'n his wisdom. You 'member the story of Prometheus? The Greek God who stole fire from heaven and gave it to the folks and those folks made tools, weapons, and other stuff with that fire? See, without that fire Prometheus stole, we wouldn't have no blacksmith and no tools. We wouldn't have no fire ta'cook or food or gunpowder ta'shoot our guns. That's kinda what the Devil did. Remember, he's the brightest angel Lucifer. It's said that Lucifer gave the light of heaven ta'us folks so we would have us wisdom. He's the snake in the Garden of Eden who taught us free will.

That candle flame is also the magic fire in the head. When you start feel'n your magic and you're connect'n with the spirits, you might feel a burn'n or fire in your head. It's that too. It's also the torch that gives you light in the darkest of times.

I bet you're wonder'n where we got these stories. See, common folk often hear stories and mythologies and they can't 'member what story belong ta'who and who did what with what. So, sometimes folks start put'n stories together from differ'nt places and differ'nt Gods. They don't mean to. They just ain't know'n where they hear stuff, so they 'member the bits and pieces of what they hear and lump it together in one story. So, the Devil might have stories from the Greek gods, the Celtic gods, and stuff from the Bible, too. It don't matter if it's right or wrong. It don't matter much where the stories comes from. What matters to witches is that they understand the power of the Devil. Sometimes, ta'understand the Devil's power, you fill in the blanks with stories from other places.

So, I 'spect you be go'n out and get'n your pitchfork or stang and summon'n the Devil. Get your candle and put it in b'tween those tines and light it. You need ta'give an offer'n of some kind, too. Maybe some church incense or maybe an apple or someth'n. When you light the candle, all you need ta'do is call the Devil in whatever way you want. What I do is I feel the Devil in my heart and see him in my mind. Then I feel him in my veins. Once I do that, that's when I call him. Momma used ta'say, "Careful, when you the call the Devil, the Devil will come." Well, I guess that's true. When you call the Devil and mean it, he always come.

If you ain't got no pitchfork you can use a stang. A stang is a tree branch that looks just like a two-tined pitchfork. You need ta'go get one from a tree, but don't be take'n it from a tree and saw'n it off or nuth'n. You see, you'll be piss'n off the tree spirits if you just saw off a branch. Best rule ta'live by is don't piss off no kinda spirits unless you have to. We 'ardy got s'much stuff ta'deal with, no need ta'have no spirits of a tree get'n at you too! Best thing ta'do is ta'find a branch on the ground or a tree that was blown over by the wind or someth'n. Those trees are gonna die anyhow. But a good walk in the woods or somewhere where there's trees, you're bound ta'find a fallen branch. Make sure it's not rotted, though. You want it strong and sturdy. First thing you want ta'do is give an offer'n of some kind. Some witches are use'n their own blood, but I don't do it like that. I take a good pour of whiskey and give it to the tree. If you can't tell which tree the branch came from, then just pour your whiskey out and say, "This is for the tree who gave this branch." You can use tobacca too, if you want. Native spirits here in the U.S. love tobacca, too. If you ain't got noth'n ta'give, then at least give some water.

Next thing you want ta'do is ta'saw the branch to the right height. 'Bout up ta'your shoulders'll do. You don't want it too tall or too short. It's the place where the Devil comes, so you want ta'make sure it's workable. When you take that branch home, make sure you sand it down real good. Get all that bark off. Once you're done with that, you want ta'set it in the corner somewhere in your house. By the fireplace will do, but you can put it anywhere. B'fore you use it, make sure you present it to the four directions and ta'heaven above and hell below. You want all the spirits ta'bless it, if they will. After you do that, you need yourself a work'n knife. Just a small one. You need the knife ta'direct the flow of the magic power you got from the Devil. You can put 'nother hook on the back of the pitchfork and tie a cord to the knife and hang it on the hook in the back of that pitchfork. Then put that candle right up there in b'tween them branches and light it. Call to the Devil and the Devil will come. Ever-time you call the Devil in your rites, you want ta'use that pitchfork or stang. Some witches be place'n it in the north, but I like ta'put it right in the middle of the work'n space so when the Devil come, he's right in the middle of it all.

See now, there's someth'n else you can do with your pitchfork. It's a way ta'work your magic on someone or someth'n. You see, you can put a small wreath on it a few inches below the fork. Just fasten it on there with a hook or someth'n. Some witches like ta'decorate it for the seasons. Flowers in spring and summer, leaves in the fall, evergreen in the winter. But that's only ta'hide what the wreath is really for. The center of the wreath is a doorway ta'your target. What you do is you get yourself in that trance, in that daydream, and call the Devil's name. Then you allow your mind ta'be filled with thoughts of what magic you need ta'be do'n. A love spell on someone for somebody, ta'change a situation, or ta'change someone's mind; to do'n what you want 'em ta'be do'n. In the center of that there wreath, you'll want ta'see what you want ta'happen. See it as clear as day. If you're have'n trouble see'n what you want ta'see, ask the Devil for more power. Do the best you can, though. Even if you don't see what you want ta'see as clear as you like, the Devil can see what you want and that's good 'nuff. You'll be able ta'see more the more magic you do with the Devil. Now, you take that work'n knife and call the magic of the Devil and 'em spirits and send the energy ta'what you see in that center, what you want ta'happen. Say what you want ta'happen, "I call upon the spirit ta'do such and such in the Devil's name!"

Now listen here. Don't be tell'n folks what you be do'n in the Devil's name. They dunno what's what and they get to think'n all types of things. Keep your work'ns ta'yourself. Folks don't need ta'know stuff, and sometimes other witches are tricky and hide themselfs. You don't want ta'be give'n away all your secrets ta'folks and then hav'n 'em undo'n what you're do'n.

4

The Well

WAKE UP...

Wake up...

I thought I heard a whisper. But it wasn't no whisper. A voice called out ta'my heart. Ta'my soul. It woke me from a sound sleep. The night was 'specially quiet. I could feel a presence outside. Someone was out there. I could feel it in my bones. Noth'n scary. It was a feel'n like I was 'wake and dream'n at the same time. The feel'n you get when you know there's someth'n go'n on outside and you have ta'know what it is. I looked out the winda' and the full moon was make'n ever-thing real bright. The little farm was covered in a silvery glow, and you could see ever-thing real clear. I was look'n out my winda, and as sure as shit, I saw a woman dressed in white, carry'n a lantern, walk'n 'cross the yard. She looked like some kinda of faery woman, or maybe even a ghost. She knew I was there 'cause she turnt ta'look at me and gave me a smile. Then the woman in white started walk'n again.

I was in'erested in what the woman was do'n on my little farm. Why was she all the way over here? It was a little ways from town, and it made no sense that someone'd come all this way unless they wanted someth'n. It was the middle of the night and most of the town folk was 'fraid of their own shadow, and I wouldn't be 'spect'n no one come'n out this way, 'specially a woman all alone at night. I went outside ta'see what she was do'n here, and I followed her to the water well. Then she stepped up on the edge of that well hold'n her lantern and then she stepped in! My heart leaped outta my chest. Why on earth would someone come all the way over here ta'jump in my water well?

I ran over to the well and called out, "Are you a'right? Are you down there?" I din't hear anyth'n. Not a sound from that well. Only the wind and the sound of the cicadas sing'n in those trees nearby. I tried ta'look down in the well ta'see if I could see anyth'n, and all I could see was the pitch blackness of the dark in that well. The well was too deep ta'see the bottom. Then I felt someth'n tug on my shirt. I looked down ta'see a ghostly pale hand grab'n me. Then 'nother hand grabbed on ta'my shirt. Then 'nother hand, and 'nother hand, and 'nother hand. The ghostly hands was pull'n me down into the well. I fought back real hard. If I fell down that well, I'd never get back out. It was too deep ta'climb and no one would hear my shout'n. I grabbed onto the bricks of the well and pulled back 'gainst 'em ghostly hands. I used all my strength try'n ta'get gone. They was too strong. The hands pulled me into the well. I was fall'n.

I felt ma'self splash into the water in the well. I was able ta'stand up. The water only came ta'my waist. Not as deep as I was think'n it was gonna be. The ghostly hands was gone. I looked up to the top of the well and I could see the moonlight flow'n down into the well. Like the moon itself was try'n ta'light the way for me. To give me someth'n ta'hope for in the place where there ain't no hope.

I stood there in that well, wonder'n what I was gonna do. Maybe tomorrow or sometime someone would come by and hear my shouts for help. Or maybe I'd die in this well alone and no one was come'n. All was quiet and still. Someth'n grabbed my feet from under the water and pulled me down. The water seemed deeper now and I had ta'swim to the surface. I opened my eyes. I was not in the well anymore. I had somehow swimmt to a small pond somewhere deep in the woods.

I walked up on the little shore of the pond. There was a little path that led from the pond down to a hill. The light of the full moon made the path glow, and I could see it just fine. The air was cool, and the light of the moon had a humm'n sound like. Kinda like the moonlight had music or was play'n a song. I felt a pull ta'my heart ta'follow this path and see where it ended up. I shoulda been more 'fraid than I was, 'cause after all, I was taken here by a strange woman in white through a well, but I wasn't. Figured if I had the protection of the Devil then there wasn't much that could do me no harm here. The big question I had was *"where is here?"* I followed that glow'n path to the hill.

When I got to the base of the hill, there were a great big stone castle on top of it. Like the ones you see in 'em faery tale books or history books. When I got outta the pond, I din't see no castle on that hill, but it was there all a sudden. Maybe it appeared outta nowhere or maybe it was there the whole time and I wasn't pay'n no kinda attention on account how I was try'n ta'figure out where I was. I was notice'n there was geese sit'n up there on that castle. A lot of 'em, too. They was ever-where. On top of that castle, beside the walls, and even on the road that led to it. You could hear 'em honk'n and make'n all kinds of noise. Maybe they was notice'n I was there. Or maybe someth'n important was 'bout ta'happen.

There was a great big wooden door that was open, so I walked on through into the castle. The castle had torches light'n the way. I couldn't rightly tell if the castle itself was black, gray, blue, or any other color. It was like my mind couldn't latch on to it. I could see the bricks of the castle, but I couldn't set my mind on the color it was. Maybe it was all those colors, or maybe it was just too dark for me ta'tell what I was look'n at. I walked into what I was think'n was the throne room of the castle. There was a big wooden chair and sit'n in that chair was a woman, dressed like she was from long time ago. A big white dress that seemed new and ancient at the same time. She got up from her chair and walked over ta'where I was. She was beautiful and yet she left me feel'n like she was made from shadows. She smiled at me and said, "Welcome."

"How d'you do?" I said. I think she was a queen or someth'n live'n in that castle, but I still din't know what I was do'n up in there in the first place. Now'd I could see the queen more close, I think that she was the same woman who was dressed in white and who jumped in that well.

"My name's Johnathan," I told her. "What's your name?"

"My name is of the stars, the moon, and of the dead," she said.

Now, I thought that was the oddest way ta'introduce yourself ta'some-one. She looked at me with the most kind smile. Kinda like how Momma used ta'look at me sometimes. "I am Fate. The Weaver of all Things. And I am Keeper of the Dead. I am the Queen of Elphame." As soon as she said that her face done flashed into a skull. For a blink of an eye, her face looked to me like death. Horrible, horrible death. That startled the shit outta me and I jumped back right quick. Just as quick as I seen her face as a skull, her face changed back again to the beautiful queen. I tried ta'get ma'self settled again. I din't wanna seem rude to the queen, act'n scared of her, but I seen the Devil and she was a lot scarier than he is. A lot.

She wasn't bothered at all by me jump'n like a scardy cat. I guess she was used ta'folks be'n 'fraid of her. "I called you here because you are the son of the Devil and brother to the dead," she said. "You are born of the stars yet tempered by the flames of wisdom. You are a child of the mysteries and keeper of the earth."

When she said all this, it made no kinda sense, but after meet'n the Devil, there was a lot of things that I was get'n used to that din't used ta'make no sense. "Where am I?"

"You are in a place between places. A world that is not a world and is under all things," she said. "Some call this place Elphame. Others call it the spirit world. I call this place home, and one day so will you when you meet death. So will you."

I felt a dreadful cold come up over me. It was like those kinda colds that creep into your bones on a rainy fall afternoon. I could hear some rustl'n over in the shadows of that big throne room. My heart was tell'n me that there was other folks in the room with us. But I din't see nobody. All I could see was some movement of yonder in the shadows. It was s'dark in that castle I couldn't see too clearly. I 'membered what the Devil said: *"Look not with your eyes, but with your heart."* I let my heart feel what was over there. It felt like ghosts. It felt like whatever was over yonder had been dead a long time. Then I used my mind ta'imagine what I think the feel'ns looked like. As soon as I did that, I was able ta'see the shadows with my mind. They wasn't shadows at all. They was the spirits of folks long dead. I got the feel'n that this is where they came when they died. They came ta'live with the Queen of Elphame.

Now that's 'nother thing I came ta'learn when I became a witch. The pastors be say'n that when we die, we go ta'heaven or hell, but that's not the long or short of it. I was learn'n that when folks die they go ta'where they be want'n ta'go. If you want ta'go ta'heaven, you go ta'heaven, but for other folks, them might come ta'live with their ancestors with the Queen of the Dead, the Queen of Elphame.

"I am Mother of the Dead and caregiver of lost souls. Some know me as Fate, others know me as Frau Holda, Hella, or Perchta," the Queen of Elphame said. "Through me, you will learn the mysteries of death and the magic of the spirits."

She gestured with her hand towards my feet and right there I saw a big cauldron. I don't think that cauldron was there b'fore, but it surely was there now. The cauldron was a lot bigger than Momma's big cook'n pot. It was big and black, and I could feel a lot of power come'n off it.

"This is the Cauldron of Life and Death," the queen said. "It is the cauldron that brings forth life with the bounty of the earth and of Elphame, and yet it is also the doorway into the realm of the dead. Through this, you can create life and healing...and bring about the Shades of the Dead."

I put my hands on the rim of this big cauldron and looked in. All I could see was blackness. I couldn't even see the bottom of the cauldron. It was like I were stare'n into the blackest hole, or maybe even the darkest night.

The queen put her hands on the cauldron's rim. She looked into my eyes, maybe even my very soul, and said, "It is through my power you will see. It is through my power you will conjure."

The queen closed her eyes and took a long deep breath. I figured I was 'sposed ta'do what she was do'n. So, I closed my eyes and took a deep breath too. I could feel her try'n ta'join with my mind, heart, and spirit. I breathed her power into my heart. I took 'nother breath and breathed her power right into my body. Then I breathed a third breath and breathed her energy into my spirit. I opened my eyes and I looked right back down into the blackness of that cauldron. It was like I was look'n into the bottom of that deep well that I fell into. I kept breathe'n slowly. In my nose and out my mouth. I stayed connected to the queen and let ma'self start daydream'n a little. After all, see'n the spirit stuff is just like a daydream. Just like when your mind is wander'n from time ta'time. When you're look'n into the cauldron ta'see the past or the future, you gotta let yourself go into a daydream. Then you be see'n stuff you be need'n ta'see. I let my eyes get heavy like and still kept look'n into the blackness of the cauldron. I know the cauldron wasn't very deep, but I got the feel'n like I was look'n real deep. Like the bottom of the cauldron was as deep as the well. My eyes got kinda blurry, and almost felt like I was go'n cross-eyed or someth'n.

Then I started ta'see it. I started ta'see pitchurs and stuff. I saw pitchurs in my head. My daydream was try'n ta'show me someth'n. The vision was blurry at first. I wasn't sure what I was see'n in the begin'n. Then the images took shape in my mind. I was see'n the past. I saw images of Momma and Daddy when they was younger. I saw 'em deep in the woods. They was speak'n with someone robed but I couldn't see who it was none. Their face was hidden from me. Daddy shook the person's hand. I got a strong feel'n that a deal was be'n made. But who was this person? What was the deal that I never knew 'bout?

The next thing I saw in my vision was the present. I saw my own home. A knock on the door. A visitor. A gift. That gift'd allow me ta'see the others. Others? What was the gift and who's the others? S'many questions left, all 'cause of my vision. All a sudden, I was see'n the future. The pitchurs of the future din't make no kinda sense. I saw a sick child. I saw a ghost. Then I saw coins. None'a this made no sense.

The energy was start'n ta'go away and I disconnected from the vision. I thought to ma'self, *what was I see'n? What did it all mean?*

"There will be a time for all your questions," the queen said. It was like she's able ta'read my thoughts in my head. Or maybe I looked like I was real confused or someth'n. "For now, you must find a cauldron such as my own. You must consecrate it to the old Gods, the ancestors, and the spirits of the land. Only then will you be able to use my sacred vessel for your magic."

I din't know noth'n 'bout no cauldron or where ta'get one. At least, noth'n like the one the Queen of Elphame had. I did have Momma's big cook'n pot. We din't have much at the house, but we had that cook'n pot. That pot Momma used for almost all our meals. That and the little iron stove we had. I could be us'n that for my cauldron. I think that cook'n pot would be just fine for a cauldron. I had ta'remember that if I was gonna work magic with the cook'n pot, then I needed ta'think 'bout the Queen of Elphame and connect ta'her like I was do'n now. The Queen of Elphame had power and I knew in my heart, in my gut, that the best way ta'be see'n somet'n in the cook'n pot or do some conjure'n was ta'call her name and bring her power into my heart. I dunno how I knew all that. Maybe the queen'd gone and put that thought in my mind, or maybe just be'n a witch you be know'n stuff like that. Either way, I was gonna do what the queen was say'n.

"Peer into the cauldron once more," The Queen of Elphame said ta'me. So, I did what she said and looked into the cauldron again. Maybe there was more visions that she wanted me ta'see. I put both my hands on the rim ta'steady ma'self and looked in.

"Closer," she said. "Look deep within the darkness. So deep that only your heart may see."

I did what she told me ta'do and I leaned over that big cauldron of hers. I felt a bony hand grab onto my neck and start push'n me down. I quickly turnt my head 'round ta'see what monstrosity was forc'n my head down into the cauldron and the Queen of Elphame, beautiful and fair, had turnt into a gruesome ghoul. Her face was rotted like an old body that'd been dug up long after she had been laid ta'rest in a grave.

I fought as hard as I could ta'get gone from this skeleton woman. *What the hell?! What was go'n on?!* I struggled and struggled and I could not get gone. I looked back into the cauldron ta'see what on earth was in there she wanted me ta'see and a rott'n corpse came at me from the blackness of that cauldron and grabbed on ta'me! That damn thing had too much strength. In the blink of an eye, I was pulled into the cauldron. Deep into blackness.

I opened my eyes. I was lay'n on the ground...somewhere.

Where'n the hell was I?

I wasn't hurt.

What happened?

I felt the cold earth under me. Seems like I fell down someth'n. Like a shaft or 'nother well. Or...someth'n. I wasn't hurt none, but I was feel'n dizzy. I picked ma'self up off that cold ground and stood up. I was in a big cave or cavern or someth'n. There was a big lake in front of me and a island in the middle of it. Or maybe it was 'nother land. I din't know what it was. Then I heard it...

Behind me there was someth'n move'n in them shadows. I stood there for a minute, wonder'n what in hell was go'n on, and then I could see it...or I should say...I saw *them*...Out of the shadows come corpses. Corpses who was walk'n towards me. I ain't never seen noth'n like that b'fore! I got this dark feel'n in the pit of my stomach. This was not a good place ta'be, and them corpses was come'n. I thought there's only a couple'a them, but as they started walk'n outta the shadows, I could see more and more of 'em. At first, I thought there was only a few, but then I could see there was hundr'ds! Hundr'ds!

Shit!

What the hell was I gonna do?!

"This way!" I heard a voice say. "Come this way if you want to live!"

I turnt 'round towards the lake and yonder was a man in a little boat at the shore. "What's taking you so long?" the man asked. "Hurry up!"

I din't see the man in the boat b'fore, but this wasn't no time ta'be ask'n questions. I ran over to the man and got in the boat. The corpses ran to the shore and was get'n closer ta'us over in the boat. The man rowed as fast as he could, but them corpses was still coming! They was gonna get us if we din't get the hell outta there!

"Row faster!" I yelled.

"I'm going, I'm going." the man said as he rowed out into the lake.

The corpses kept come'n but they was soon swallowed up by the dark waters of the lake. I guess they can't swim. But I'm guess'n they don't need no air ta'breathe neither, so they's prob'ly still down there under that water, walk'n 'round or someth'n.

"Don't put your hands in the water," the boatman said. "Corpses are known to grab on to you and pull you under."

This was the craziest shit. *What the hell?* I kept my hands to ma'self as the boatman rowed us to the other side of the shore. I felt the boat hit the ground and the boatman said, "Here we are. I'll accept payment now."

Damn it. "I don't have anyth'n ta'pay you with."

"You can pay me later," he said. "When you go to the well or to the shore of a river or lake, place two coins in the water and know the payment goes to me."

"I will."

With that, the boatman rowed off away and dis'ppeared into that darkness of the lake in the cavern.

Now where the hell was I? I asked ma'self. I started walk'n on this here island. It wasn't dark at all. In fact, there was no fires, no lamps, no torches, and the island was still all lit up like. Like it was glow'n or someth'n. There was this path lead'n deep into a fog that was surround'n the island. It was the strangest thing. The fog was s'thick, I wasn't sure where I was or where I was go'n. I walked on that path anyhow. I was listen'n ta'my gut and my gut said I should keep follow'n this path. I was feel'n it had ta'go somewhere, but after the fall'n in the cauldron and be'n chased by corpses, I wasn't sure if this was a place I wanted ta'go.

After a bit of walk'n, the fog cleared up a bit and I could see this mighty big dark building. It was like a castle or a fortress or someth'n. But this castle was differ'nt than the Queen of Elphame's castle. This castle was old as hell and was fall'n apart. It looked like someone just left it 'bandoned long ago and no one never came back. Its walls was crumbl'n down and there wasn't noth'n but darkness here. This was a lonely place. Someone in their right mind woulda left, but I knew I was 'sposed ta'be here. I knew I was 'sposed ta'go inside this awful place. I walked up to the big door. There wasn't no door handle, and far as I could tell, there was no way ta'open'n it. I was wonder'n what the hell I was gonna do. I was sent ta'this great big castle for a reason, and I was hope'n it was a good reason. But with ever-thing that's been happen'n the last couple'a weeks, I wasn't sure anymore. It felt like I was stand'n at that big door for a long time. I pounded on the door but there wasn't no answer. I pounded again. Nuth'n. *Fuck it.* I was leave'n.

I turnt ta'go back down that path ta'see what else I could find in this strange place, and that's when I heard the creak'n noise. The door was open'n and it was loud as hell. I guess someone was there after all. I went inside and it was like I 'spected it ta'be. Like the inside of a big castle, lit up with candles and torches. The castle was real big. Huge. The great hallway when you walk in went on for miles it seemed, and the ceil'n was the highest ceil'n I've ever saw. I started walk'n down the big hallway and was hope'n whoever was here would come out soon, 'cause I ain't never been in a place like this and I din't know where I was go'n.

All a sudden, I was in a big room with a real big wooden table. It was long and had lots of chairs 'round it. There was food on the table, but I had the feel'n this food was for the dead.

"Sit." a woman said from the shadows.

The voice echoed in the big halls of the 'ole castle. I pulled out a chair and waited for the woman ta'come out. After a minute or two, a woman hidden 'neath a dark cloak came outta the shadows. She pulled back her hood and it was that skeleton lady who was push'n me in that cauldron from b'fore. I din't say noth'n. I wasn't 'bout ta'say noth'n.

"Welcome to the Land of the Dead," she said. Her face was a skeleton, but I got the odd feel'n that this was the Queen of Elphame again. It was a woman with noth'n but a skull and no face, but I had this know'n that this was 'nother face of the Queen of Elphame. In my mind, I kept see'n the beautiful face of the queen, but my eyes saw noth'n but a bone lady.

"Are you the Queen of Elphame?" I asked. It had ta'be her. It was her! I think...

"I am known as Fate. I am Hella. I am Holda. I am the Queen of the Dead and of Life." I wasn't understand'n what she was say'n. I guess she was both. Maybe she's the Queen of Elphame and Queen of the Dead. I din't know what she meant by "Fate" though. Maybe she could change a person' fate. Or maybe she was the one you was call'n when you wanted ta'see your own fate.

"I am Johnathan Knotbristle," I learnt you need ta'introduce yourself ta'all the spirits; good, bad, or otherwise. You don't want ta'be offend'n nobody, and you never know who was gonna get their britches in a knot for not be'n polite. Remember what I said, don't go piss'n no spirits off and you don't have ta'worry 'bout spirits come'n after ya.

She looked at me with her boney face. "I've known you in dreams. You have been dreaming of me throughout the ages."

B'fore I could figure out what she as talk'n 'bout, I heard someth'n move'n 'round. I looked behind me, and there was bone men bring'n in food for the dead and sett'n it on the table. They was dressed in fine clothes but they was bone men. Men who was noth'n but bones. I tried ta'steady ma'self and act like none'a this bothered me. "Why did you bring me here?"

"This is the home of the beloved dead. A place of healing and warmth. A place of love," she said.

All I could see in this lifeless place was darkness, shadow, and them skeleton men that wandered these here great halls of her castle. It was cold and lifeless. It din't make no sense. "Heal'n? Warmth? There's only darkness here. And death."

"You see the profane," she 'splained ta'me. "Your eyes deceive you. You only see this place as shadow because you fear death. You fear the grave and the end of things. You forget your dead after you place them into the earth." She leaned forward and I could feel her cold black eye sockets in her skull look'n deep into my heart. "You abandon your dead to the cold earth, and it is I who embraces them and give them a loving home here with me. The dead are forever in my care. They love me and I love them. Forever."

I sat there on that wooden chair try'n ta'understand what she was talk'n 'bout. She was right. I understood death, but I was 'fraid of it. I wasn't ready ta'die, and I wasn't ready for Momma, Daddy, or my brothers ta'die. I don't think die'n is like they say in church, with angels and Jesus come'n ta'get ya, but I know it's a bad, horrible thing. Someth'n we want ta'avoid if we can. Seems like there's always someth'n try'n ta'kill us somehow. The world is hard and then we die and there seems like there ain't no sense ta'any of it. But for right then, in that place, I was surrounded by death. It seemed a'right right then 'cause the Queen of Death was there. I figure if she was protect'n them dead folks then she'd be protect'n me. I hope.

"As you walk upon the crooked path of the witch, you will learn the mystery of the dead, and through the shadows you will learn to live," the Queen of the Dead said. "When the time comes to face the dead, do not be afraid. Find your power, your true self, within your heart and face death not with fear, but with love."

I opened my eyes, and I was back home in my bed. It was morn'n and the sun was come'n up. Birds was chirp'n and I wasn't sure what time it was. Hell, I wasn't sure what day it was. I sat there in my bed wonder'n what'd happened ta'me. It was a dream. All a dream. I was becom'n more 'wake and come'n ta'my senses. Was it real or was it noth'n but a dream? Well, if them daydreams are real, then I guess my nighttime dreams are real too.

5

The Full Moon

AS THE WEEKS PASSED, I was start'n ta'get used ta'life as it was. I was work'n at the market with Mr. Picklesworth and that was go'n a'right. I did my daily chores and he paid me once a week. Folks would see me work in that little store, and after a while, they must have figured I was a'right 'cause they quit say'n stuff 'bout me. Or at least noth'n ever got back ta'me that folks was say'n stuff n'more. It was like s'long as the town folk saw me work'n hard and keep'n outta trouble, then no one had no reason ta'be think'n anyth'n was wrong. I think there would always be someone who din't trust me 'cause they thought I was cursed, or that my family died 'cause we wasn't godly 'nuff. Folks is always say'n someth'n anyhow, so I don't pay much mind, but I like it just fine if I din't have ta'worry much 'bout folks say'n stuff 'bout me.

I got to think'n. Everyth'n seemed ta'get better when I met the Devil. My life got better. I wasn't cast'n no spells, 'cept ta'get this here job at the market. I only did it the one time, and I 'spose I would do more spells if I needed it. It seemed like ever-thing was go'n the way it was 'sposed to. Maybe 'cause of the Devil. Maybe he made ever-thing a'right. Well, whatever it was, I wasn't gonna be argue'n 'bout it. Long as ever-thing worked out, it was gonna be fine.

I got the pitchfork and Momma's cook'n pot, just like the spirits told me ta'do. Well, when I say "spirits," I mean the Devil and the Queen of Elphame. I still think the Queen of Elphame and the Queen of the Dead is one and the same. But I guess it don't matter much. If I need ta'talk to the Queen of Elphame, then I'll talk to the Queen of Elphame. If I need ta'talk to the Queen of the Dead, then I'll talk to the Queen of the Dead. Either way, s'long as it works, it don't matter much ta'me. Anyhow, I got ever-thing set up like the spirits'd told me. I put the pitchfork on one side of the fireplace and Momma's cook'n pot on the other. It's been real quiet the last couple'a weeks. That's a'right by me.

Now'd it's October, the leaves is turn'n all sorts of colors. With fall, it seems like things are change'n and the cool air gets folks all move'n, get'n ready for winter. Folks is harvest'n their crops now and sell'n the extras to the market or to their neighbors. Some folks be put'n stuff in jars. I get ever-thing I need from the market. I'll harvest the crop Daddy and me and my brothers planted last spring. It won't be much, but if I jar some of it, I'll be fine this winter. I hope. This'll be my first winter by ma'self. Mr. Picklesworth gives me some money off at the general store, so things don't be cost'n me s'much. I think he's start'n ta'like me. He'd never say that though. So, I got ever-thing I need. I guess if anyth'n happens this winter, I'll call to the Devil like I was told ta'do.

The full moon that year in October came on a Sund'y. The day was the same as any other Sund'y. The town folk go ta'church and then go home and have their Sund'y supper. Not much happens here on a Sund'y. Matter fact, not much happens any other day neither. I go ta'church ever-Sund'y with ever-body, and this seems ta'make folks feel a little easier 'round me. I 'spose they think a man who goes ta'church and listens to the gospels ain't got much a mind ta'do no harm ta'nobody. Well, they dunno I was talk'n to the spirits though. I can't be tell'n 'em things like that. That'll scare their good Christian hearts. Plus, you have ta'remember, simple folks be think'n in simple ways. They listen to the pastor and that's good 'nuff for 'em. I heard a man say once that "complicated things lead ta'complicated life." I 'spose he was right 'bout that.

After church, I went home like I do ever-Sund'y. I made my own Sund'y supper just fine. Wasn't too fancy, but it was good 'nuff. The whole day I was feel'n someth'n quite odd. Like my bones was try'n ta'tell me someth'n. Now ever-body in this here town knows that the full moon has spirits and things of that nature. The pastor be say'n that s'long as you pray and have faith in Jesus, then you ain't got noth'n ta'worry 'bout. Most folks, I think, are of sound mind and don't pay attention ta'old superstitions. No one thinks witches are fly'n in the air no more. But still, there's this feel'n I been feel'n all day. Someth'n ain't quite right.

When night came, I lit my oil lanterns and was read'n some books. Mr. Picklesworth'd gave me some books that he said he din't want no more, and if I din't take 'em home, he was just gonna throw 'em away anyhow and I might as well take 'em ta'avoid him the hassle of throw'n 'em out hisself. I was read'n one'a them books and I heard the wind pick up a little. Maybe a storm was com'n. I went over to the windas and made sure that they was latched. They was locked good and tight. They won't be bang'n if a storm comes real quick. Even though the windas was locked down, I had a bad feel'n. Like someth'n was gonna happen. You know that feel'n you get when you're know'n someth'ns gonna happen? When you feel it in your bones? That feel'n s'strong in your heart, it goes clear down to the bone? That's what I was feel'n that night.

I stood there look'n out that winda' into the night. The tree branches was shake'n mighty terrible. Like a giant was just shak'n away at 'em. I could see that full moon shine'n bright outside. Them clouds out there was mov'n real fast. Too fast. I tell you what. I never saw no clouds move s'fast. Not ever. I figured I best be stay'n away from that winda'. A branch could come off one'a them trees and slam right into the winda'.

All a sudden, the wind stopped. It din't die down. It just...stopped. I thought that was the strangest thing. I stood there, wait'n for someth'n ta'happen. I dunno what, but someth'n. That's when I heard it...

Tap

Tap

Tap

What inna hell? I said to ma'self. That wasn't no tree branch hit'n that winda'. Someone was out there. I went over and looked out that winda'. I din't see noth'n. Even though the full moon was out, it was dark as hell. The clouds was cover'n that moon so there wasn't much light shine'n down. It was dark as hell.

Tap

Tap

Tap

Damn it! Who inna hell is out there? I was get'n kinda scared. I dunno why. When you is follow'n the Devil, ain't noth'n scares you s'much nomore. But for some reason, I was kinda worried 'bout what was outside. "You best be get'n the hell outta here!" I yelled. I was a bit nervous. Ain't no one never come out this way in the middle of the night unless they had to. Someth'n wasn't right. Through the winda', I thought I saw a faint outline of a woman. I could kinda see her, but at the same time, I couldn't. It was almost like she was there and not there at the same time. When I done saw the Devil and the Queen of Elphame, I saw 'em clear as day. This was someth'n differ'nt. Someth'n strange. I went over to the front door ta'make sure it was locked. *Damn it!* It wasn't locked. I swore I locked that door just like I do ever-night. Tonight, it was unlocked! How the hell could that be? Did someone unlock it from the inside or am I lose'n my mind?

As soon as I was 'bout ta'lock the door, someone pushed it open. I quickly pushed it back shut. Whoever was on the other side was try'n ta'push it open again. It took all of my strength ta'keep whoever was push'n on this door out. I was push'n real hard. As hard as I could. Then they overpowered me. The door came a fly'n open and three women on brooms came fly'n in my house. They knocked me to the floor and I hit it hard. A little too hard. The fly'n women laughed like they'd lost they damn minds. Like they was mad. *Crazy as hell!*

"Get the hell outta my house!" I yelled. "In the Devil's name, get outta my house!"

"In the Devil's name!" the women laughed at me like that was the silliest thing they'd ever heard. "We are *here* in the Devil's name!"

As I was lay'n on the floor, try'n ta'recover my wits, one'a the women jumped on top of me, straddl'n me.

"It's time you come with us and join the sabbat!"

"Get off me!" I yelled, try'n ta'swat her off me.

She was strong as hell. "The Devil has called you forth and you do not listen."

"Get the hell off me!"

She looked deep into my eyes. I could feel her gaze penetrate'n my heart. For a minute, I was wonder'n why it was when a spirit be look'n at you, it's always in your heart; in your soul. She leaned down ta'my ear. "You are one of us now. The Devil calls you to the sabbat. You don't want to disappoint him, do you?" And then with that, she leaped off me and the three women flew outta my house on their brooms.

My front door slammed shut.

My kitchen broom fell and slammed on the wooden floor. I got up off the floor and brushed ma'self off. Damn, them women was strong. *What the hell just happened?* I saw my kitchen broom on the floor. That was the craziest thing. After I calmed down a little, I got to think'n 'bout that full moon. Maybe the Devil was call'n me. I figured I was 'sposed ta'join 'em at the sabbat. Superstitious folks be talk'n 'bout witches on the full moon. Maybe the Devil was call'n me ta'some full moon ritual. I wasn't quite sure what I was 'sposed ta'do. How would I get to the witch's sabbat? How could I fly like them women? I figure you can't just grab any 'ole broom and jump on like it's a horse or someth'n. There had ta'be more to it.

I think Old Henry might be know'n what ta'do. I took the cat skull outta the box and lit the candle that I was use'n just for Old Henry. When I lit that candle, Henry knew that it was time for him ta'come out. Also,

Henry said that he likes the energy of the candle flame. He said ever-time I light the flame, the power of the flame feeds him. He also has me feed him whiskey or beer from time ta'time, too. Keep'n Henry well fed and happy has been real good for me. Whenever I need someth'n, I just light the candle and he come. So I lit that candle and said, "Old Henry, Old Henry, I call to thee, Old Henry Old Henry, I summon thee. Old Henry, Old Henry come ta'me."

"It's time for the full moon, isn't it?" Henry said from behind me. He likes ta'do that. Whenever I summon Henry, he never appears in front of me. I dunno why he does that. These spirits seem ta'really like ta'be sneak'n up on me.

"I was visited by three women," I told Henry. "Witches, I 'spose."

"Indeed, they are." Henry seemed real excited by this. "The Devil has called you to the sabbat. You mustn't keep the Old One waiting." He saw the broom still lay'n on the floor. "I see you have your broom. Let us be going."

Hmmm. I wasn't know'n how ta'be ride'n no broom ta'no sabbat on the full moon. I've seen Halloween drawings of witches on fly'n on broom sticks on a full moon, but I never thought noth'n 'bout it. Well, not 'til now. I guess it is true. I've been notice'n that some things that the town folk say 'bout witches are mostly untrue, but some things is true. Maybe this is one'a the true things. "How do I use the broom ta'get to the sabbat?"

"Oh, that's easy!" Henry said. "You travel to the sabbat in spirit. You must leave your physical body and allow your spirit to fly to where the witches meet."

Where the witches meet? Well, wherever witches be meet'n, it had ta'be both wonderful and strange. "Where's that?"

"On a mountain. On a beach. In a church yard. In a cemetery." Henry answered.

I was still confused. Where was I go'n and how do I get there?

"You see," Henry said, "to get to the sabbat, you must use the broom to wisp you away. The broom will aid you in taking flight in spirit form. Take the broom and hold it right-side up, as if you were about to sweep the floor. You can sit in a chair or lie down on the floor. Place the broom between your legs. Allow the bristles to touch the floor. When the bristles of the broom touch the floor, they pull up the energy of the earth. This gives it a type of energy or fuel that will help carry you to the sabbat. Grab onto the broom handle with both hands. Then place the broom handle on your forehead between your eyes. Close your eyes and imagine that the broom is taking your spirit away from your physical body. In your imagination, see the broom take your spirit into the air."

I did what Old Henry said. I picked up the broom and sat ma'self on the chair next to the fireplace. I held it with both hands with the bristles touch'n the floor. I placed that handle on my head b'tween my eyes. I took some deep breaths. I took some more deep breaths, and 'magined that as I was doi'n that, I was breathe'n in the energy of the earth, the energy was fill'n the broom with magic. I kept on breathe'n that earth magic into the broom. After a few breaths, I felt the broom start ta'get real hot like. It was the power fill'n up the broom. When I figured the broom was filled with energy, I 'magined that the broom was help'n me leave my body. I'd seen ma'self rise up from my body in my 'magination and I was float'n in the air.

"Splendid!" Old Henry said with excitement. "Now you can leave through the window or a door, but it might be better if we leave through the fireplace."

"We?" Henry rarely went anywhere with me. The only time I've seen him leave my house is if I be need'n him ta'do someth'n for me. "Are you come'n with me?"

"Oh yes! When the Devil calls, one must not keep him waiting," Henry changed hisself into a bird. I'd never seen him do that b'fore. "Through the fireplace!"

I had never left my body b'fore. It was the strangest feel'n. I was fly'n over my body on this here broom and I felt light as a feather. At the same time, I was in spirit with my broom, and I was feel'n my physical body, too. Like I was in two places at once. I could feel my physical body, but I was also fly'n at the same time. I was wonder'n if I was do'n it right. Was

I 'sposed ta'feel my physical body at all or was I 'sposed ta'be concentrat'n on my spirit body? "I can feel my physical body. Is that right?"

"Oh yes," Henry said. "You see, your body and brain are still functioning as normal. It's only your spirit that is leaving your body. You will be aware of your physical body. Don't worry, the more you practice flying in the spirit, the more you will feel safe enough to focus only on your spirit. As of right now, your physical body needs to feel safe, so an aspect of your awareness remains with your physical body. I suppose this allows you to remain safe enough to allow your spirit to leave. If anything goes wrong or you are in danger in the physical realm, you will be aware of it and can return to your physical body any time you like."

As strange as all this sounded, it did make me feel a little better. I can fly to the witch's sabbat but I can also return home at any time if I be need'n to.

"Allow me to lead the way." Henry, in his bird form, flew up the chimney and into the night. Us'n my mind, my 'magination, I followed him. Henry flew higher and higher into the sky. The full moon was shine'n real bright right now, and the light was s'bright it looked almost like it was daytime. Well, almost. That moon was s'big and s'round I felt like I could reach up and grab some of that moonlight and take it home with me. That moon made me feel real powerful like. Magical. I was in a deep trance and wide 'wake at the same time. Right 'bout then, I was aware of other witches fly'n in the night sky. I couldn't really see 'em, but I knew they was there. I figured they was go'n to the witch's sabbat, too. Maybe I'd see 'em there.

We flew and flew and flew. I had no idea how long we was flying. All I knew is that Old Henry was lead'n the way, and I figured he knew where he was going. I certainly din't. I was real happy I had a guide like Henry. I din't know what I would do without him. In the clouds in the distance, I could see a mountain top. I dunno where or what mountain this was, but it was surely a mountain. There was no mountains where I'm from, so this had ta'be far, far away. How fast was we going? I dunno, but fly'n in spirit must be real fast if we was fly'n to a mountain that was s'far off.

Old Henry flew down to the mountain and I followed. As we landed on that mountain, I could see what looked to me like campfires. There was lots and lots of campfires. I sat my broom down on the ground and walked over to the light of the campfires. I was hear'n drumbeats in the distance. Henry turnt hisself back into a person and led the way. As we got closer to the fires, I saw folks dance'n, drum'n, and play'n music. Some folks had fiddles while other folks had bells and others had small drums. Ever-body was sing'n. The songs was more like chants than any songs I'd ever heard. I don't even think they was in English. I wasn't too good with folks talk'n from other countries. There was some folk who once moved into town from Germ'ny, but the language they was speak'n din't sound noth'n like that. "What language is that?"

Henry smiled, "That's a spirit tongue."

"What's a spirit tongue?" I was real confused 'bout what he was talk'n 'bout.

"A spirit tongue is a language that is spoken by the spirits and magical folk. It's a language that is not found on earth spoken by humans. To speak a spirit tongue is to open yourself to the magical energies of the spirits. Great spells are cast using the spirit tongue."

I was real in'erested in this idea of spirit tongue. I was wonder'n what kinda power spirit tongues'd give you. What'd happen if you casted you a spell with a spirit tongue? "Can you teach me?"

"I can introduce you to someone who can." Henry led me into the center of the festivities. Ever-one was hav'n lots of fun dance'n and sing'n in their spirit tongue. There was folks eat'n some good food, too. There was a strange thing 'bout all this. I was wonder'n...if I was in spirit, then was ever-one else in spirit too? And if we was all in spirit, then how could they be eat'n food and ever-thing else that was go'n on?

I couldn't tell how long we was there. It seemed like it was just a minute and at the same time it felt like we'd been there for hours. There was so much go'n on, I couldn't keep up with it all. There was s'much hustle'n and bustle'n. Folks come'n and go'n and what not. It also seemed like there was folks from all 'round the world. Or at least places I ain't never been. There was both men and women dressed in plain ever-day clothes, but then I saw folks with strange hats and gowns and things like that. Maybe they was in spirit from other countries. Or maybe they was folks from the past, or even the future. We was in a strange place of spirit, so you can never be tell'n what's what.

After a while, there was a great hush that fell over ever-body. It was seem'n like someth'n important was 'bout ta'happen. All the dance'n and chant'n stopped and ever-one gathered in a big circle. There was a mighty big bonfire that was lit in the middle of the circle. Then folks carry'n drums walked over to the great fire. They started drum'n again. This was the most beautiful and enchant'n music I ever done heard. The drumbeats vibrated in such a way that I was feel'n like I was float'n on water. The music seemed ta'speak ta'my heart and my very soul. Ever-one began ta'shake and sway a little bit. Like we was all float'n in a stream and the water was tak'n us away ta'someplace magical.

Then the great bonfire became real bright and got even bigger. The fire was s'bright, for just a minute it looked as if it was day. Then, step'n outta the flame, it was the Devil hisself. He looked a little differ'nt from both the times I'd saw him before. He was in his form of the Old One. The Horned God of the witches. The Devil. He walked outta 'em flames like he was walk'n through a door. Maybe he come from hell or maybe he come from the Otherworld. Either way, it din't seem ta'matter ta'nobody anyhow. When we saw the Devil, we was overcome with joy. Our hearts was filled with s'much love that some of us was in tears. Others placed their hands over their heart and enjoyed the love they was feel'n. The Devil started dance'n ta'that drumbeat. He started move'n and turn'n and shake'n and sway'n. The other witches started dance'n in a big circle 'round him. I'd like ta'say I joined in the dance, but I din't join. As I watched those witches dance 'round the Devil, my heart was connect'n with 'em. I was connect'n ta'those witches like I'd known 'em my whole life. You know someth'n? Maybe I was know'n them witches my whole life. And maybe I knew 'em from other lives. In this place of the witch's sabbat, it din't seem ta'matter. We was all connected, and we was all joined...in magic.

As the witches danced, I was filled with a joy that took hold of me. I had s'much joy in my heart and b'fore I knew it, I was dance'n too.

Now, you gotta know, ta'get me dance'n is someth'n special. I ain't never danced, and that was fine by me. But them drums and that sing'n! Someth'n took me like I was possessed by the Devil hisself. I dunno how long the dance lasted. Like I said, time was strange here and it din't seem ta'matter ta'nobody much. We danced 'til I couldn't dance no more. We danced 'til my legs was gonna break off, and my heart was beat'n s'hard it felt like it was gonna beat right out my chest. I never wanted the dance ta'end. I managed ta'break free from the dance'n that compelled you ta'dance, too. I walked over yonder ta'where I saw 'nother campfire, much smaller than the main bonfire, a'course. There I saw ma'self a small group of witches. There was four of 'em sit'n 'round that fire, talk'n in that spirit tongue I had heard. They seemed friendly 'nuff.

"Mind if I join you?" I asked.

"Of course," the older of the four said. "We would love to have you. Please sit down. My name is Alma."

"Johnathan." I replied.

Alma gestured over to the other three witches, "These are my coven mates; Clara, Harriet, and Viola." Clara was middle-aged and was wear'n her a bright purple dress. Harriet was younger'n the rest and wore red. Viola wore green. They each looked like they was from long ago; from a time that wasn't a time. A place that wasn't a place. Look'n at 'em, I couldn't help but to be reminded of my little brother's book, *Mother Goose*. Their dress seemed two hundr'd years old, yet as new as the rise'n sun. I felt at ease with 'em. I felt like I've known 'em for quite some time, and yet they was strangers. I'm learn'n that with the magic of the witch, the strangeness is what is normal. It's what folks think is normal that I find odd.

"The language you are speaking. Is that a spirit tongue I was hear'n 'bout?" I asked.

"There are many spirit tongues," Alma said. "This one is the language of the spirits that we work with in our magical practice. This is the language we use to summon our spirits and ask them to do magic for us."

"Yes!" Harriet spoke up. "It's the spirits that do the greater works of magic." Harriet was full'a energy, and it seemed as though ever-thing was fun ta'her. Ever-thing was excite'n. She reminded me of those folks who never care 'bout no consequences. But them folks usually knew what they was do'n, or they was reckless. I din't know Harriet, so I couldn't be tell'n which of 'em she was yet. She gave me a sly look, "I can see that you already have spirits at your beck and call, don't you?"

I din't know how ta'answer that. Where I'm from, I would never talk 'bout magic or witchcraft with nobody. I kept quiet 'bout anyth'n I did with the spirits. I just looked at her without say'n nothin'.

"Oh, leave him be," Viola said. "He's new. The Devil will teach him things he needs to know."

Alma looked deep into my eyes, "Would you like to know how to call to the spirits in the spirit tongue?"

"Yes, I would." I said, try'n not ta'sound too excited.

"It's very simple," Alma said. "Close your eyes for a moment and take some nice deep breaths. Relax your thoughts and your mind. Take some more deep breaths and connect to the energies around you. Connect to the land. Connect to the stars above. Feel the energies in your body, and as you breathe in, allow yourself to go into a light trance. You have been in a trance before, right? It's like a daydream. When you start thinking about other things. Imagine what a trance feels like, and as you take each breath, allow the energies to take you deeper and deeper into a trance."

I did 'zactly what Alma said. I 'membered the feel'n I got once after a summer rain. I was stand'n in the barn, watch'n the rain come down, and I could smell them trees and that loamy ground 'neath my feet. Everyth'n was refreshed and smelled like the earth itself. I 'member that feel'n bring'n me to a daydream. A daydream that had me think'n I was connected ta'that smell of rain and earth. I breathed that feel'n in, just like Alma'd done said. Then I 'membered one time when I was look'n up at the stars at night. I had just had a glass of whiskey, and for the first time in a long time, I was relaxed and was do'n noth'n but look'n up at them stars. Them stars was out in the cosmos somewhere, giv'n light. Things come and go, but them stars was always there with a certain kinda magic all their own. I connected my heart ta'those stars, and I felt ma'self a power, a energy, all through ma'self. I 'membered that feel'n of those stars and breathed the stars into my body. Then, as

I breathed, I was all relaxed like. The more I breathed in those feel'ns of the earth and the stars, the more deeper I went into a trance. It felt like I was get'n hypnotized or someth'n.

Alma saw me go'n deeper and deeper into a trance. "Good. Now focus on your heart. Feel the energies of the stars and the land coursing through your body and feel them balance at your heart. Now, speak. Don't speak in English or some common language. Say syllables, sounds. Say consonants and vowels. Don't worry about making sense. The spirits will know what you are saying."

I started ta'make noises. "*Wa wa wa, bo bo bo, go de te che, may gay fay lay.*"

"Excellent!" Alma seemed happy, so guess I was do'n it right. "Don't correct yourself. Take the sounds you make and experiment with different sounds and pretend words."

I kept breathe'n in the energies of the stars and land so I wouldn't be lose'n the trance. So Alma was tell'n me not ta'make words that make sense and ta'put consonants and vowels together, make'n up 'maginary words. "*Wa bo go che may lay. Su bo ko foozl lay te.*"

"He's doing it!" Clara seemed real happy for me. "Sisters! Let's join him!"

The four witches started say'n 'maginary words with me. None'a them made no kinda sense or had mean'n ta'me, but I could hear all four of 'em speak'n their whole other secret language.

"*Keta lo wanna may dia que le*"

"*Fo muta nay lay gonnonna me le way*"

"*Haya me say chelay may tonna nay*"

"*Hi incha may sikka lippo wanna*"

As I was in my trance, I couldn't right tell who was say'n what words. I din't care. It was helpful ta'hear 'em speak'n their spirit tongue while I be I practice'n mine. We said the 'maginary words all at the same time, so I wasn't that embarrassed ta'say my spirit words. They said don't worry 'bout what I was say'n, but it's hard ta'be self-aware of what you is try'n ta'do. I tried real hard ta'just focus on my heart and let the energy course through my veins. I kept say'n the 'maginary words over and over again. Myself and them four witches said them spirit words louder and louder. I could feel the energy 'round us becom'n filled with power. I opened my eyes and I saw the strangest, happiest thing. There was spirit creatures fly'n all 'round us. The spirits was in all shapes and sizes. Some looked all whimsical and silly like, while others looked downright serious and frighten'n. Some of the spirits looked like perhaps they'd be live'n in nature, while others looked as if they was from a far-off place, ain't never seen by humans. Them spirits was ride'n the energy that we called up with our spirit language.

"Now that the spirits are here," Alma said, "what do we want to ask of them?"

"We never call the spirits without having a purpose," said Harriet.

I couldn't think of anyth'n I wanted the spirits ta'do for me. I'm sure I could'a thought of someth'n later, but right now I was put on the spot, and I wasn't sure what ta'ask of 'em.

"I'm sure there's something you need," Clara said.

"Some deep desire you never allow yourself to wish for?" Viola clearly'd saw right into my heart. There was a desire I had.

I din't say anyth'n for a second. I was try'n not ta'be embarrassed at the desire I was ask'n for. "I want the town folk ta'like me. Ta'not be scared of me. Not ta'treat me like I'm cursed."

"Don't tell me," Alma said, "tell the spirits. And tell them in the spirit tongue."

Quickly, I took ma'self a deep breath and brought back ta'mind the trance those witches'd taught me. I connected to the stars and the land and then focused on my heart. I tried my hardest ta'let go my fears of sound'n dumb or stupid. I focused on the energy of them spirits and allowed 'maginary words ta'come outta my mouth from the heart. When I was say'n them spirit words, I was 'magine'n that ever-body in town was like'n me. "*Teka miya wa doya de mi monna mekka delayjo whatechio.*"

And with that, the spirits dis'ppeared.

It was mighty quieter now. The witch's sabbat was still go'n. The witches was dance'n in the circle 'round the great big bonfire and the Devil was have'n his fun, dance'n with the witches. I dunno how much time I was with the four witches. It seemed like hours, but it was prob'ly just seconds. This here was a place of no time, yet a place where all times met. I felt proud of ma'self for learn'n how ta'do the spirit tongue and talk'n to the spirits. I felt more powerful than I have ever felt b'fore. I also felt more secure. Mighty strong in my own body. Strange how one day you can feel like you're right lost to the world without no friend in sight and the next you be feel'n like you can conquer the world.

"Thank all of you for teach'n me how ta'speak in the spirit tongue," I said to the four witches.

"You show great promise," Alma said. Clara, Viola, and Harriet was in agreement. If noth'n else from tonight, I made new friends and called the spirits. I think this was a night ta'remember.

"Why do we come here?" I asked the witches. "I mean, why do we come to the sabbat?"

"The sabbat is between this world and the spirit world," Alma 'splained. "It is the place where all witches and magical folk meet. We come from all the ages and all places around the world. This is a place where we gather to honor the Old Ones and learn the secrets of witchcraft."

"Why here?" I asked. "Why in spirit form does we come to the sabbat? And why on the full moon?"

"We come here to the spirit lands in spirit because it is safer. Long ago, there were those who sought to kill us. This keeps us safe. The world thinks we are tucked away in our beds, and yet we ride with the Devil. Also, some of the witches are from our own present time, while other witches are from hundreds of years ago. To us, they are long dead. But from their point of view, they are very much alive. From their point of view, it is *we* who are from the future. This intersection of time and space allows us to dance freely with our brother and sister witches and gives us the gift of sharing our witchcraft with those from the long-forgotten past and the future that has yet to come."

That night was filled with dance'n, feast'n, and share'n magic spells. The more I danced, the more I had forgot ma'self. The more I danced

as the night went on, the more I couldn't right tell who I was and who
them other witches was. The more I danced, the more I seemed ta'melt
into the minds and hearts of them other witches. The more I danced, I
was no longer dance'n. I was soar'n into the night sky. The drumbeats
done melted into the moonlight. I wasn't no longer dance'n, I was fly'n
to the rhythm of the moon herself. I danced ma'self deep into a trance,
and all I could see were the shadows and shapes of them witches from
other places and other times. But I 'member be'n able ta'focus on my
heart. My heart was the only thing that kept me sound. If I forgot
ma'self, I could think of my heart and I was me again.

Through the dance'n...or was it fly'n? I dunno now. Maybe it was
both. Or maybe it was neither. Anyhow, through the dance'n, I could
feel me a constant presence in my heart. I closed my eyes and focused
on my heart and there they was. The Devil and the Queen of Elphame.
They was sit'n on a throne made'a twisted and gnarled trees. They was
watch'n me with smiles of delight on their faces.

"Come to us," the queen said.

Wait! What was happening?! I was still in spirit form at the witches'
sabbat in the Otherworld. But at the same time, I was someplace else.
Somehow, I'd traveled to a place deeper into magic. It was a dream
within a dream. A secret place deeper into the Otherworld that was
meant for no one but them witches and that was called upon by the
Devil and the Queen of Elphame.

"Come closer," the Devil said.

I walked up closer to the Devil and the Queen of Elphame. I was
in awe of their presence, and yet I had me a sense of fear and dread. I
wanted ta'be with 'em and far away from 'em at the same time.

I walked up to 'em real close. The Devil never scared me none, but
tonight was differ'nt. Tonight, there was someth'n 'bout the Devil and
the queen that gave me a sense of fear all the way ta'my core.

"It is time for you to know our names," the Devil said. "I am Lucifer,
the Old One, Tubal Cain, Witch Father, Master, or the Man in Black."

"I am Frau Holda," the queen said. "I am also the Old Dame,
Perchta, Hella, or even Diana."

"Where is this place?" I was real confused. "Am I still at the witch's sabbat?"

The Devil gazed up to the skies and them stars was turn'n faster and faster. "This is the place where magic lies. This is the place of creation that is connected to dreams."

The queen, or Frau Holda, gazed to the ground. I saw wavy lines of energy move'n through that ground. The ground opened itself up ta'show folks who was long dead. "This is the place where magic lies. This is the place of formation that is connected to all life."

The words of the Old Ones resonated through my heart and touched my spirit. It was not the words themselfs but the energy, the magic, they was teach'n me. Their words was a mystery that'd unfold one day. Not today. Today I was in a dream inside a dream. A place that was within the spirit world and was a secret place even ta'some witches. The journey was begin'n ta'become deeper than I'd thought. I hope I would visit this place again. How I would I get back here, I don't rightly know. I figure when the Old Ones want me, they'll come and get me. 'Til then, I'll float on the dream.

I opened my eyes, and there I was on the floor next to the fireplace, still hold'n my 'ole broom. The sun was rise'n and the birds was chirp'n like someth'n had gotten 'em all riled up in the night. The fire wasn't noth'n more than a few embers dy'n out. I stood up the best I could. I hadn't had a drop of whiskey but I felt like I was have'n ma'self a bad hangover. Like I had gotten drunk all night long. I din't have a drop a whiskey. Maybe it was the magic of it all last night. Maybe the trance was a kinda drunk that stayed with ya 'til the next day. Or maybe it was the Old Ones who took me deep into some part'a magic that I dunno where.

I opened the front door and I could smell the morn'n. You know what the morn'n smells like. Like a cool breeze be'n warmed up by the ris'n sun. Like the smell of the dew on the grass. Like the cold earth was be'n woke up. I wasn't in a trance no more, but I could still feel the magic. I could feel the magic energy flow'n on the wind. I could feel the magic energy in the earth 'neath my feet. I could feel the magic of a new day.

6

The Ghost Road

⚜⚜⚜

OCTOBER'S ALWAYS A NICE TIME here on the farm. The trees are turn'n lots of differ'nt colors and there's a cool breeze that's always welcome. It gets real hot down here in the South. Even in September, it's real hot. After months and months of hot days, you'd be wish'n there was a rainstorm or a cool wind. It does rain here from time ta'time, but the cool of the rain don't last too long. Soon as it clears up and the sun comes out, the humidity is someth'n terrible. You get used to it I guess, but sometimes hot is just plain 'ole hot. Now'd fall was here, I had ta'make sure the cow, chickens, and goats was taken care of for the winter. They'd be a'right, but I had ta'make sure the barn's ready. Make sure there ain't too many holes in the roof or the walls. It don't get as cold as it does up North, but on some Janu'ry nights it gets real cold out here. I don't need no chickens or noth'n die'n on me. They'd be a'right though.

After the witch's sabbat on the full moon, things started ta'change a bit for me. Maybe it was the spirits I called up use'n that spirit tongue, or maybe it was Mr. Picklesworth talk'n good 'bout me to the customers, but folks started ta'treat me a little differ'nt. They din't seem s'scared of me like they was while back. Maybe it was magic or maybe folks tend ta'forget stuff after a while. I ain't bothered nobody, and sometimes that's good 'nuff for folks ta'leave you alone. Maybe if 'nuff time's passed, folks'd be start'n to think'n you're a'right. Either way is fine by me. I'd like ta'say I ain't never needed nobody, but the truth is we all need each other from time ta'time. I'll be 16 years old this year, and other men who is 16 get wives and stuff. I ain't never had no think'n for no wife, but sure would be nice ta'have someone help me 'round the farm and the house. Right now, I'm do'n ever-thing ma'self, which is just fine, but sometimes some help 'round here might be nice. But I'm make'n friends with the town folk. Folks are be'n nicer ta'me, so I guess I'm just fine for now.

I'm wonder'n if them spirits is help'n me with those town folk though. I'm also wonder'n if it's the same kinda power ta'call the spirits in the wake'n daytime as it is in the witch's sabbat. When you're in the witch's sabbat, you is at the very center of magic, of witchcraft. You ain't gotta visualize noth'n too hard, 'cause you is right in the middle of the spirit world. Spirits is 'ardy there, so you ain't gotta try s'hard. Alma said you do the same magical technique in the wake'n world as you do in the spirit world. I'm gonna have ta'try call'n them spirits with the spirit tongue from time ta'time. I'm pretty reliable when it comes to get'n stuff done. Mr. Picklesworth at the store pays me good 'nuff, so I'm not starve'n, and what I don't have at the farm I can buy from the store with a discount. But sometimes a person be need'n someth'n he can't get from work'n for it. Sometimes you be need'n some kinda help and the spirits be provide'n it for you. Harriet made sure ta'tell me that anytime I call up the spirits and ask for someth'n, I best be give'n 'em an offer'n of some kind. She said I can give whiskey, tobacca, food, or if noth'n else, then water'll do. Ain't noth'n for free she said, 'specially magic.

My town has a small tavern that some of the men go to from time ta'time. I always thought it was strange that you hardly never see no women over there drink'n and holler'n and play'n cards. But I guess women have more sense than men do. Women don't waste their money on whiskey and drink their lifes away. Most women I know gots ta'take care of the children anyhow. Why the men don't come right away home and help 'em, I'll never know. Maybe sometimes it's good though, 'cause I know sometimes the wives might need time away from their husbands' nonsense from time ta'time.

I don't like ta'waste money on drink'n neither. I don't make a lot of money at the store and Momma used ta'say ta'save what money you can, 'cause you never know what's gonna happen tomorrow. Might be good, might be bad. Never can tell. One night, I got ta'think'n it might be a'right for me ta'go over ta'that tavern and have ma'self a drink of whiskey. One ain't never hurt nobody. Besides, now'd the town folk wasn't scared of me no more, it might be nice ta'be make'n some friends.

I went over there ta'that tavern and I ordered me a whiskey. There was 'bout six or seven other men in that tavern and ever-body seemed ta'be have'n a good time. There was a couple'a men at the table play'n cards. Barkeep said those men are there ever-Frid'y night play'n 'em cards. Sometimes one wins and sometimes the other wins. Those two boys been friends a long time, so they don't get mad s'much if they lose, 'cause they know they'd win their money back the next time.

I sat there drink'n my whiskey when a fella named Samuel Toberson sat right down at the bar beside me. He ordered him a whiskey. He took a few sips and then looked at me. "You're the Knotbristle boy, ain't ya?"

"Yes," I said. I felt a little sheepish 'cause I wasn't sure which way this conversation was gonna go.

"It's a shame what happen ta'your family," Samuel said. "A right shame."

"Yeah, it's a shame," I said. "Momma, Daddy, and my brothers are in heaven now I 'spose, so I ain't gotta worry 'bout 'em much."

"I 'spose you're right," Samuel said. "What brings you here tonight?"

"Nothin'," I said. "Thought I might see what ya'll boys are up to."

"Nothin' good!" Samuel laughed and asked for 'nother whiskey.

I was there for maybe an hour or so talk'n ta'my new friend Samuel when the tavern door opened and a man dressed in fine black clothes walked in. He wore him a black flat-brimmed hat and had black hair, black as midnight. When he walked on that wooden floor of the tavern, you could feel the vibration of his walk'n. He was graceful but with the weight of a hundr'd horses. He carried a black case with him. He sat hisself down next to Samuel at the bar and asked the barkeep for a whiskey. When he paid him, he paid him with a gold coin. Like someth'n a ship pirate'd have.

The barkeep looked at the gold coin and said, "What's this?"

"A coin of gold," the man said. "I assure you, it is worth much more than any coin you may have seen." The man had an odd smile on his face. "My gift to you."

The barkeep took the coin. I'm sure he ain't never seen no gold coin b'fore. Hell, I don't think anyone in this town had ever seen them a gold coin b'fore.

Samuel was get'n pretty drunk after a while and patted the man on the back. "What's your name, stranger?"

"The Stranger," the man replied.

Samuel let out a big belly laugh. I don't think he thought it was real funny. I just think he was real drunk. "The Stranger! No! Really, what's your name, friend?"

"The Stranger," the man said again with a great big smile on his face.

"Then 'The Stranger' your name will be!" Samuel said, laugh'n. "Come drink with us!"

The Stranger scooted his bar stool closer ta'us and ordered 'nother whiskey. Again, he gave the barkeep a gold coin. Samuel told his stories and laughed at his own humor. Me and The Stranger laughed with Samuel. Samuel had one'a them laughs that you couldn't help not ta'laugh with him. After tell'n one'a his stories, Samuel noticed the black case that The Stranger had next ta'him. "What's in the case?"

"Why, a fiddle!" The Stranger said.

"A fiddle!" Samuel said, laugh'n.

"A fiddle!" The Stranger said again.

By this time, Samuel's get'n real drunk. He was drunk 'nuff ta'slide off his stool, but sober 'nuff ta'know he was slid'n off and he needed ta'steady hisself. "Then play for us, Stanger!"

The Stranger opened up his case and in it was a golden fiddle. This fiddle was the most beautiful thing I had ever done seen. The fiddle was look'n like it was made from sunlight or even a star. The other men in the tavern noticed The Stranger was take'n someth'n outta the case, and them men looked over, see'n the golden fiddle.

"That's a fine look'n fiddle you got there," one'a the men said. "You gonna play that?"

"Why, of course," The Stranger said.

The whole tavern stopped drink'n and carry'n on ta'see what The Stranger was gonna do with that magnificent fiddle. The Stranger carefully took the fiddle outta the case and started play'n the most beautiful music I ever did hear. The music filled my ears and my heart with such joy and sadness, I din't know what I was gonna do. The music was like noth'n I had ever heard b'fore. It was beautiful and sad, and it seemed ta'be speak'n right at me. Like the music was tell'n me things I needed ta'hear. The music made me think of Momma, Daddy, and my brothers. It made me think of all the happy times together. The music also made me think of lose'n 'em and all the sadness I had after they died. The music also made me think of the hope for the future and that ever-thing was gonna be a'right...s'long as I had this music played on this golden fiddle.

The Stranger finished his song, and I looked 'round at the men in the tavern and ever-damn one'a 'ems was smil'n and had tears in his eyes. Now, these was not the kinda men who go 'round cry'n over some feel'ns. These was the kinda men who was farm folks and was tough as nails. I dunno what happened, but whatever it was, The Stranger was able ta'affect these men just like he was able ta'affect me.

"Play again, Stranger," Samuel said. "Play for us again."

The Stranger lowered his fiddle and looked Samuel right in the eye and smiled. "Oh, but to play again there must be a price."

Someth'n din't seem right ta'me. The music was beautiful, and I'd say even magical, but someth'n was tell'n me someth'n ain't right.

"Whatever price you ask, I'll pay," Samuel said, and I think he really meant it.

The Stranger gave Samuel a sly look once again. "Perhaps for payment I will take your soul."

Samuel din't speak. He said nuth'n for a long while. Then he burst into laughter! "My soul!" Samuel laughed s'hard I thought he might piss his britches. "My soul!"

"Well then," The Stranger said, "if you don't want me to play, then I'll be on my way."

"No!" Samuel couldn't stop laugh'n. "No, no, no. Please play. I'll pay your price."

This wasn't a good idea at all. I grabbed Samuel by the arm and shook my head no. "Samuel. This might not go s'well."

"Don't worry, my new friend," Samuel was stagger'n, and how he managed ta'stay up right is an act of magic in itself. "I don't believe in no Devils, faeries, and pacts. I don't believe in God or the Saints. So let him take my soul if he can!"

"Do we have a deal?" The Stranger asked.

"Why not!" Samuel answered. "My make-believe soul is yours."

The Stranger began play'n his fiddle and he once again started play'n the most beautiful music I'd ever heard. The music filled me with s'much joy that I was moved beyond heaven and earth. Then the music began ta'play faster. I wanted ta'dance. I wanted ta'jump outta my seat and dance to the magic of the fiddle. But I knew that if I got up I would fall down, 'cause I was get'n drunk ma'self. Samuel was overcome by the joy of the music. He leaped outta his seat and began ta'dance. The music played faster and faster.

"Faster! Faster!" Samuel shouted. His joy was take'n over his body. "Yes! I must dance!"

Them other men leapt outta their seats too and joined Samuel in the dance of the fiddle. This was the funniest sight I ever did see. Watch'n these grown ass men dance'n and carry'n on like this. They was dance'n s'hard they was knock'n over drinks and tables and chairs. The barkeep din't mind s'much, though. He was dance'n behind the bar, too. This was the craziest shit I ever did see! Then The Stranger started ta'dance hisself. He fiddled and danced and fiddled and danced. He danced over ta'one side of the tavern and then fiddled and danced to the other side of the tavern. And you know what? Those men was dance'n and follow'n him 'round that tavern, knock'n down shit as they went. Then The Stranger fiddled and danced right out the front door. Sure 'nuff, Samuel and those men followed him right out the door. They was fiddle'n and dance'n right in the middle of the marketplace, right in the road. It was a good thing it was late and ever-body was in bed. They'd never hear the end of it if folks saw 'em carry'n on like that. Then without no kind a warn'n, The Stranger stopped his fiddle play'n. Ever-body was outta breath. There was a sadness that overcame the men.

"Play again!" Samuel shouted. He was breathe'n s'heavy I thought he was gonna pass out right there. I thought he was gonna be faint'n right here in front of ever-body.

"Alas," The Stranger said, "I must take my fiddle and bid you all a good night." The Stranger put the bow on those strings one more time and the sound wasn't like the music from b'fore. It sounded like the song of specter or a ghost. It sounded like a song that could be heard in the spirit world.

Samuel started breathe'n real heavy. He grabbed at his chest and fell hisself right down to the ground. The look on his face was terrify'n, he was in s'much pain. Such agony. Then he just stopped. No shout'n, no pain, no agony. No noth'n. Samuel was dead.

We ran over to Samuel ta'see if we could do anyth'n, but he was dead. The men couldn't believe what they was see'n. Samuel had danced hisself ta'death. I looked over to The Stranger, but he was gone. The Stranger had gone dis'ppeared.

A few days after, we had a funeral for 'ole Samuel. I'd offered ta'help dig the grave back on his family's land. One'a his friends built a casket for him. Noth'n fancy. Just a simple wooden box. Ever-one in town came to his funeral. The pastor said him some nice words and the women done cried. No one asked what happened, and them boys at the tavern said noth'n 'bout The Stranger. It's a funny thing 'bout folks sometimes. You can show 'em magic as clear as day and they'll be see'n some strange things, but the very next day they'd be rationalize'n ever-thing.

They'll either 'magine some reason why it happened that wasn't magic, or they be forget'n the whole thing in the morn'n.

I spent the next few days kinda quiet. Din't say much to Mr. Picklesworth when I was work'n at the market. Noth'n much ta'say. I made ma'self a friend, and that friend died that very same night. I was think'n why The Stanger came ta'take Samuel and why he took him that night? I don't think it was just a coincidence. I got to wonder'n if The Stranger was really there for me and Samuel got in the way. Was it the Devil who decided ta'come and take me away? Or maybe the Devil wanted ta'come and show me his power? Or maybe The Stranger got to feel'n some witchcraft and got hisself attracted to it. Maybe simply by be'n me, my magic attracted The Stranger and Samuel was just crazy 'nuff ta'take on The Stranger's challenge and lost. I wasn't feel'n up ta'talk'n ta'nobody, so after work'n at the market, I'd just walk home. I had the kinda loneliness that I hadn't had since Momma, Daddy, and my brothers'd gone. I was do'n real good and then Samuel went ahead and died. Magic or no magic, it wasn't my fault, and I don't care much what was attracted ta'what.

The days went by, and ever-morn'n, I'd wake up and open the door and smell me that fall air. Ever-day it was a bit cooler than the day b'fore. The leaves was fall'n off real good. Harvest time was almost over, and the few vege'ables that I done growed on my little piece of land was jarred and put away in the cupboard for the winter. There was someth'n more to the air than just fall and jar'n. There was a smell of death. Not like the smell when an animal dies and you be smell'n that rotted animal like. It's the smell of the earth over a new grave. This's what I 'magine ghosts'd smell like. I dunno what ghosts smell like, but if they had them a smell, it'd be the smell of leaves on the wet ground on a fall morn'n. Whatever smell it was, it was pretty clear. Death was come'n soon.

Couple nights later I was sit'n in my rock'n chair, and I heard the wind pick up real good. Kinda like the wind on the night of the sabbat, but I could tell that this wind was differ'nt. The wind on the night of the witch's sabbat was excit'n and magical. This wind seemed ta'have the voices of a hundr'd souls. Storms bring wind all the time dur'n this time of the year, so I don't pay much mind 'bout no strong wind. Most the time, wind's just wind. I only pay attention when the wind feels differ'nt. Like there's witchcraft on the wind. Thing you gotta 'member 'bout the wind, it carries witchcraft on it sometimes. Like when a stream be carry'n off a leaf, sometimes the wind be carry'n witchcraft on it. Sometimes the witchcraft is excite'n and sometimes it carries messages. This wind was carry'n death.

All a sudden, I heard a ruckus in the barn. Like there was a fox or someth'n bother'n them chickens up in there. I took my rifle and ran over to the barn. Whatever it was, I couldn't let 'em kill my chickens. I'd be need'n meat come dead of winter. I ran over to the barn door and slung it open. I din't see noth'n. Ever-thing was real quiet.

Well, hell, I thought. Maybe whatever it was'd gone. Or maybe someth'n blew a tree branch at the barn and got them chickens all riled up. I put my rifle down and looked 'round. Noth'n. I had left the barn door open in my hurry'n and the wind was still blow'n. Albeit wasn't bad as it was b'fore. Then I felt it again. Death.

Someth'n in my belly told me ta'take a step back and get outta the way, so I did. The wind picked up again and then I saw forms that looked like folks made'a fog, walk'n right through my barn from outside. I couldn't see nobody's faces, but I knew they was folks. There must have been twenty or thirty of those foggy look'n folks. I stood close to the barn wall ta'give 'em some room ta'do whatever the hell they was do'n. They was walk'n in line to the other side of the barn. Them chickens and goats was carry'n on someth'n terrible. Like they was be'n attacked or someth'n. Then they walked right through the other side of the barn like they was walk'n down a path or a road or someth'n. Then the wind stopped and the animals quieted down.

I din't know what the hell that was, but as strange as it was, noth'n surprised me no more. One thing I learnt ever since I became a witch was that things is strange. Hell, normal folks who ain't witches is strange. Add witchcraft to the mix and you got strange shit that happens almost ever-day. I stood there for a short while, wait'n for someth'n else ta'happen, and it never did.

The next night, I was sit'n in my chair again, and again I heard that wind pick up. I opened the front door ta'my house and again I could smell the smell of death. This time I was gonna see what was go'n on. I ran over to the barn and stood where I did b'fore, 'gainst the wall, outta the way. The wind picked up and them animals started carry'n on again. This time though, I decided ta'put ma'self in a trance so I could see the fog folks better. I took a few deep breaths and put my thoughts aside. I connected to the land and them stars, just like I did at the witch's sabbat. I took slow, deep breaths, allow'n my mind and my heart ta'go deeper and deeper into a trance.

Then they came. The foggy look'n specters came in the barn, walk'n straight through like they was walk'n on the road or someth'n. In my trance, I looked at the fog and it turnt out it wasn't no fog. It was ghosts. Spirits of folks long dead. Ever-body walk'n through my barn was somebody that'd died. Some of those ghosts I recognized and some I din't. I looked for Momma, Daddy, and my brothers, but they wasn't there. I was both relieved and heartbroken at the same time. I din't want 'em ta'be a part'a some ghostly train, but at the same time I'd do anyth'n ta'see my family again.

The ghosts walked by me, one by one. Some'a them ghosts looked at me and some even seemed ta'know who I was. The expression on their faces was somber, but nobody looked like they was in no kinda pain or noth'n. At the end of the ghostly train, that's where I saw him. My friend Samuel. He followed them other ghosts like he was compelled ta'do so in some way. I wanted ta'reach out ta'him. To grab him. But for some reason, I couldn't. I dunno if I was 'fraid or if it was the magic of the ghosts or someth'n, but I was froze where I was. Then, like the night b'fore, the ghostly train walked through the other side of the barn door and dis'ppeared.

All the next day I kept think'n 'bout it. Why was Samuel in that ghostly train and how could I help him get gone from it? I din't know noth'n 'bout no ghost trains but I could feel in my bones that this wasn't a place that Samuel should be. I din't know what I should do, so I decided ta'ask Old Henry. I took down the cat skull from the shelf I kept him on and I lit the candles. Then I conjured him just like I did b'fore, "Old

Henry, Old Henry, I conjure thee, Old Henry, Old Henry, I summon thee." I did the conjuration three times and Old Henry appeared.

"Hello, Johnathan," Old Henry said.

"It's good ta'see you, my friend," I said back. Even though Old Henry was a familiar spirit sent ta'me by The Devil, I considered him ta'be my friend. When I din't know or understand someth'n, it was Old Henry who always helped me when I needed.

"What can I do for you?" Henry asked.

"I need your help with someth'n," I said. "The last few nights I'd been see'n a ghostly train walk through my barn. They be come'n after midnight when that wind picks up. I saw my friend Samuel who died a few days ago."

"I see," Old Henry walked to the winda' and looked over ta'my 'ole barn. He nodded his head like he knew someth'n. "You have a ghost road that leads straight through your barn."

"What's a ghost road?" I asked him. I ain't never heard of no ghost road b'fore.

"A ghost road," Henry 'splained, "is a path of energy that the spirits of the dead walk upon. Usually, it's created by the funeral procession from the church to the graveyard. You see, mourners of the dead radiate an energy as they are carrying the casket from the church to the graveyard. As they carry the casket down, their thoughts and energies are focused on death. The energy that they radiate from their bodies creates an energetic path that attracts the spirits of the dead."

Old Henry has a way of 'splain'n things that make sense. I can always count on Henry ta'be teach'n me things I need ta'be know'n. "Where are they go'n?"

"They go to different places," Henry said. "Sometimes they are traveling to the world of the dead. Sometimes they are visiting the living. Other times they are simply walking the final road back and forth from the grave to the church."

That was a bit confus'n ta'me. The ghost road wasn't go'n to the church and the graveyard. It was go'n right through my 'ole barn. "But there ain't no church here, only my 'ole barn. Why are they come'n over here?"

Old Henry thought for a minute. "Come outside with me."

I followed Henry outside over to the barn. He looked 'round, or I might say he was "feel'n" 'round.

"Let's see what used to be here. Come, we can look into the past and see what this little farm of yours used to be." Henry said. "Go into your trance just as you have done before. Imagine your heart expanding itself over the barn, your house, and the land. Close your eyes and reach back into time with your imagination. Allow your thoughts into the past before you were born, before your mother and father were born, and back even further. Keeping your physical eyes closed, imagine opening up your spirit eyes. Your thoughts are in the past. What do you see?"

I did 'zactly what Old Henry told me ta'do, and when I opened my spirit eyes, I saw the land I was on, but the 'ole barn and my house wasn't there. But there was a small 'ole church. I din't know what year it was, but I could see men carry'n a casket down the way to a little graveyard. In my thoughts, I had my spirit follow'n those men with the casket. They took the casket to a little cemetery, not real big at all. In fact, I'd say it was real small. I got the feel'n that this was the first church they'd done built a long time ago when this here town was just a settlement. There *was* a church here at one time. Then again, so was there a little graveyard. That 'ole graveyard wasn't on my land, but the ghost road sure was. And I'm guess'n the graves's still there.

After Henry was tell'n me the things I needed ta'know 'bout the ghost road, I gave him an offer'n of whiskey and tobacca. I blew out the candles and wrapped up that cat skull and put it back on the shelf where I was keep'n it safe. I couldn't stop think'n 'bout that ghost road and I couldn't stop think'n 'bout poor Samuel. I'm wonder'n if he was forever condemned ta'walk the ghost road.

That night, I waited again for the ghostly train ta'walk on that ghost road to the barn. Just like them other nights, the ghosts came walk'n on that ghost road. As them spirits come towards the barn, I started ta'hear a familiar sound. I was hear'n that beautiful otherworldly music of the fiddle. That music done filled the air with a magical sound, and it looked ta'me like the wind was blow'n to the music. Then I saw him, as plain as daylight. The Stranger was lead'n the ghostly train. The dead was follow'n him down the ghost road. I knew The Stranger was up ta'no good, but I couldn't help but ta'be listen'n ta'that fiddle. The wind was blow'n like all the other nights. I was wonder'n, was it the fiddle play'n to the wind or was the wind blow'n to the fiddle? It din't matter much what was happen'n with that fiddle. All I was think'n is that I had ta'save poor Samuel.

I wasn't gonna stand aside from the ghostly train like I did them last few nights. This time I was gonna confront The Stranger ma'self. I din't want him ta'get gone. I stood in the back of the barn right where them spirits walked b'fore. If they was gonna pass through the barn, they was gonna have ta'pass right through me. The Stranger led them spirits right into the barn and was head'n straight for me when The Stranger stopped play'n his fiddle and looked directly at my eyes. "Sir, you are standing in the way of my train. Would you care to move aside?"

"You're the fiddle player who took away my friend, Samuel." I tried ta'sound strong, but I'm sure The Stanger knew that I ain't never confronted no ghost train b'fore.

"Indeed," The Stranger said. "A bargain is a bargain."

The Stranger put the bow to the strings of the fiddle and was 'bout ta'start play'n again. "How abouts do I release Samuel from you?"

The Stranger sure seemed in'erested in my idea. He had that same look on his face as he did the night he gone and took Samuel away from the world of the living. "With a wager, of course."

"A wager?" I din't trust The Stranger for one minute. He was up ta'no good, and if I wasn't careful, I might be walk'n behind him on the ghostly train too.

"Yes," The Stranger lowered his bow and fiddle and peered into my soul. "If you can outplay me, then Samuel is free to walk to the shadowlands. If you cannot, then you must join my spirit train and take your place by Samuel's side."

I din't know what ta'say. I din't know how ta'play a fiddle. Even if I learnt how, I wouldn't be able ta'play better than The Stranger. There had ta'be a better way. There had ta'be someth'n I wasn't think'n 'bout. The

Stranger could tell I wasn't gonna take his bet. At least not tonight. He smiled in his dark way and then started play'n that fiddle again. He and his train of spirits walked through the barn wall and done dis'ppeared.

The next day, I conjured Old Henry again. When he 'ppeared, I told him 'bout the bet with The Stranger and how I couldn't no way outplay him and his fiddle. Old Henry a'course had an idea. He always be know'n ever-thing what we should be do'n. He told me that we should be go'n to the graveyard tonight. We oughta wait 'til way after midnight when ever-one in town was sleep'n. Henry was know'n of an 'ole fiddle player who was lay'n dead in that 'ole graveyard. His name was Arthur Tomtable. Arthur'd been dead by the time I was born, but he did still have family liv'n in town. I heard tell some stories that Arthur was the best fiddle player there ever was. Folks used ta'say that 'ole Arthur was s'good at the fiddle, he might could out play the Devil hisself. Well, tonight, Arthur might get his chance.

Old Henry and me waited 'til it was real late at night. It was s'late that even the cicadas was asleep. We walked down over to that graveyard next to the church. I was carry'n a bag of stuff that Henry'd told me ta'bring. We was gonna do a ritual ta'raise the dead. I ain't never done someth'n like that, so I was glad Henry was with me. There was a odd stillness that night. Like the spirits was know'n that we was gonna do someth'n powerful. Someth'n real strong. I was a little nervous like, but Henry was with me, and he'd help me if anyth'n went wrong.

The church was dark and silent. When we got to the church, I was notice'n that at that moment, at that time, the church felt like it were a thousn'd years old. I happen ta'know that church was built only twenty years ago, but that night, it was ancient and had seen the come'ns and go'ns of the world and it stood right there, watch'n ever-thing. The graveyard was out 'round back. It wasn't real big. Most folks out on them farms buried their dead on thems own property somewhere. Folks liked ta'keep their family close, even in death. Other folks, though, was the religious type and wanted ta'keep their dead on hallowed ground. You know, ground blessed by the priests. I asked somebody once why be'n buried on hallowed ground was s'important ta'some folks, and they said it was 'cause when a priest blessed the graveyard, God protected it from demons and evil spirits, and even witches. Well, we was 'bout ta'find out if the church graveyard was protected from witches.

Henry led me to the grave of 'ole Arthur Tomtable the fiddler. The grave had a small marker on it that simply be say'n "Arthur Tomtable." Most of them grave markers was small and simple, just like this one. I got the feel'n that we was not alone. No, not one'a the townsfolk spy'n on us. I got the feel'n that the spirits from those graves was watch'n what we was do'n. Maybe that's how call'n the dead works. When someone is trapes'n 'round their grave they know.

"Are you ready to begin?" Old Henry asked.

"Yup," I answered.

"Take everything out of the bag," Henry said.

B'fore we left my house, Henry had told me ta'bring a small bag with one candle, matches, whiskey, mullein, and a small piece of coal. I took ever-thing outta the bag like Henry said. We put the candle down on top of the grave first. Then we lit the coal with the matches and placed that on the grave, too.

"Light the candle," Henry said, "and say 'I call upon the Queen of Death, Bone Lady, Lady both Foul and Fair, Lady of Fate. We ask that you open the gates of the Otherworld and allow Arthur Tomtable to come to us this night.'"

I did just like Henry said. When I called to the Queen of Death, I pitchurd her down in the Otherworld, open'n the gates and tell'n 'ole Arthur ta'come ta'see us.

"Now, put some of that mullein on the coal. When it smokes, visualize the smoke going into the spirit world and calling to the dead." Henry said. "Say, 'Arthur Tomtable, come to us from the spirit world. Join us this night so that we may speak with you.'"

I did that too. When the smoke of the mullein went up to the sky, I 'magined them spirits see'n that smoke and it lead'n him ta'us like a smoke signal.

"Pour the whiskey on the grave as both offering and magical energy so Arthur can manifest before us," Henry said.

As soon as I poured that whiskey, I seen a faint fog appear'n over the grave. I poured a little more and the fog started ta'take shape. I went into my trance and I could see that it was a man take'n shape. "Are you Arthur Tomtable?"

The spirit of Arthur looked both surprised and happy that he was be'n called to the world of the living. "Yes, my name is Arthur Tomtable. What is your name?"

"My name is Johnathan, and this is Henry," I said. Henry'd told me ta'always make sure that you tell the spirits who you are. He said we don't keep secrets from the spirits none. Hell, most spirits know who you are and what you're do'n anyhow. Spirits like ta'be treated good, just like liv'n folks like ta'be treated good. Henry said it's better ta'get on the good side of spirits 'cause they be help'n you when you need it. If you piss off them spirits, they won't help you that much and you never know what a pissed off spirit is gonna do ta'ya. Best be be'n nice to the spirits. Best be make'n friends with 'em.

"Why do you call me to the world of the living?" Arthur asked us.

"I hear you can play the fiddle real good," I answered him. "I hear that you can even out play the Devil hisself."

Arthur laughed and smiled real big. "Where did you hear a tale like that?"

"The folks in town be say'n that 'bout you for years."

Arthur nodded his head, "Well, it's the damned truth! But I never played against no Devil. But why do you need me to play the fiddle?"

I told Arthur the story of Samuel and how he'd lost his soul to The Stranger, and how he was now part'a that ghostly train, destined ta'forever walk along the ghost road, follow'n the music of The Stranger's fiddle. The story made Arthur sad, and I think he understood why I needed his help. "Only thing is," I said, "if we make a wager with The Stranger, I think he's gonna want me ta'wager my soul. And I can't play no fiddle."

"I could out play him, of course," Arthur said. "But I'm sure he wants the soul of the living. Not someone who's been dead the last twenty years."

Old Henry interrupted, "I have a wonderful idea!"

Both Arthur and I was in'erested in what Henry had ta'say.

"Arthur, you can possess Johnathan's body and you can play the fiddle against The Stranger!" Henry was real pleased with his idea.

I wasn't so sure this was a good idea. "Wait, what? You want Arthur ta'take over my body?"

"Not forever," Henry said. "Just long enough for Arthur to play the fiddle and win back Samuel's soul."

Arthur looked uneasy, "I've never done that before. Hell, this is the first time I've been back to the world of the living since I died."

"I'm happy to teach you," Henry said. "Johnathan, are you in agreement?"

"Well, unless one of ya'll has a better idea, I guess this's our only choice," I said.

"Splendid!" Henry was all too happy 'bout this. "Johnathan, the first thing you must do is go into a trance. Then open your heart and your mind. You do this by imagining the energy surrounding your body opening up like a flower. Then imagine Arthur stepping into your body. He steps into your legs like britches, then he places his arms into your arms like long gloves. Then he places his chest in your chest and then his head into your head. Imagine your two hearts connecting and your two minds connecting. Then he sees with your eyes, hears with your ears, and can speak with your tongue. Once Arthur is in your body, you can allow your mind to lose a little bit of control. Then, allow Arthur to take control of your body. Arms, legs, everything. You are in full control if you want to be, Johnathan. You can gain control whenever you like. You can also release Arthur whenever you like."

Old Henry 'splained ta'me that the reason you want ta'imagine the spirits join'n with you is that it gives you all the control. Imagin'n the spirits do'n stuff like join'n your body gives 'em the permission ta'do it and it gives 'em the energy and strength ta'do it. Henry said that spirits can't do noth'n with the live'n unless the live'n allows it. The only time a spirit can possess the liv'n is if somewhere in their head they either want the spirit ta'possess 'em or they don't care if the spirit possesses 'em anyhow. Either way, the spirits must have permission.

"Let's try it now," Henry said.

I did what Henry had taught me and opened up my energy and 'magined Arthur join'n with my body. I have ta'say, this was a strange feel'n. I've never had no spirit in my body b'fore. I did take comfort in know'n that if someth'n wasn't right, then Henry was there ta'help me make it right again. When I felt Arthur be fully join'n with my body, I let go of my own control'n and let Arthur fully take over. I was along for the ride in my own body. Just a passenger, but I could still see, hear, and feel ever-thing that Arthur was do'n. Arthur walked 'round in my body a little bit ta'get used to hav'n a physical body again. I could hear Arthur's thoughts and he could hear mine. Arthur was happy ta'be in the world of the live'n again, but there was a sense of sadness. His thoughts was on his wife and daughter who'd gone moved on since his death. I learnt real quick that I could take a peek into Arthur's mind, even if he din't want me to. From Arthur's thoughts, I was see'n that Arthur be miss'n his life on earth and that he's hav'n many regrets of how he done lived his life. He had many things that he felt was undone and unsaid. Know'n this, I felt a little closer to Arthur. I think this closeness helped us stay connected even more. We opened our hearts and mind ta'each other. This made the magic more powerful.

After practice'n this for a while, it was time ta'release Arthur back into the grave. I regained my control of my body by just think'n it. I 'magined Arthur separat'n from my mind, then my head, then my heart, then my arms, then my legs. I 'magined Arthur stepp'n outta my body and then he stood next ta'me. I took a few deep breaths and made sure I wasn't dizzy or noth'n.

I took a small shovel and took me some dirt from Arthur's grave. I could use it ta'summon him again at home instead of come'n all the way over to this here churchyard. I put the dirt in a little pouch, and I put ever-thing back into the small sack. I went on home that night. Now, all I was need'n was a fiddle.

The next day, I went dig'n through Momma's 'ole trunk. I 'membered that Momma kept Daddy's 'ole fiddle in that 'ole trunk. Daddy got the fiddle from his Daddy, but he ain't never played it none. When Grampa died, the fiddle was one'a the few things that he owned that he gave to Daddy. I don't think Daddy even could play the fiddle. When he got it, he told Momma ta'put it in her trunk. Momma kept all kinds of things in her trunk. Blankets, candle stick holders, some clothes, and that fiddle. Anyth'n that was in that trunk was important to Momma. Me and my brothers ain't never opened it up. No reason to. 'Til now.

That night, I got ever-thing ready. The graveyard dirt ta'call Arthur, the cat skull ta'summon Henry, the candles, and that fiddle. I figured I'd summon ever-body b'fore the ghostly train started. It came at the same time ever-night, so I knew 'zactly what time ta'start. Right b'fore midnight. When the time came, I summoned Henry first. If I needed help with anyth'n, he'd be the one ta'help. Then I put that 'ole graveyard dirt on a small dish and lit the same candle that I used last night ta'call Arthur. I got the coal and the mullein and said the incantation. Arthur appeared just like last night. I poured some whiskey out in a small glass as an offer'n. "Arthur, are you ready?"

"I am ready," Arthur said.

I put ma'self into a trance and opened ma'self up, allow'n Arthur ta'take control of my body. Once Arthur was in control of my body, he picked up that fiddle and started play'n the prettiest music I ever did hear. We was all ready for The Stranger.

We walked us out to the barn with the fiddle and was wait'n for the ghostly train. Sure 'nuff, it came just like it did those other nights. The Stranger led the dead through the barn, play'n his fiddle. *"That's him,"* I told Arthur in his thoughts, *"it's time."*

"Hold on there, Sir," Arthur said through my voice.

The Stranger stopped and put his fiddle ta'his side, "Oh, hello sir, it is you again. Have you come to wager?"

"I have!" Arthur said ta'him. "I have come to wager for Samuel's soul."

"Then let us play against one another." The Stranger said. "Whoever plays the best fiddle will win. You will play for the soul of Samuel, and I will play for your soul. Do we have a deal?"

"We have a deal," Arthur said.

The Stranger gone played first. His song was a song of magic. The notes soothed them winds and calmed all them night's creatures. It was seem'n to me that all God's creation stopped ta'listen to The Stranger's music.

Then it was Arthur's turn. Arthur played a song that was fast, and them ghostly spirits of the train began ta'dance. They danced with each other or danced with themselfs. But either way, they danced the ghostliest dance I ever did see.

The Stranger was seem'n to be a little annoyed by Arthur's song. But it was The Stranger's turn again, and he'd not be outdone. He played his song, and this time the walls of the barn started shake'n and the ground was move'n to the music. The Stranger was not gonna lose to Arthur. When he finished, he looked at Arthur like he knew he 'ardy had done won.

Arthur put his fiddle under his chin again and put that bow on those strings and he started play'n again. His song was s'good that more and more ghosts showed up. Arthur's song called the ancestors of those ghosts in that train. The song went to the spirit world and called 'em right up. Now, that was a sight ta'see. My barn was filled with ghosts dance'n away ta'that fiddle.

Now The Stranger was mad as hell. He was madder than I ever did see anyone be mad. He played for a third time. This time, The Stranger played a song that called the birds outta their nests and the coyotes was howl'n away. This was a strange song. Instead of joy and bliss like b'fore, it was a song of darkness and shadow. This song was call'n ever-thing that was alive ta'come ta'that barn. The chickens was riled up, the birds come, and frogs be come'n, too!

Arthur picked up his fiddle one more time. This time, he played a song that I swear went through time and space. This song went through the spirit world and back again. All them ghosts in the barn was dance'n away. They was dance'n and dance'n and dance'n. They was dance'n s'hard that someth'n happened to 'em. Whatever was keep'n 'em trapped in The Stranger's ghostly train wasn't trap'n 'em no more. Joy came back to 'em and they stopped dance'n. They was real mad at The

Stranger. They stood there in dead silence, give'n The Stranger an awful look like they was want'n revenge or someth'n. Then all the spirits was gone.

"No!" The Stranger was s'mad he started beat'n his fiddle on the ground, tear'n it ta'pieces. His beautiful golden fiddle had no more power over the dead. The Stranger put hisself back together. "Well, sir, it seems that you have won."

Arthur looked The Stranger right in the eyes and said, "Samuel's soul please."

The Stranger dis'ppeared and where he was stand'n, Samuel appeared. Samuel looked mighty grateful. "Thank you, Johnathan."

I let Arthur separate from my body and said to Samuel, "If you want ta'thank anyone, thank Arthur here."

Samuel bowed his head for a second and said, "Thank you, Arthur."

"My pleasure," Arthur said.

And with that, the two spirits returnt to the land of the dead.

7

Mother Goose

THE FALL RAINS'D STARTED. Once we get into fall, the rains come. The days are cool, but not s'bad. But when the rains come, it'll send a chill down ta'your bones. Momma used ta'say that sometimes the fall rains was s'cold that you'd get a chill down ta'your very soul. Momma used ta'say a lot of things like that. Now'd I'm older, I was realize'n that half of what she said was old wives' tales, and the other half was just know'n stuff from know'n stuff. I think part'a it is live'n out here in the country. City folk dunno the same stuff as us country folk know. We know when the rains come'n 'cause our bones start ache'n. We know when the animals start look'n for shelter on a clear day, a bad storm is come'n soon. We know when we get lost in the woods that if we just listen to the earth and the trees we can find our way home.

Ever-day the rains come and it was just a storm'n. Winds blow'n the leaves off those trees. They was almost bare now. Soon 'nuff, the winter'll be here. Here in the South, we might get some snow, but noth'n too terrible. It usually leaves a dust'n or melts the same day.

I think I'd rather have that snow than this rain. Sheets and sheets of rain just fall'n down. Rain s'hard, sounds like someone's bang'n on the windas. Although with the way things was go'n the last few weeks, I wouldn't be surprised at all if someone was bang'n on the windas.

When I wasn't work'n at the market and I was home, I'd sit by my fireplace in my rock'n chair read'n a book. Mr. Picklesworth gave me a new book ta'read. He has a shelf in his house full'a 'ole books. Some'a them he's read and others he ain't. I think he gets a kick outta loan'n me books ta'read. Hell, I think he's just happy that someone in this town *can* read! Anyhow, if I'm sit'n at home on one'a those rainy November days, I just sit here in my 'ole rock'n chair by the fireplace, read'n one'a Mr. Picklesworth's books. The book I got now's called *Journey to the Center of the Earth*.

One day, I was sit'n in that rock'n chair, read'n by that fireplace, and all a'sudden I got a strong feel'n in my bones. Somebody's here.

A knock at the door.

Nobody ain't ever come ta'see me. Things was do'n better for me with the town folk. They don't be whisper'n 'bout me s'much as they used to. But still, I live down and outta the way of ever-body else. When Daddy built this house, he wanted someplace where we wasn't gonna be bothered. And sure 'nuff, nobody ain't bothered us.

'Nother knock at the door.

"Holt on! Holt on!" I shouted at the door. I put my book on the little table next to the rock'n chair and walked me to the front door. Who inna hell would come out here in the middle of the rain? I opened the door, and I was surprised ta'see there, stand'n outside with umbrellas, was the witches from the sabbat; Alma, Harriet, Viola, and Clara.

"Well don't just stand there!" Clara said, "Let us in!"

"A'course! A'course!" I said, a little embarrassed that my surprise'd made me forgot my manners. "Please come in!"

The four witches shook off them umbrellas on the front porch and put 'em outside next to the door. There was a little roof over the porch. Not 'nuff ta'keep you dry dur'n a rainstorm mind you, but good 'nuff for keep'n umbrellas outside. The four witches followed me inside and seemed grateful ta'be outta that rain. Alma carried her a leather bag and sat it down on the floor next to the fireplace.

"Please sit down," I said to 'em, pull'n out some of the chairs that was 'round the table. "Would you like some coffee?"

"Oh, yes," Harriet said, "please."

I had just made'a large kettle of coffee that was on the stove keep'n warm. I took out four cups from the cupboard and poured 'em all a cup of coffee. "I din't know y'all lived s'close by. I thought y'all might live in faraway lands."

Alma laughed, "No, we live in the next town over. Only a few miles away. Not far at all. We were almost here when the rains started."

"All of you live in the next town over?" I asked.

"Oh, yes," Viola said. "That's how we know each other."

"What brings ya'll out here ta'my little house?" I asked. The four witches was helpful ta'me at the witches' sabbat. I bonded with 'em in a way, and I think they was bonded with me. I was glad ta'see 'em. When I woke up from the sabbat, I thought I might only see 'em again at the next sabbat.

"We saw magic in you, Johnathan," Alma said. "We think it's time for you to have more training."

Alma was a bit older than the other three women. She was their leader, I guess you'd call it. She had a presence 'bout her. Like when she walked in the room, ever-one could be feel'n that she was there. She commanded attention. I could tell that Alma knew more 'bout witchcraft than the other three women. Oh, don't get me wrong! Them other three knows what they was do'n! 'Specially compared ta'me. But Alma. She looked like she lived and breathed witchcraft.

"What kinda training?" I asked.

"Spirits, Devils, and ghosts will give you a certain type of experience," Alma said. "In fact, the spirits will teach you more things than any witch can teach you. But there are some basic things that every witch must learn and understand before they can develop their relationship with the spirits."

"Whatever you have ta'teach me, I'm will'n ta'learn," I said.

We sat by my fireplace, keep'n warm and drink'n coffee and talk'n a bit. We talked 'bout where they lived and how we all became witches. I told 'em 'bout the ghost road and how Old Henry helped me help Samuel. The four witches told me that almost ever-witch had a familiar. The Devil, or sometimes the Old Dame, gave it to 'em. Alma told me that sometimes we call the Queen of Elphame, "the Old Dame." She's called Perchta or Hella also, depend'n upon where you are in the world or who your teachers is. She also was tell'n me that the Devil has other names, too. Sometimes we call him the Devil and sometimes we call him Old Horny. Sometimes we call him Witch Master or Witch Father. She said she's heard of him be'n called The Stranger. I thought that was mighty odd. The Stranger did seem like a devilish spirit, but he weren't the Devil that I met. And how come The Stranger din't recognize me then? Alma said that the Devil's known ta'play tricks on us witches. He loves play'n tricks on Christians, 'specially boastful Christians. She also said that the spirit world is filled with things we don't be understand'n and that maybe there's more than one Devil. *More than one Devil? Is that possible?* She sure gives me a lot ta'think 'bout.

Alma also told me that sometimes witches hide magical things in plain sight. She said that witches is clever and learnt how ta'keep magical things outta the sight of them Christians who don't understand our ways, but in plain view, too. She said that witches do that ta'teach other witches things without have'n ta'say nuth'n. She said that a witch'll always know when they see someth'n magical. Like the broom, pitchfork, and the cook'n pot. All these things is used ta'call the Devil and the Old Dame, but ta'other folks, they look like ever-day items. Witches started do'n this dur'n the witch persecutions. Instead of have'n fancy magic tools that'd give you away as a witch, witches used ever-day things that ever-body had in them houses. It was harder ta'know if a witch was a witch or not. Alma said that even though the witch hang'n days was over, you never did want ta'anger the Christian town folk. They start blame'n you for ever-thing that happen. Some old man dies, and they say a witch did it. A hailstorm come and they say a witch did it. Alma said that even if folks be know'n you a witch, best not ta'call yourself that or folks will start come'n up with stuff you did wrong, even if you din't do noth'n.

Alma went over ta'her leather sack and took out a book. She put it on my lap. *Mother Goose.*

"Mother Goose?" Momma used ta'read me Mother Goose all the time when me and my brothers was little. "This is a children's book. I still might have this book in my Momma's 'ole trunk."

"A children's book, yes," Alma said. "But it's much more than that. Remember, witches hid things in plain sight. This is not only a children's book. This is a spell book."

"A spell book?" This din't make no kinda sense ta'me. Momma used ta'read Mother Goose ta'us all the time when we was little. Never once did she say anyth'n 'bout no spells or 'bout no magic. "What d'you mean spell book?"

"You see, Johnathan," Alma said, "Frau Holda, or the Dame as we sometimes call her, is pulled through the air on her chariot by magical geese. Some say she rides a goose through the night sky. The goose is her magical familiar. Whenever you see a flock of geese flying through the night, be sure that Holda is near."

Clara took the book outta my lap and turnt to a page that was 'ardy marked and started read'n, "Old Mother Goose, when she wanted to wander, would ride through the air, on a very fine gander."

I sat there for a minute, think'n 'bout it. I seen some strange things these last few months. Things I couldn't 'splain ta'nobody...well, 'cept 'nother witch. So, I thought maybe there was someth'n ta'this Mother Goose book.

Viola took the book from Clara and flipped through the pages, "Here's an easy spell. It's to stop the rain."

"Dear Viola," Alma said, "instead of telling him, why don't we show him?"

Alma, Clara, Viola, and Harriet stood up from their chairs and walked outside. The rain was pour'n away, but they was a'right 'cause of that porch roof. Then they all took a deep breath and said, "Rain, rain, go away, come again another day, Little Johnny wants to play." They gathered their power and their witchcraft and spoke in unison again, "Rain, rain, go away, come again another day, Little Johnny wants to play." Stand'n side by side they grabbed hands and said the rhyme one more time, "Rain, rain, go away, come again another day, Little Johnny wants to play."

I tell you what, that rain stopped! I ain't seen noth'n like it. The rain clear stopped! The four witches came on back inside the house. I stood out there on that porch just beside ma'self. "Tell me how you did that!"

Alma, Clara, Harriet, and Viola all went back ta'where they was sit'n and started drink'n their coffee again. "You see," Alma said, "not just anyone can pick up Mother Goose and make magic happen. The first thing you must do is summon energy from the earth and the sky into your body. Instead of using it to go into a trance, you make it your intention to send it out to influence the world. One witch is good, three or more is better. The power is stronger. Then as you send the power out into the world to change it, you say the rhyme. One time is good, three times is better."

"Another thing to remember," Harriet said, "is that witches have been adding power to the rhymes for a long time."

"What d'ya mean?" I asked.

"There is a magical current in the spirit world. Think of it as like a stream, but instead of water, it's magic," Harriet said. "Every time a witch uses one of the rhymes, they add their power to the stream that is connected to Mother Goose. The magical stream empowers the words of the rhyme."

"Here's one of my favorites," Viola said. "On Saturday night, shall be my care, to powder my locks, and curl my hair. On Sunday morning, my love will come in, when he will marry me with a gold ring?"

"A love spell?" That one seemed pretty obvious ta'me.

"A marriage spell," Viola said.

Alma took the book back from Viola and turnt ta'nother page. "This one many folks know but don't realize it comes from this book:

"Monday's child is fair of face
Tuesday's child is full of grace
Wednesday's child is full of woe
Thursday's child has far to go
Friday's child is loving and giving
Saturday's child works hard for its living
But the child that's born on the Sabbath day
Is bonnie and blithe, and good and gay"

I 'member one'a the town folk, Mrs. Binniton, was pregna't and her Momma told her that rhyme. I 'member 'cause she told it ta'us one day when she was in the market buy'n stuff. "That one's ta'tell what temperament your baby'll have."

"Yes," Alma said. "What day a baby is born will tell you what kind of personality it will have. Not all the rhymes are spells to change something. Some are wisdom sayings and others are a magical mystery. Some are portals to open doors to other worlds. And some are curses. Some are stories of history turned into a clever rhyme. But all can be used for magic."

Me and them four witches spent the rest of the afternoon go'n through the Mother Goose book and talk'n 'bout what rhymes could maybe be used for what. Alma said that it wasn't s'much the words, but the magical power and intention behind 'em. It was good ta'have visitors in my house. Like I said b'fore, I lived at the edge of town, and ain't nobody ever came out this far unless someth'n was wrong. I like spend'n time by ma'self. I never really feel alone. I got Old Henry if I need. I also got the Devil and the Old Dame if I need someth'n. Also, as the days go by, I'm know'n that more and more spirits are 'round. They prob'ly 'ardy been 'round and I'm just now know'n that they's there. Makes me wonder how long they been there. Maybe for all time. Maybe they came when I became a witch. Either way. I never feel alone.

When night came, I lit the candles and the oil lamp so the house wouldn't be too dark. Alma wanted ta'show me someth'n else b'fore the four witches went on their way home. She picked up her leather bag and took out a large cup, a loaf of bread, a bowl, and a bottle of wine. "Let's do a housel."

"What's a housel?" I asked.

"A housel is kind of like the lord's supper, but for witches," Clara said.

"Wine and bread as an offering is an ancient practice," Harriet said. "Christianity is but one of the religions that give offerings in this way."

Me and the four witches went outside. It was cool out, but not too cold. No one never came out here, but Alma be say'n that we oughta go behind the barn just in case. Witches don't like pry'n eyes, and you never know who's got pry'n eyes. I took my lantern ta'light the way. I din't need no light. I knew this little farm good, but Alma said we needed a light ta'represent the light of Spirit. We found us a nice spot behind the barn. Alma had me put down the lantern and we all stood in a circle 'round it. We put the bread in the bowl and Alma opened the bottle of wine and started pour'n some in the large cup. She put the cup next to the bowl and told us ta'hold hands in our little circle.

"Take a deep breath," Alma told us. "With each inhale, connect to the land. Open your heart and connect to the spirits of the land. Allow the power of the earth to fill your body. Turn your eyes to the stars. Take a breath. As you breathe in, allow the power of the stars to fill your body. Now, take another breath and connect with each person here in this circle."

We spent just a little while connect'n to the land, the stars, and ta'each other. It felt real nice be'n in the little circle, connect'n with the four witches. I felt connected, protected, and at peace like. The more I practiced connect'n to the land and the stars, the more I felt like I was understand'n the power that Alma was talk'n 'bout. Each time I connected was like I was get'n ma'self a little piece of the puzzle. Like each time I connected, the spirits was tell'n me more and more who they was.

Alma picked up the cup of wine, "I call to you, Devil, Witch Father, Old One, He of the Cloven Hoof, come! Place your power, your essence into this sacred vessel!"

Alma told us ta'imagine that we done see power come'n from the stars in white light into the cup. "Dame Holda, Lady Both Foul and Fair, Keeper of the Gates of the Underworld, come! Place your power, your essence, into this sacred vessel!"

We 'magined Dame Holda put'n her power into the cup. We 'magined white light fill'n the cup with power.

"Pass this vessel of wine widdershins, against the path of the sun," Alma said. "We do so because as witches, we go our own way in our own time. Also, because going with the sun is the way of the common folk. We witches go in between the worlds, so we go against the sun." This made sense ta'me. In my short time as a witch, I've learnt that witches be do'n things in the night when the common folk be do'n things in the day. The good town folk listen to the pastor and do what they's told. Witches do what we want and listen ta'our heart and not some preacher man. Common folk fear the spirits. Witches dance with 'em.

"As the vessel is passed to you, take a deep breath and slowly breath your power, your magic into the wine so that your magic mixes with the magic of the Old Ones," As Alma spoke, I could right feel the power in her voice. We passed the cup widdershins and when it came ta'me, I took me a deep breath and slowly breathed out my magic into that there vessel. Each of the four witches did so, too.

When the cup got back ta'her, Alma placed her hand over the cup and made a circ'lar motion. "By the power of alchemy, of transformation, do we stir the essence of the Witch Father and the Witch Mother with the essence of each one of us."

Maybe it was the light of the lantern or maybe I was in a trance, but I could'a swore I saw red and white energies mix'n in that cup. There was other energies, too. I could'a swore I saw sparkly lights in that wine.

Alma handed the cup to Harriet. She picked up the bowl that was hold'n the bread and she said, "We call to the spirits of the land. Elves, fey, and land wights. Place your power, your essence into this sacred bread."

When she done said it, I could smell the loamy earth. I could smell them trees, the grass, and the dirt too. We was just behind the barn, but the feel'n we got was just like we was in the deepest forest. I guess the land spirits was there. We all 'magined the land spirits put'n their energy in the bread.

Alma poured a little of the wine on the bread. "We combine the essence of the Gods and ourselves with the essence of the land to make this sacred meal."

Alma would later 'splain that the "Red Meal" may have been folk memory of when our pagan ancestors'd sacrifice an animal and be share'n in the sacred meal. She also done said that it also could'a been a symbolic way of reject'n our Christianity. For us, she'd say, it wasn't neither of these things. The Red Meal was the share'n of energies of the land and the Gods with each other, on account'n for magic and fellowship like.

"Each of you tear off a piece of the Red Meal and eat," Alma said. "By eating the red bread, you are sharing your energies with the energies of the spirits of the land."

We all took us a piece of that bread. It tasted sweet like with the wine that was on top of it. Alma poured just 'nuff of the wine on that bread ta'make it red, but not soggy like. When we all took us a piece of bread, Alma took the bowl and put it back on the ground.

"As we drink from this vessel we say, 'I drink in fear and dread'. We do this because by drinking the essence of the Old Ones, we agree to be transformed and changed by them. We agree to become better and wiser. We agree to allow the Old Ones to teach us the ways of magic. But the Old Ones work in their own way. They do what is necessary. But what is necessary isn't always pleasant to us. This is why we drink in fear and dread."

Alma stood quiet for a couple'a seconds. I could tell she was really try'na connect ta'what the mean'n of the housel, the Red Meal, was. "I drink in fear and dread." After she drank, she passed the cup 'round and we all said "I drink in fear and dread," b'fore take'n a big swallow. The cup went 'round the circle couple'a times 'til it was emptied.

After the housel, the four witches packed up their things in that 'ole leather bag of theirs and rode away in their wagon. It wouldn't take 'em too long ta'get home in Alma's wagon. They din't live that far away. I watched them four witches ride off and, maybe it was the magical wine, but it looked to me like them horses was pull'n that wagon real fast. Like real fast, the horses looked like they was trot'n normal like but the speed was otherworldly fast. I'm gonna have ta'ask Alma how she did that. Maybe witches can be change'n space and time. Maybe.

Now, let me tell you 'bout Old Mrs. Fossey. Old Mrs. Fossey was married to Mr. Fossey who owned the only bank in town. I've never had no cause ta'go ta'no bank 'cause I keep my money in a box in a closet. Yup, that box is right next to Old Henry's cat skull, so I figure ain't nobody gonna bother it none. Mr. Fossey was the richest man in town, so Mrs. Fossey, as you can prob'ly guess, was used to get'n her way. Also, Old Mrs. Fossey was the worst kinda rich, the kind that went ta'church and thought her Jesus was better than ever-one else's Jesus. What I mean by that is that ever-body be see'n and believe'n in Jesus they own way. The pastor tells us stuff 'bout God and the Bible and Jesus, but still, common folk has they own way of pray'n and see'n Jesus. Old Mrs. Fossey thought that how she saw Jesus was the right way and had no problem tell'n ever-body 'bout it. Most folks let her say her piece and then did their pray'n their own way. Sometimes, Old Mrs. Fossey would get on her high horse 'bout someth'n and this was one'a them times.

One day, Old Mrs. Fossey came into the store and was look'n at me like I was worser than dirt. She gave me such a snarl. Now, I never did do noth'n to Old Mrs. Fossey, or anybody else for that matter. But that pa'ticular day, she was not like'n me one bit. She brought her things to the counter and b'fore she paid her money, she said to Mr. Picklesworth, "Mr. Picklesworth, I didn't know you were partial to heathens."

Mr. Picklesworth knew she was talk'n 'bout me. He never paid no mind ta'what most folks thought of noth'n. He had the only store in town, and he knew that folks had ta'come ta'his store whether if they liked him or not. Mr. Picklesworth kept ta'his own business and never minded no-body. "Will that be all today, Mrs. Fossey?"

"Mr. Picklesworth," Old Mrs. Fossey raised her pitch, "this is a Christian town, and we want to keep it that way, wouldn't you agree?"

I kept sweep'n up the floor, act'n like I wasn't listen'n ta'what they was say'n. Mr. Picklesworth knew I was try'na hear the conversation. "Mrs. Fossey," Mr. Picklesworth said real calm like, "I try to mind my own business. I'd advise you do the same."

Old Mrs. Fossey's temper flared up real bad. I could tell she was mad as hell, but she considered herself too much of a lady ta'start yell'n at Mr. Picklesworth. Also, she was rich. The rich folks I know always be act'n like they'll get their way sooner or later, so they ain't gotta need ta'be hoot'n and holler'n 'bout someth'n, 'specially in public. Rich folks got a thing 'bout how folks be see'n 'em in public. "We'll just see what the pastor says about this. You wouldn't want anyone closing your store, would you?"

Mr. Picklesworth had known Mr. and Mrs. Fossey for a long time. He knew they's the richest family in town. Most folks in town was poor farmers or tradesmen of some kind, so I 'spose that made Mr. Picklesworth the second richest person in town. Either way, he din't scare easy. He had the most even temperament I'd ever seen. I woulda loved ta'see Mr. Picklesworth tell off Mrs. Fossey, but that wasn't the kinda man he was. "Good day, Mrs. Fossey."

Mrs. Fossey left in a huff, but that wouldn't be the last we heard of her. I guess Mrs. Fossey followed through on her threat, 'cause the pastor, Rev. Howard was his name, came over to the store ta'talk to Mr. Picklesworth. I was work'n back in the storeroom that was behind the front counter and I could hear ever-thing the pastor was say'n.

"Mr. Picklesworth, Mrs. Fossey came to see me yesterday about a young man that you have working for you," the pastor said.

Mr. Picklesworth sounded like he was 'bout ta'get real mad. He rarely lost his temper, but I could see it come'n. "Rev. Howard, who I hire and have work in my store ain't no one's business but my own. Johnathan Knotbristle has done noth'n wrong and attends church now and again, which is more than I can say for most of your congregation."

"Now, Mr. Picklesworth–" the pastor tried ta'interrupt.

"And further," Mr. Picklesworth continued forcefully, "Mrs. Fossey has nothing to do all day but bother poor boys who have lost their family 'cause of tragedy. If going through hard times is a sin, then we'd all be going to hell."

I ain't never heard Mr. Picklesworth talk like that ta'nobody, 'specially the pastor. I ain't never really thought of me and Mr. Picklesworth as friends, but I figure over the last few months I was grow'n on him. He was nice 'nuff ta'me, but you could say he was nice 'nuff ta'ever-body who walked into his store. I wasn't sure if he was say'n this stuff ta'be nice ta'me or 'cause he was not have'n no busybody rich woman tell him what's what. Either way, I 'ppreciated Mr. Picklesworth's kindness.

"Now, let's be reasonable," the pastor said. "Mr. Knotbristle and his whole family never did anything but get into trouble and folks are saying he's a witch."

"A witch!" Mr. Picklesworth was get'n sick and tired of this nonsense. "There ain't no witches here and there never was. This ain't the 1600s."

Rev. Howard was try'n ta'reason with Mr. Picklesworth and he could tell he wasn't do'n too good a job. "Please understand. When a prominent woman–"

"You mean the banker's wife," Mr. Picklesworth said firmly.

"Well, yes," the pastor said. "When a prominent and pious woman believes that the Devil is working against God in the community, we must listen to her concerns."

"We will not have a witch-hunt in my store or my town," Mr. Picklesworth was try'n real hard ta'hold back yell'n at the 'ole pastor. I made sure ta'stay in the storeroom. I din't want ta'come out to the store, no way. I kept listen'n, though. Mr. Picklesworth continued, "You go back to Mrs. Fossey and tell her that she can take her make-believe 'pious' stories and stick 'em where the sun don't shine!"

Rev. Howard stood there for a minute, not know'n what ta'say. I don't think he'd be able ta'change Mr. Picklesworth's mind anyhow.

Once he made up his mind 'bout someth'n, that was it. There wasn't no change'n it. He was truly a stubborn man.

That very next Sund'y, I figured I should go ta'church. Even b'fore be'n a witch, I wasn't the church go'n type. Truth be told, our little town din't have lots of folks who was the church go'n type. Yes, there was those families that thought they was better'n anybody else and they made sure ta'be in church ever-Sund'y. Momma used ta'say that church go'n folks and folks who was good wasn't always the same thing. She said that sometimes there're folks who go ta'church ta'be seen and then there are those folks who don't care 'bout shit like that and do good just 'cause. This Sund'y, it might be best if folks see me in those pews. Most folks was start'n ta'like me, so I ain't had no cause ta'worry 'bout noth'n. But Mr. Picklesworth was have'n problems, and I figured I should go ta'church ta'make things easier on him.

I walked into that church and 'em town folk was just a stare'n at me. Like I was some kinda crim'nal on the loose. I was guess'n that Mrs. Fossey'd been talk'n their ear off. Mrs. Fossey and her lady friends was sit'n in the front pew. Seemed like they was the kinda church go'n folks who wanted ta'be seen, just like Momma talked 'bout. They was look'n back at me, give'n me the nastiest looks. I was try'n ta'act like I din't notice, but them looks felt like nails hitt'n me right in the face. After ever-one got into church and sat down, the pastor started his sermon. He started with the welcomes and such, just like he did ever-Sund'y, but the sermon was, as you'd 'spect, 'bout witches. He talked on and on 'bout how sometimes folks is seduced by the Devil and how folks forget 'bout God. He talked 'bout how we must stay diligent in our Christian faith and keep up our prayers. At one point, he even said that we oughta keep an eye out for witches.

At the end of the service, ever-body left and went outside. Mr. Picklesworth and his family came over ta'me and said hello. I wasn't sure if I was 'sposed ta'bring attention to 'em by say'n hello, so I'm glad he came up ta'me first. We was talk'n 'bout the day and what I was gonna do on my day off when Mrs. Fossey walked straight up ta'us.

"Mr. Picklesworth," Mrs. Fossey said, "I see you don't enjoy listening to reason."

"When someone is being reasonable," Mr. Picklesworth said, "I'll be sure to listen."

You could see how mad Mrs. Fossey was gett'n ta'be on her face, "We'll see just how reasonable you are when no one comes to your store because you are kind to witches."

Mr. Picklesworth was get'n real tired of Mrs. Fossey, "And how much did you put in the church coffers to make Rev. Howard part of your nonsense?"

Mrs. Fossey din't say noth'n 'bout that and walked away. I could tell that Mr. Picklesworth was glad for it. We said our goodbyes and I went home that day. Walk'n home, I was wonder'n how much trouble all this was gonna cause. I din't want ta'cause no kinda harm to Mr. Picklesworth or his store. Noth'n ta'do but see how things go. I was just hope'n this'd all pass soon 'nuff.

The next day, I went back ta'work at the store. It was a Mond'y like any other Mond'y. Noth'n too special 'bout it. It wasn't rain'n that day, so business should be good. I did ma'daily chores of sweep'n, stock'n the shelves, and any other thing that Mr. Picklesworth wanted me ta'do. Sometimes he had me haul'n in grain or corn when one'a the farmers was sell'n to Mr. Picklesworth. After a few hours, I was notice'n that ain't nobody come into the store. No one at all. This was kinda strange, 'cause somebody always come into the store buy'n or sell'n someth'n. Today, noth'n.

"Kinda strange how ain't nobody come in today," I said to Mr. Picklesworth.

"Strange indeed," Mr. Picklesworth said. He had a look on his face that he was know'n someth'n wasn't right. Someth'n was go'n on. He looked outside the winda' and said, "Goddammit!"

I hurried to the winda' ta'see what Mr. Picklesworth was upset 'bout, and there she was. Mrs. Fossey was stand'n on a wood crate, holler'n 'bout someth'n. Mr. Picklesworth ran outside ta'hear what she was say'n and I followed him.

I couldn't hear much of what she was say'n none 'til we got closer. "–and to allow ungodly folks in our town! Near our children!"

Dammit, I thought to ma'self. This wasn't no good at all. Mrs. Fossey was try'na turn the town folk 'gainst me and 'gainst Mr. Picklesworth, too. I wasn't sure what we was gonna do. Mrs. Fossey was hoot'n and holler'n 'bout witches and Satan and all kinda things she din't know noth'n 'bout. The next thing I heard was not good at all. "Mr. Picklesworth is allowing a witch to work in his store!" Mrs. Fossey was point'n directly at us. I wasn't sure if she was point'n at me or Mr. Picklesworth, but either way, it wasn't good, no way.

Mr. Picklesworth stormed out the door of the store and marched right up to Mrs. Fossey stand'n on that crate. I figured I best be follow'n him, 'cause he looked s'mad I thought he might have a mind ta'take a swat at her.

"Now you wait a minute!" Mr. Picklesworth shouted at her.

"Good townsfolk," Mrs. Fossey was plead'n with the folks now. "Knowing that Mr. Picklesworth is allowing a witch to work in his store, we couldn't possibly step foot inside, could we?"

The small crowd of folks was agree'n with ever-thing she had ta'say. They was get'n real wound up and started look'n mad as hell. I figured we best be get'n away from this crowd, 'cause who knows what they's gonna do ta'me or Mr. Picklesworth. Mr. Picklesworth pulled me away and we walked back to the store. He din't say one word rest of the day. I'm not sure if he believed I was a witch or not, but he seemed ta'want ta'put up a fight just ta'spite Mrs. Fossey. As the week passed by, there wasn't one customer in the store. There was a small group of folks stand'n near the store, and anytime someone tried ta'come inside, they'd start shout'n 'bout witches, the Devil, and sin. No one came into the store that week.

On Frid'y night, I walked home feel'n real bad for Mr. Picklesworth. He done noth'n but help me and it was my fault this was happen'n ta'him. Mrs. Fossey was a cruel woman and hellbent on cause'n trouble for someone she don't know and ruin'n the business of a kind man.

Someone need'd ta'stop her. I could stop her.

When I got home, I decided I was gonna cast me a spell on Mrs. Fossey. Even better, I was gonna send her a curse. The best way ta'do a spell like this was call'n the Old Gods and have'n 'em help me with my magic. I propped my two tined pitchfork on the right side of the fireplace and put me a candle in the center of them two tines. I put my 'ole broom on the left side of the fireplace. It was time ta'call the Old Gods.

I had the fire in the fireplace go'n real good. I connected with that fire with my heart. When I was connect'n with that fire, I felt like it wasn't no fire at all. It was the power of the Old Gods. The magic of the ever-thing. You ever be know'n stuff and not know how you be know'n it? I was connect'n ta'that fire, the magic of ever-thing, and all a sudden, in my head, I was think'n that ta'better call the Old Gods I was need'n ta'call 'em with the spirit tongue.

I took a few deep breaths and put ma'self in a trance. I 'membered what Alma and the three witches'd taught me 'bout how ta'talk in spirit tongue. I focused on my heart, and with each breath, I done got deeper and deeper into a trance. I 'magined the power of the stars and breathed that down into my heart. I 'magined the spirits of the earth and breathed that power into my heart. Then I focused on my heart. My heart was feel'n ever-thing: the cosmos, the land, and the Gods. I 'magined that I could speak in the ancient spirit tongue by just feel'n the power in my heart. In my mind, I thought 'bout call'n the Devil. I lit that candle in b'tween them two tines on that pitchfork. I let sounds come out my mouth. I knew what I was want'n ta'say, and I just let syllables and pretend words come out my mouth with the hope of call'n the Devil. "*Wata ka-noma-yanna-so-mile-ya-se.*" After I said that I 'magined the Devil appear'n over the pitchfork.

I connected to the broom lean'n 'gainst the wall next to the fireplace. I 'magined in my mind call'n to the Old Dame, to Holda, Queen of Elphame. I let the syllables and pretend words come out my mouth. "*So-la miya-se-loggo, wanna, bay-yalta mina-ya. Coma be-yalto-my-ka.*" I 'magined Holda appear'n over the broom. The Old Ones was here.

I lit two candles I had on my wooden table. Next to 'em, I had the Mother Goose book that Alma'd gave me. It was time ta'use one'a the spells from this book. I knew just the one ta'use ta'get rid of Mrs. Fossey. I took a cup outta the cupboard and trapped me a spider that was hang'n up in them rafters of the house. I put that spider in the cup b'tween the candles and kept a book on top so that spider wouldn't escape none. *It's time for Mrs. Fossey ta'learn her lesson,* I thought to ma'self.

I know just the spell for her. I opened up the Mother Goose book and turnt to the page with the rhyme "Miss Muffet." I 'magined the power of the stars come'n down on me and fill'n up my body with power. I focused on the land, the trees, and ever-thing on earth and 'magined the power fill'n up my body. I focused my attention on that spider. I breathed more and more power into my body 'til I couldn't stand it no more. Then I said the rhyme.

Little Miss Muffet
Sat on a tuffet
Eating of curds and whey
There came a big spider
And sat down beside her
And frightened Miss Muffet away

When I was say'n that rhyme, I used my mind and 'magined a big spider crawl'n up next to Mrs. Fossey in her dreams. I said the rhyme a second time and I 'magined the big spider weav'n a big web and captur'n Mrs. Fossey. I said the rhyme a third time and I 'magined the spider weav'n a web 'round her head and mouth, leav'n her silent. I focused all the power I could ta'this here spider. I sent the spider's spirit out ta'do the work I needed it ta'do. To silence Mrs. Fossey. I let them candles burn for a while, and when I felt ready for the spell ta'be done, I put that cup up to the rafters and let the little spider out. It scooted away.

The follow'n Sund'y, I decided ta'go ta'church and see if my spell'd worked any. I walked up in that church and I din't see no hide or hair of Mrs. Fossey. That was strange, I thought. I figured she'd be in the front pew, just as she always was. I saw Mr. Picklesworth and said hello ta'him and his family. But no Mrs. Fossey. I sat down in one'a the pews and ain't no one said a word. The pastor saw me too, but he din't say a word neither.

I got a strange feel'n like. Ever-body was wrapped up. It felt like the church was nestled right snug in a blanket. When the pastor started his sermon, he welcomed ever-one just as he always do. Then I heard the big church door creak open. Mrs. Fossey and her husband came in, late. The whole congregation turnt ta'see 'em come in late. This wasn't like Mrs. Fossey at all. She was always early ta'church. But not today. Today, she held her head down and sat herself in the back. She could'a sat anywhere in the pews, really. There was plenty of seats left, but I guess she din't want ta'draw no attention ta'herself. She sat in church, not say'n a word. After the sermon, she and her husband left without s'much as a word. Noth'n.

I walked outta the church and all those folks who was hoot'n and holler'n 'bout witches the other day just looked at the ground when I did pass by. Just for fun, I said hello to 'em as I was walk'n by, and they din't lift their eyes from that green earth. They was silent, too.

I said goodbye to Mr. Picklesworth and headed home. It was look'n like the spell done worked. Maybe too well. When I got home, I pulled ma'self out a chair and looked up in them rafters for that spider. Sure 'nuff, that little spider had built hisself a new web. I looked a little closer at the web and I saw me four flies wrapped up in that spider's web. Silent.

8

The Ghost
and the Gate

HARVEST TIME WAS ALMOST OVER. I jarred ever-thing I was gonna jar. Be'n by ma'self, I din't need ta'grow a whole lot on my little farm. It was just 'nuff ta'last me 'til spring, and maybe a bit more. The trees still had some leaves on 'em. Be'n in the South, the trees had leaves almost all year 'round. They was mostly brown. Where I live, leaves don't get all them pretty colors like up in the North. Just brown leaves. The air was get'n real cold, 'specially with the breeze. Now'd it was Halloween, there was a feel'n in the air. Ever-where I went there was a feel'n that there was spirits in the air. Walk'n back and forth from my house to the store, I felt like someone was watch'n me. Maybe it was ghosts or maybe it was witches. I never could tell.

I got to the store early in the morn'n and Mr. Picklesworth was put'n up paper pumpkins and ghosts in the windas. He wasn't one for celebrate'n most holidays 'cept for Christmas, but today he was make'n a 'ception. My family never celebrated Halloween. Momma and Daddy was quick ta'have us all go ta'bed early. One'a the Halloween traditions is ta'tell spooky stories 'bout ghosts, but Daddy said it ain't no use get'n all bent up 'bout no ghosts when there ain't no ghosts. Halloween wasn't celebrated a lot in town neither. There was some families that had their own celebration and maybe'd invite friends, but my family was never invited, and Daddy was just fine with that.

"Does your family celebrate Halloween?" I asked Mr. Picklesworth.

"Oh, I think a good ghost story and apple eating never hurt anyone," Mr. Picklesworth said. "Besides, we all need a good scare from time to time. It reminds us we're alive."

I never really thought 'bout it like that b'fore. The times I've been scared 'bout someth'n in my life I was always happy when it was over. I 'member one time I got lost in the woods by my house when I was 5 or 6 years old. I was play'n out there in those trees, just have'n a good 'ole time, not think'n 'bout where I was or what time it was. It was get'n dark and I got ma'self lost. I was try'na find my way home but din't know where I was go'n. The darker those 'ole woods got, the more scared I got. I started call'n for Daddy and all I saw was the shadows of them trees. Them 'ole, ancient trees. I started run'n but din't know if I was even run'n in the right direction. Finally, I heard Daddy call'n my name and I went run'n towards the sound of his voice. I ain't never been s'happy ta'see him in all my life. So I guess Mr. Picklesworth was right. When you're scared ta'tears, you 'preciate things more when it's all over.

"This came in the mail for you, Johnathan." Mr. Picklesworth took out a small brown package from behind the counter. "It came yesterday, after you'd left for the day."

I took the small package and was amazed anyone'd sent me someth'n. Who in the world could it be from? There wasn't no return address. I opened up the package and inside a small box was two sticks fastened with red string, make'n an equal armed cross. There was a note inside that said, "You may need this tonight. Best, A." Alma. It had ta'be from Alma.

"Looks like two rowan twigs," Mr. Picklesworth said. "I wonder who sent that to you?"

"I dunno," I said. I was wonder'n if this was for protection from ghosts or spirits or someth'n. It was Halloween, after all. Anyth'n could happen. I put the little rowan cross in my trouser s pocket. I had a feel'n I might need it b'fore the night was over.

Later that day, Mrs. Miller came into the store look'n for a few things for a party her and her husband was have'n for Halloween. I din't really know the Millers, but they always seemed like a right happy family. They went ta'church ever-Sund'y just like ever-body else and never bothered nobody. They had a big house that was close to the town square. They was not the richest folks in town, but they sure did have money. Mrs. Miller brought several apples to the counter and some brandy wine, too. She had me go into the storeroom and fetch more fruit, cheese, meat, bread, beer, and whiskey. Ever-thing you needed for a Halloween party.

"Looks like your Halloween party is gonna be wonderful," Mr. Picklesworth said. He had been know'n the Millers for a long time. The Picklesworth family and the Miller family was some of the oldest families that settled this town. I think they've known each other since they was children.

"Oh, yes," Mrs. Miller said, "it's sure to be a fine time." Mrs. Miller watched me get all her stuff and place it in a bag.

"I can deliver these ta'ya Mrs. Miller," I said. "I don't want you hav'n ta'carry all this home yourself."

"Thank you, Johnathan," Mrs. Miller said. "Johnathan, if you aren't busy tonight, would you and Mr. Picklesworth like to come to our Halloween celebration?"

"Oh, no," Mr. Picklesworth said. "I'm gonna stay inside tonight, away from all the mischief. But you should go, Johnathan."

No one ever invited me to a party b'fore. Like I said, me and my family lived s'far at the edge of town and we was the type ta'keep ta'our own business. I was kinda jealous of folks who had parties like the one Mrs. Miller was have'n. It sounded like a fine time. "If you don't mind, I'd love to."

"Of course!" Mrs. Miller was a real social type of woman. She and her husband loved have'n parties and entertain'n guests. I get me the feel'n that part of it was that they liked ta'have fun, and the other part was that they liked show'n off their wealth. Either way, it'd be a good time. "Mr. Miller and I will be very happy for you to attend."

I took Mrs. Miller's bag 'cross the town square ta'her house and then came back to the store as soon as I could. It was get'n dark early and the air was noticeably cooler than dur'n the day. As I walked up the steps of the general store, I got a cold feel'n in my gut. Someth'n wasn't right. I turnt 'round and looked at the other buildings in the town square. Maybe I was get'n all caught up in the Halloween feel'n of ghosts and stuff, but I couldn't stop the cold feel'n in my belly. Somethin's not right at all.

Mr. Picklesworth closed up the store early. It was dark and the winds was start'n ta'blow the cool air. I din't want ta'go all the way home ta'change clothes and come all the way back ta'town again, so I went straight from the store to Mr. and Mrs. Miller's house. I knocked on the door and was greeted by their youngest daughter, Sarah. Sarah was 'bout 10 years old, and she was excited 'bout the Halloween party. "Are you here for the party tonight?"

"Yes, I am," I said.

"Johnathan!" Mrs. Miller yelled from inside the house, "Is that you?"

"Yes, Mrs. Miller," I yelled back at her.

"Good! Do come in! You can help me with the party before everyone gets here." Mrs. Miller was busy decorate'n the dine'n room in her house. I ain't never seen a house with a formal dine'n room b'fore. The Miller house always seemed s'big ta'me. Sarah Miller let me inside and Mrs. Miller instructed me ta'hang up paper pumpkins and ghosts in the windas of the house. She also had me put bowls of fruit and nuts and be place'n 'em on the dine'n room table. I helped her carve Jack O' Lanterns and put 'em in the dine'n room and in the windas of the house. While I was do'n all this, Mrs. Miller was finish'n with the cakes and candies that she was make'n in the kitch'n. I enjoyed help'n Mrs. Miller get'n ready for the Halloween party. I was alone most the time. I don't mind be'n alone too much, but this was real nice.

In no time at all, the party guests started ta'get there. The house was filled with relatives and friends. Some of them folks there I knew and some I din't. I was wonder'n if any of 'em was friends with Mrs. Fossey and maybe woulda had them a problem with me be'n there. I din't see nobody from the group of folks who was say'n I was a witch. Good. I wanted ta'enjoy the party without worry'n who was gonna say what. The party was go'n well and ever-body was have'n a good time. Folks was eat'n and drink'n and laugh'n. I hadn't laughed with nobody in a long time. It seemed like for tonight, ever-body was forget'n work, responsibilities, and arguments that they was hav'n with each other. Tonight was Halloween, and we was all together ta'celebrate the ghosts and spirits of the day.

Mr. Jones walked up ta'me, carry'n a glass of brandy wine. I din't know him that well 'cept for his orders from the general store. "Johnathan, you're not gonna go mischief making tonight?"

"Mischief?" I had 'nuff trouble the last few weeks ta'last me a while. The last thing I needed was find'n ma'self in trouble. "No. I think I'm good and fine stay'n here where it's safe."

Mr. Jones laughed a good belly laugh and took a drink of his brandy wine. "Just as well, Johnathan. No need of stealing gates from a fence or moving the outhouse."

"Why'd anyone steal a fence gate?" I just thought that was the strangest thing. Seemed like a lot of trouble ta'me.

"Young folk do things like that for a good laugh," Mr. Jones said. "Halloween is a time of chaos and mischief. It's a day that is said to be between the worlds. At night the spirits come out and cause havoc. So, some folks decide to play tricks on each other and blame it on the spirits."

Isn't that the luck, I thought to ma'self, folks always blame things on us magical folk.

"One Halloween," Mr. Jones laughed, "someone took Mr. Fossey's wagon apart and put it back together on his rooftop!"

"Wouldn't that take all night ta'do?" I asked, wonder'n who'd do such a thing.

"Yes!" Mr. Jones laughed s'hard I thought he wasn't gonna be able ta'breathe. "That greedy 'ole man deserved it! I'm sure the look on his face when he went out on November morning to fetch his wagon was worth every minute of it."

When it started ta'get late, Mr. Miller gave instructions for the dine'n room table ta'be cleared. Mrs. Miller brought her a large bowl that was filled with chopped fruit, nuts, raisins, and little metal trinkets. She poured the brandy in the bowl, cover'n ever-thing that was in there. She took a match, struck it, and lit the bowl of brandy on fire. The light from the oil lamps was put out. It was dark 'cept from the flame of the brandy. The flame of the brandy gave an otherworldly look to ever-one.

"Let's play snapdragon!" Mr. Miller said with such joy in his heart. "Everyone, gather 'round the bowl. You must plunge your hand into the burning flames of the brandy and retrieve the fruit, nuts, and trinkets from the bowl. At the end of the game, whoever has the most items from the bowl wins!"

This was surely a game I ain't never played b'fore. It was funny as hell watch'n ever-body put their hands in the bowl and get'n burnt up by them flames. Not real burnt up like that. You din't catch on fire, but it was hot as hell and folks kept say'n "ow!" or "oof!" or "damn, that's hot!" Ever-body took turns try'na get stuff outta the bowl quick as they could. I tried a few times, but the flames was just too hot for me. I'm not sure the flames was all that hot, but stick'n my hand in a bowl of burn'n fire made me think twice. Maybe that's part'a the game, get'n over your mind, get'n over your fear of things. In b'tween all the "ows!" ever-one was laugh'n and have'n s'much fun. At the end of the game, anyth'n that someone took out was theirs ta'eat and enjoy. It was Mr. Miller who won the game. Mrs. Miller whispered in my ear, "He always wins, that's why he insists on playing this game every Halloween and Christmas."

"Who is ready to talk to some ghosts?" Mrs. Miller said with a smile like she wasn't up ta'no good. Well, it was Halloween and I guess ever-one was do'n mischief tonight. "Follow me, everyone."

Mrs. Miller led the party-goers into the parlor room. The room was draped with curtains with the color'n of burgundy. In the center of the room was a round table. There was several chairs all 'round the table and it was draped all over with a black cloth. There was a single candle and a small oval mirror stand'n upright at the center of the table. I would later find out that that 'ole mirror was a gift from Mrs. Miller's granny who left it ta'her when she died. "Those of you who would like to participate in the séance, take a seat at the table, please. Those who wish to watch, stand around the table and keep silent."

A few folks took a seat at the table. Mrs. Miller sat herself at the far end, face'n the door. Mostly it was the women who was sit'n at the table. The men seemed ta'be just fine stand'n behind the chairs, just watch'n. I was fine to stand'n up. Some of them town folk 'ardy was think'n I'm a witch, so I thought best not ta'have someth'n happen and prove 'em right. Mrs. Miller lit the candle with a match and the parlor door got closed.

"Let us hold hands," Mrs. Miller said as she was grab'n the women's hands who was sit'n next ta'her. "Turn off the oil lamps, please."

Mr. Miller done put out all the oil lamps and any other candles that was light'n up the parlor room. The only light was the single candle sit'n in the center of that table. The little flame lit up the room just 'nuff so the ladies' faces had a ghostly look to 'em. I could see Mrs. Miller close her eyes. She looked like she was focus'n real hard on the séance. "Everyone in the room, suspend any disbelief. For any disbelief will cause an energy block and the spirits cannot cross over into our world. Ladies. Take a deep breath with me. Now open your minds and your hearts to the spirit world. Imagine that your mind is allowing the spirits to come through for us. Let your heart open. Feel the presence of the spirits. You may see the spirits in your mind or you may gaze into the mirror. For the mirror is a window into the spirit world."

The ladies did what Mrs. Miller was say'n. I think all them women'd done a séance b'fore, 'cause it looked like they was know'n what they was do'n. One'a the ladies at the table spoke up. Her name was Mrs. Brown. I only knew Mrs. Brown from church, and she sometimes'd come into the store from time ta'time. "There is a spirit here who wishes to speak."

"Can you see them, Mrs. Brown?" Mrs. Miller said.

"I cannot," Mrs. Brown said. "I only feel them with my heart."

"Gaze into the mirror," Mrs. Miller said. "Don't look at your reflection or the reflection of any other living person. Look deep into the mirror as if you were looking deep into a well. Imagine your mind moving from this world into the spirit world."

Mrs. Brown must have done what Mrs. Miller was tell'n her 'cause she said, "Yes, I see them now."

"Good," Mrs. Miller said. "What do they wish to tell us this night?"

Mrs. Brown's voice was sound'n real strange. Like it was her voice and someone else's voice talk'n at the same time. What I know 'bout talk'n with ghosts in a seance is that the trick is you wanna connect real good with the spirit. Imagine your heart and your mind is join'n with the heart and the mind of the spirit. Open'n your life force to 'em. Let 'em connect with ya. You don't need ta'worry 'bout get'n possessed or noth'n. That only happen's if you is sick or in a bad way or someth'n. You is live'n and they is dead, so they can't hurt you none if you don't want 'em to. That's the only trick you need. Mrs. Brown had joined her heart and her mind to the spirit, so they was talk'n like they was one person. "We have returned to the world of the living to give you this message..."

There was a long pause. Mrs. Miller still had her eyes closed and she said, "Yes? What is the message?"

"There are those among you," Mrs. Brown and the spirit continued, "who do not wish you well."

"Who?" Mrs. Miller asked. "Here at the party?"

"No," Mrs. Brown and the spirit said.

"Who then?"

Mrs. Brown and the spirit din't say noth'n for a while. "Witches."

Witches? When I heard that, first thing I thought was that the spirits was know'n I was a witch and was warn'n Mrs. Miller. Damn it. I was hope'n those spirits wasn't gonna say noth'n. That'd sure spell trouble for me. I din't say a word. All I could do was hope noth'n more'd be said and this'd be the end of it. Only thing is, the spirit said there was a witch that din't wish Mrs. Miller well. I liked Mrs. Miller just fine and din't wish her no harm, so maybe the spirit wasn't talk'n 'bout me. Maybe they was talk'n 'bout 'nother witch. So...was there 'nother witch in town that nobody knew 'bout?

"There is more," Mrs. Brown and the spirit said.

"Yes?" Mrs. Miller was get'n excited. "Tell us more."

All a'sudden, it was like all the energy went outta that room. Like someone sucked the life right out the whole place. Mrs. Brown looked straight at Mrs. Miller and her face turnt white as a sheet. Like someth'n had scared her awful. "They're here."

Mrs. Miller looked like she din't know what inna hell Mrs. Brown was talk'n 'bout. She din't say a word though, I figure 'cause she felt that feel'n in the room, too. Hell, we all did. Someth'n was real wrong.

There was a knock on the door.

Mr. Miller looked at the front door of the house. "Whoever could that be?"

No one said noth'n. I guess they was tryna figure out what in high hell was go'n on with a witch and what did the spirit mean say'n, "they're here"?

Mr. Miller left the parlor ta'open the front door of his house. When he opened that door, stand'n right in front of him was a corpse. A godamned corpse! Not a ghost. A damned corpse. Like someth'n just crawled out the grave. Mr. Miller took a step back and slammed the door, latched it up tight. The corpse knocked on the door again. Some of the men heard the commotion and ran to the front door where Mr. Miller was stand'n. All the blood ran outta Mr. Miller's face. "It's a damn corpse!"

One'a the men looked out the winda' and saw the corpse just stand'n there, knock'n on the door. He noticed that the gate to the Miller's wooden fence was gone. "The gate is gone! Someone must have pulled a prank and stolen your gate!"

I din't know this at the time, but fence gates is more than a doorway inside and outta your fence. It's also a magical boundary that keeps the bad spirit outta your property. If your gate is removed, then all kinds of spirits and ghouls can get through. That's a lesson we need ta'know. Always keep your gate closed. Never let noth'n in that don't belong. It's true that the miss'n gate allowed the corpse ta'come to the house, but how'd the corpse get there in the first place?

Mr. Miller fetched his rifle, loaded it, and opened the front door again. He pulled the trigger and shot the corpse square b'tween the eyes, but that bullet went through the corpse like it was go'n through fog. It went clear through 'em. Mr. Miller shut door again and latched it tight. Bullets wasn't stop'n these things.

The ladies came outta the room and joined the men ta'see 'bout the commotion. Mrs. Miller looked out the winda' and saw the corpse too, stand'n at her front porch. She could see the neighbors' houses from the winda' along with their fences. "The neighbors' gates are all gone too!"

'Nother corpse come walk'n through the hole in the fence where the gate used ta'be. Mr. Miller pulled Mrs. Miller back. "Stay away from the windows!"

Mrs. Miller din't take her gaze away from the windas. She was determined ta'see what was go'n on. She saw more corpses walk'n in her neighbors' yard, too! "They're everywhere!"

Kock. Knock. Knock. Knock.

"Everybody be quiet," Mr. Miller whispered.

Knock. Knock. Knock. Knock.

A hush was on ever-body in the house. Ain't no one said a peep. I don't think no one breathed neither. We all stood there, hold'n our breath.

Knock. Knock. Knock. Knock.

"They only seem to be knocking," Mrs. Miller said.

"Nobody open the door," Mr. Miller said quietly. "Stay away from the windows and stay quiet. Maybe they'll go away."

We stood there for a while, and that corpse just kept knock'n. I took a peep out the winda' and I could see corpses at all them neighbors' houses, too. They wasn't do'n noth'n but knock'n. No one knew why them corpses was here and what they wanted. I, on the other hand, knew one thing right certain...this here's witchcraft, plain and simple. I think I was the only one who was able ta'do someth'n, but I had got no clue for what inna hell ta'do. The only thing I could think of is that them corpses came out the grave, so it was the graveyard I was a go'n to. I quietly walked over to the back door. I unlatched it real quiet like and opened just 'nuff ta'where I could see outside. No corpse knock'n here. I guess they was only at the front door. I slipped out the back door and started run'n to the graveyard. As I was run'n, I saw one or two of them corpses knock'n on ever-bodys' house. At ever-house with a corpse, the fence gate was clean gone. Someone'd stole 'em!

I ran as fast I could. I din't understand much what was go'n on and who could'a done this type of magic. When I got to the graveyard, the gate was gone there, too. I tried ta'catch my breath b'fore I went in. In the dark, I heard someone say'n someth'n. It sounded to me like a chant. I slowly walked closer, and that's when I saw it. A man wear'n a black hooded cloak. I crept closer and I heard the man speak'n in a spirit tongue. *"Oro ubano may-kyo lantana say ko mio."* I frozen in place for just a short while. *Holy shit!* I thought. There's a witch conjure'n in the graveyard! Maybe this was the person who done conjured the corpses ta'attack the houses. I heard the chant'n again, *"Iba so-yoto, mina a-co-lee-yo, bo-naya-te-lay!"*

I slowly got closer and closer to the cloaked person. Shit, what was gonna happen?! *Shit shit shit!*

Fuck it, I thought. I needed ta'see who this was, "Who's there?"

The chant'n stopped and the cloaked person turnt 'round ta'face me, lower'n their hood. *Holy shit!* It was Mr. Picklesworth! I sat there try'n ta'figure out what inna hell was go'n on. Mr. Picklesworth...is a witch? All this time I was work'n for him, Mr. Picklesworth was a witch! I din't know much what ta'think. The man who I worked for was secretly do'n magic. "Mr. Picklesworth..."

"Johnathan," Mr. Picklesworth looked relieved ta'see me, "I'm glad you're here. I need your help to put these spirits back into the grave."

"Wait," Now I was even more confused ta'what inna hell was happen'n, "you din't conjure them corpses out the grave?"

"Of course not," Mr. Picklesworth said. "As soon as I saw the spirits, I came over to the cemetery to put them back in the ground."

"How'd they get outta them graves?" I asked.

"A witch conjured them tonight. In fact, it was most likely a coven of witches," Mr. Picklesworth said.

A coven'a witches. In this town? It seems like ever since I became a witch, witches was come'n out the woodwork. "What do we do? How'll we be get'n them corpses ta'come back to the graveyard?"

"They're not corpses," Mr. Picklesworth said. "They're simply spirits of the dead. But these aren't the spirits of the ancestors who have passed on to the spirit world. These are the leftover spirit fetch of the dead that rot along with the actual physical body."

"I don't understand, I seen 'em, Mr. Picklesworth. They look like rot'n bodies. We all heard 'em knock'n on the doors of the house."

Mr. Picklesworth figured that if I was gonna help him with the spirits, then he needed ta'come clean and tell me what they was 'zactly and how ta'put 'em back in the ground.

"We have our spirit, yes, but we also have a *fetch*, or spirit of darkness. This is an energy body that is lower than our spirit. It's what helps us shapeshift. Or we can send our fetch out to do things for us. When we die, our spirit moves on to the spirit world, but the fetch is attached to our physical body. So when our physical body rots, so does our fetch body."

"Ok," I said, "then how'd this happen?"

"A powerful witch, who knows how can conjure and summon the fetch of someone who's died to do their bidding," Mr. Picklesworth looked worried. "There's too many of these spirits loose to be the work of just one witch. It has to be a coven. A powerful one. One that is up to no good."

Now this din't settle with me too good. All this time, I thought I was the only witch in this town, and the closest witches I knew 'bout was Alma, Harriet, Viola, and Clara, but they was clear in the next town over. I figured I had a lot ta'learn.

"I need you to help me put these spirits back to where they belong." Mr. Picklesworth said. He had a black cloth bag behind one'a the grave markers. He took stuff out the bag, one by one. He had a pouch of tobacco, a jar of cow's blood, a piece of coal, a rowan stick, and a jar of mullein herb.

"What do I do?"

"Take this cow's blood. You're gonna pour a straight line of blood from the road up there to the entrance of the graveyard," Mr. Picklesworth said. "Dark spirits are attracted to blood 'cause it's a living being's life force. They need the life force of the blood to stay manifest on the physical plane. It's important that you start at the road and pour a line to the entrance. The direction is important. You want the spirits to come to the grave and not away from it."

"Ok," I said as I picked up the jar of blood.

"Once that's done," Mr. Picklesworth said, "we'll place mullein on a lighted piece of coal. The mullein calls to the spirits. I'll use the rowan wand to summon them here. Rowan controls spirits of all kinds. Before the spirits return, we'll place tobacco on each of the graves as an offering. The tobacco will entice the spirits to stay at the grave. Once they enter, we'll place a small piece of rowan wood on each grave to seal the spirits in."

Me and Mr. Picklesworth hurried fast as we could and put tobacca on each of them graves. Then he lit the coal with a match and put the mullein herb on it, so it'd smoke real good. I ran out to the road and opened the jar of cow's blood and started pour'n it on the ground. Not too much at once. There needed ta'be a thin bloody path from the road to the graveyard entrance. As I poured, I 'magined that the dead was be'n compelled ta'follow the trail of blood back to the graveyard. Once that was all done for, I ran over to Mr. Picklesworth's side.

Mr. Picklesworth'd closed his eyes for a minute and gathered his power. I was think'n he called up the power of the stars and the power of the earth, just like Alma taught me. He pointed the rowan wand of his towards the center of town where them spirit fetches roamed. "By the powers of the Witch Father, I call to you spirits of the dead. In the Devil's name I command you to return to the grave! You, who walk with the living, by the powers of witchcraft and the powers of the Devil himself, I command you. Return to the grave!"

The mullein herb on the coal started smoke'n a whole lot. The smoke done rose up from the coal and moved through the air. It moved through the graveyard and right down to the center of town. The spirit corpses stopped their knock'n and took them notice of the mullein smoke. I think they heard Mr. Picklesworth call'n 'em. They'd just stopped what they was do'n and started walk'n towards the graveyard. Mr. Picklesworth said his conjure'n again, "By the powers of the Witch Father, I call to you spirits of the dead. In the Devil's name, I command you to return to the grave! You, who walk with the living, by the powers of witchcraft and the powers of the Devil himself, I command you. Return to the grave!"

It was work'n! The spirits was walk'n to the graveyard! Once they all got to the road, they must'a smellt that cow's blood or someth'n, 'cause they all followed that trail of blood in a straight line. I counted ma'self nine of 'em. I din't know that many spirits was out knock'n on folks' doors. I was relieved that Mr. Picklesworth was there, and he knew what he was do'n. I dunno what I woulda done if I was have'n ta'do that all ma'self. Someth'n I don't want ta'think 'bout. The spirits was almost at the entrance of the graveyard when we heard a scream.

"What the hell is that?!" The group of boys who had stolen the gates was come'n down the road. There was six boys and they wasn't much younger'n me. They's maybe 14 or 15 years old. They saw the spirits of the dead walk'n in a straight line and must'a been scared by the sight of corpses walk'n back to the graveyard.

Then, the spirits stopped...

They just stopped...

"Holy fuck!" 'Nother one'a the boys screamed. "It's the dead! They really came from the grave!"

All at the same time, the spirits turnt, face'n the group of boys, and stood there all silent like.

No, no, no, no, no! Shit! The spirits was distracted from Mr. Picklesworth's incantation. They wasn't be'n called no more by his spell. Instead, they's be'n called by the boys' screams! "Mr. Picklesworth, what do we do?"

"Dammit those boys!" Mr. Picklesworth was pissed off at them boys. They wasn't noth'n but trouble. "I have to say the spell again."

"Hurry!" I screamed.

Mr. Picklesworth said the spell again but this time sound'n more powerful like and command'n. "By the powers of the Witch Father, I call to you, spirits of the dead. In the Devil's name I command you to return to the grave! You, who walk with the living, by the powers of witchcraft and the powers of the Devil himself, I command you. Return to the grave!"

The spirits of the dead wasn't listen'n to Mr. Picklesworth's spell no more. They was focused in on them boys. You would'a thought them boys would'a run off, but they just stood there. They was transfix'n on the eyes of them corpse spirits. As if they was hypnotized or someth'n like it. They just stood there without say'n a word. The spirits was slowly walk'n closer and closer. Them boys stood there, not move'n a muscle. The spirits walked closer and closer to 'em. Still, those boys stood there, look'n at the eyes of them corpse spirits.

"Johnathan, don't let them spirits touch those boys!" Mr. Picklesworth yelled at me. "We don't know who conjured them or what they are capable of!"

"Fuck!" I wasn't even think'n right. I ran fast as I could over ta'those corpse spirits and stood b'tween 'em and the boys. "Stop!"

The corpse spirits stopped walk'n. They must'a been startled by my scream'n at 'em. They only paused for a moment and then they started walk'n closer ta'me and the boys again. *Fuck, fuck, fuck, fuck! What do I do?* I leaped b'fore I looked and I din't know what I was fix'n ta'do. Mr. Picklesworth said not ta'touch 'em, so I couldn't well fight 'em off with my bare hands. Then an idea came ta'me! The rowan cross with the red thread that Alma'd done sent me in the mail. I fished it out my trousers pocket and I held it up for them corpse spirits to see it. "Stay back!"

Noth'n. The corpse spirits kept walk'n closer and closer. They was real close now. Close 'nuff ta'reach out and grab us if they had the want'n to. I must'a been real scared or someth'n, 'cause without even think'n 'bout magic or trance or noth'n, I realized who I was! I was a witch, capable of magical powers given ta'me by the Devil and the Old Dame. *I am a witch!* With plain instinct, I focused on the power of witchcraft that swirled in my belly. Like a flash of lightni'n, I felt my blood burn'n with the fires of the Devil. My blood burnt with the fires of all them witches that ever was and all them witches that'd ever come after me. I took ma'self a mighty deep breath from my belly, and in that moment, I connected ta'all of witchcraft. I forced the magic outta my belly, up through my heart, through my arms, outta my hands, and empowered the rowan cross. I yelled out the magic in my belly as forcefully as I could, "I said, stop!"

The corpse spirits stopped.

"Now, walk back ta'your fuck'n graves or I will destroy you!" The magic came over my whole being. I was no longer Johnathan. I was Johnathan Knotbristle the Charmer! The witch! "Go! And never come back!"

The corpse spirits heard my magical command and walked back to the graveyard along the path of cow's blood. My yell'n must'a broke the boys' trance, 'cause they all looked at me now. Quickly I turnt to 'em and said, "Go, home and stay there. Lock your doors!"

They boys ran s'fast home I bet they ain't never run s'fast again in their whole lives.

I ran fast as I could into the graveyard. I had ta'help Mr. Picklesworth seal the corpse spirits back into the grave.

Mr. Picklesworth said the last part'a the spell, "In the name of the Devil do I compel you to return to your grave. Return to your resting spot to sleep forever in the arms of the Old Ones. Sleep forever in your graves. Let no one awaken you. By the Devil's name, I command it!"

The corpse spirits walked to their own graves. As each spirit corpse found its fit'n grave, it turnt into vapor and settled back inside their rest'n place.

Mr. Picklesworth gave me a handful of rowan sticks. "Plunge these sticks into every single grave! It'll seal the spirits back in! Hurry!"

I did what Mr. Picklesworth'd told me ta'do. I took the sticks and stabbed 'em into the dirt over the graves of each person. When I put 'em in the ground, I 'magined the power of the rowan wood keep'n the spirits in their graves. Every single grave had a rowan stick stick'n up halfway in the ground and halfway in the grave. Mr. Picklesworth had a hammer, and he gone 'round ta'ever grave and hammered the rowan all the way into the ground. When he did that, he said, "I bind this spirit to the grave! May they forever be bound in the name of the Devil!"

I was s'relieved when the last of the rowan sticks was pounded into the grave. I wasn't 'spect'n all this ta'happen my first Halloween as a witch. If noth'n else, I sure learnt how ta'seal an unruly spirit back into the grave. Mr. Picklesworth was relieved, too. There was s'much commotion go'n on that it sunk into me right then and there. Mr. Picklesworth was a witch, and a damned good one. He knew 'zactly what ta'do and how ta'handle the spirits. If it wasn't for him, we'd prob'ly still be haunted by them spirits. Mr. Picklesworth put his hammer back into his bag and took a deep, long breath. "All done. Every spirit is back into the grave, but there's still the remaining question. Who brought them out of the grave in the first place?"

That was a damned good question. It wasn't me and it wasn't Mr. Picklesworth. Alma and her witches din't do it, neither. So that means there was 'nother witch in town. A witch who wanted ta'hurt folks. Or at least scare 'em out their damn minds. I got a strange feel'n in my gut. This wasn't the last we'd be hear'n of this witch.

That night when I got home, I had all kinda dreams. I was think'n I might be dream'n of ghosts and corpses and things like that, but that wasn't what happened at all. I walked home feel'n good. Like I helped do someth'n important. I was a part'a someth'n bigger'n ma'self. Jonathan Knotbristle the Charmer. I dunno where that came from. I guess with all the excitement and the power run'n through my veins and such, it just sorta came ta'my head. I liked how it sounded, though. Mysterious and powerful like. When I got home, I went right ta'sleep. I had dreams of witches and the Devil. I had dreams of folks who'd been long dead. I had dreams of the Queen of Elphame, the Old Dame. I had dreams of the witch's sabbat and of Alma, Harriet, Clara, and Viola. I din't have no kinda dreams of Momma, Daddy, or my brothers. I wish I did though. I dunno why I din't.

The next day was Tuesd'y and I had ta'be at the store just like any other day. The whole way walk'n into town, I was think'n 'bout all the questions I wanted ta'ask Mr. Picklesworth. How long was he a witch for? Why din't he tell me? He obviously knew I was a witch, so why'd he keep it a secret? How'd he know how ta'seal the corpse spirits back into the grave? S'many questions I had for him.

When I got to the store, Mr. Picklesworth was busy go'n over the finances and things like that. "Ah, Johnathan, good! We have a lot to do today."

Mr. Picklesworth handed me a list of chores ta'do for the day and then went to the storeroom. We never talked 'bout what happened that Halloween night. We went back to do'n things like we'd always done 'em. Mr. Picklesworth was a mysterious man indeed.

9

A Hunt on Christmas

THE DAYS AFTER HALLOWEEN was, strangely, pretty much the same as they always was. Many of the town folk saw the corpse spirits knock'n at their door, but ain't no one mentioned it or talk'd 'bout it ever again after that night. You gotta understand that most folks is taught not ta'believe what their own eyes be see'n. You can see a ghost right up in your house, have a full conversation, and the next day they be think'n in was a dream or their 'magination play'n tricks on 'em. I been learn'n that folks want ta'believe what they want ta'believe, no matter what you tell 'em and no matter what they see. You see, some folks want ta'live a certain kinda life free of demons, ghosts, and devils. They think life should be a certain kinda way and they don't wanna see no differ'nt. When they see someth'n like a corpse ghost, they'll sure as hell convince themselfs I ain't real so they can go back live'n a simple life that they believes they should be live'n. I guess that's the differ'nce b'tween simple folk and us witches. Us witches know what's what. We be know'n 'bout demons, devils, and ghost and don't feel no kinda need to pretend'n it ain't real. See, see'n spirits ain't always 'bout be'n psychic or be'n magic. It's 'bout be'n a'right with the truth and not be'n scared if someth'n come up in your house at night. The days and weeks passed and ever-thing went back ta'normal for most folks. Folks went 'bout their business, act'n like noth'n had changed and noth'n will change.

The town was get'n ready for Christmas. Mr. Picklesworth was decorat'n the store with bows of evergreen branches. He was sell'n Christmas ornaments, too. He said that this was the first year he'd ever be sell'n Christmas ornaments or cards, 'cause folks din't used ta'do things of that nature 'til recently. I 'member at Christmas time, Momma would make a special meal for us. It wasn't much, but for us it was special 'cause Momma wanted it ta'be special. Momma and Daddy din't have much money and Daddy would say that you ain't need noth'n ta'celebrate Christmas. He would say that you just need ta'go ta'church and be pray'n for good health for the winter and you'd be a'right. Mr. Picklesworth was say'n that after the Civil War, many folks started celebrate'n more things like Halloween and Christmas 'cause they was thankful ta'be alive and that the war was over.

The town folk was decorate'n the town square with evergreen bows and there was big ribbons tied to 'em, too. Ever build'n in town had some kinda evergreen or ribbon decorate'n it. Mrs. Fossey had done paid someone ta'decorate her husband's bank, both inside and out. I noticed that there was folks come'n in the store, buy'n little gifts for 'em children, and husbands buy'n things for 'em wives. Most folks celebrated Christmas in their own way. Mr. Picklesworth said that religious folk went ta'church and came home ta'cook a nice meal. He also said non-church go'n folk usually drank the day away and'd regret it the next morn'n with a headache.

After we closed up the store on December 21st, Mr. Picklesworth said that he had someth'n for me he wanted me ta'take home. He'd gone into the storeroom and came out with a small log. "I made you a Yule log for Midwinter."

"A Yule log?" I never heard a no Yule log b'fore. I took the little log and put it in my satchel. I was take'n home some food and a few supplies that I got from the store that Mr. Picklesworth let me buy at a real cheap price. I guess 'cause it was Christmas and he wanted me ta'have someth'n special.

"You never heard of a Yule log?" Mr. Picklesworth asked. "Most folks around here use them. On Christmas, you make your fire in the fireplace and put this on top. Burn this log and you'll have warmth and light in your house all through winter."

"Thank you, Mr. Picklesworth," I said.

"When the darkness comes," Mr. Picklesworth said. "You'll have light."

I put that log in my satchel and walked on home. It was dark and real quiet. Walk'n home was unusually quiet. This was an eerie silence in the air tonight that I sure wasn't used to none. It felt like the whole world'd stopped. It din't feel right, so I walked home faster'n I usually do. I wasn't scared or noth'n. I had a feel'n in my bones that I best be get'n inside soon. When I got home, I lit my oil lanterns and a couple'a candles. I took the Yule log outta my satchel and set it by the fireplace. After I ate my supper, I was read'n a book when I heard ma'self the strangest sounds. I heard coyotes just a howl'n away. They was howl'n someth'n terrible. Most of the time when you heard coyotes, they was howl'n at each other like some kinda nightly song. This was differ'nt. These howls wasn't no song. They was a warn'n.

I stepped outside on my front porch. I wanted ta'see what all the fuss'n was 'bout. Those coyotes was not happy 'bout someth'n. I thought it might be best if I made sure the barn door was locked up tight tonight. An open barn door and coyotes on the loose wasn't never good. It would be a big mess in the morn'n if a coyote got inside there and killed them chickens. The barn was latched up and I went back over ta'my porch. All a sudden, the howl'n stopped. It was like all at once them coyotes knew someth'n was 'bout ta'happen.

That's when I saw it. Up in the sky, there was scream'n and shout'n and howl'n. I was stand'n up there on that porch try'n ta'figure what inna hell was go'n on. Up there in that sky was a terrible sight of spirits and critters fly'n through the air. It looked like a wild pack of ghostly animals, shreik'n through the night sky, all be'n led by an old lady dressed in rags. I couldn't figure out quite what it was I was see'n. I thought maybe it was witches fly'n to the sabbat, but it felt differ'nt than that. It felt...deadly.

BAM! BAM!

I heard gunshots come'n out the woods near my little farm. *What inna hell? Was someone out there hunt'n at night? What was they shoot'n?*

BAM! BAM! BAM!

The ghostly scream'n spirit and animals moved outta the way as quick they could.

Someone was shoot'n at them spirits!

BAM!

The spirits dived down into the woods and I heard ma'self a man scream'n. A terrible, terrible scream. I ran over ta'them woods as fast I could. I wasn't scared of them spirits at all. Maybe I could help whoever was scream'n like that. I ran ta'those screams and that's when I saw a man stand'n over 'nother man, lay'n on the ground. I watched those spirits swoop down and then fly right back on up into the air. They was gone. All they left behind was the faint sound of shrieks in the air.

"Are you a'right?" I called out to the man.

The man dropped down ta'his knees right next to the other man who's lay'n on the ground. When I got over ta'him, he was in shock. "They killed him!"

"What?" I saw the man lay'n on the ground. His belly was ripped open, and the ground was right covered in blood. It looked like some-one'd took a big knife and gutted him.

"We was out in the woods hunt'n," the man said. "We lost track of the time. It got dark real early tonight, so we started walk'n back home. On the way home, he started talk'n 'bout Midwinter and the monster Perchta."

I decided he couldn't just be stay'n there with his friend lay'n dead on that ground. I wasn't sure if an animal had attacked him or if someone had gone murdered him. Either way, I had ta'get this man away from these here woods and back ta'my house. "Come with me. I'm take'n you back ta'my house. What's your name?"

The man stood up and started walk'n with me. He was shake'n someth'n awful. "John. John Wessnell."

"Johnathan Knotbristle," I told him.

"You're the witch Mrs. Fossey was warn'n us 'bout," Mr. Wessnell said, matter of fact.

I wasn't gonna say noth'n either way. I just needed ta'get this man in a warm house. "What happened ta'your friend?"

"That's my friend, Phillip Gullmann," Mr. Wessnell said. "On the way home from hunt'n he started tell'n me this story. A story that his grandmother told him back in Germ'ny. There's this spirit who lives in 'em mountains. On Midwinter, after the sun goes down, if you ain't had all your work done b'fore it's dark, she comes. The monster Perchta. She comes and slices open your belly."

Damn, I thought. I never want ta'see this creature.

"Phillip said that we was in trouble 'cause we din't get our hunt'n done b'fore dark," John was scared ta'death and confused at the same time. "He even said a rhyme that his grandmother had told him ta'say on Midwinter's Eve:

'If the work of the year
Is left undone
As the sun will set
And the darkness comes
Frau Perchta will ride
With the hunt so wild
She will ride the skies
And search for the child
Whose chores are undone
Frau Perchta will come
Frau Perchta will come
Everybody, run!'"

I walked John back ta'my house, and I gave him some whiskey ta'calm his nerves. After a little while, he was calm 'nuff ta'walk into town with me ta'get us some help from the men. We went to the tavern and John told his story. Ain't no one believed him when he said that he'd saw an 'ole hag who led a ghostly train in them skies and that she right murdered his friend. The men figured that an animal done attacked his friend and that was that. They thought it was prob'ly a bear or a coyote. Now, I ain't never seen a bear out in those woods, so I can't be say'n I think it was a bear. The men in the tavern called on the town doctor, Doc Taylor, ta'go out and look at the body. After we told Doc Taylor all what happened, he hitched his wagon so he could take the body back ta'his office. Myself, Doc Taylor, and two other men rode in the wagon ta'fetch that body. When we got there, we loaded it up on the wagon for Doc ta'take a look at. He said the cut din't look like no animal claw or bite. Doc said it looked like a knife'd sliced open Philip's body.

The next day, John Wessnell came into the store ta'tell us that him and his friends William Ricket and Jim Nelson was gonna go back in them woods after dark and would be wait'n for the 'ole hag who'd killed his friend. Mr. Picklesworth din't say a word but looked at me like he thought John'd lost his damn mind. I believed John. I saw me that ghostly sight ma'self, but in all my years on this earth I ain't never seen it b'fore. I wondered that maybe you din't see it unless you was a witch or maybe you din't see it unless you was damned. Still, I din't think it was a good idea for nobody ta'go out in 'em woods tonight. I walked home after work, and I kept ma'self a good eye out for any spirits, ghosts, or hags up in there in that night sky. I din't see anyth'n and I din't hear anyth'n.

When I got home, I latched my front door, turnt on the oil lamps, and lit some candles. I lit the fireplace, made my supper, and settled in ta'read my book. Then, just like the night b'fore it had, the coyotes was just a howl'n away. B'fore I came inside tonight, I made sure the barn door was all locked up so there wasn't no need for me ta'go outside and check it. I din't even look out the winda' ta'see what was go'n on. Best business was none'a my business. The coyotes stopped their howl'n and all was quiet.

Knock! Knock! Knock! Knock!

Someone was bang'n on my front door! I knew there was gonna be trouble. I ran to the door, unlatched it, and opened it up. John and Jim Nelson was stand'n there, pant'n like wild animals, and both was covered in blood! "What inna hell happened?"

"She came!" John screamed. "The 'ole hag Perchta came!"

John and Jim came inside. Jim was as white as a ghost and din't say a word.

"Where's William?" I had a feel'n that someth'n terrible'd happened to Mr. Ricket.

"She got him!" John screamed. "He's dead!"

I din't know what ta'say. If it was the 'ole hag Perchta, she had more power than I'd ever seen b'fore. Maybe she even had more power than the Devil hisself. I din't know what we was gonna do. Then I heard William mumbl'n someth'n under his breath. John and me stopped talk'n and looked at William.

"If the work of the year
Is left undone
As the sun will set
And the darkness comes
Frau Perchta will ride
With the hunt so wild
She will ride the skies
And search for the child
Whose chores are undone
Frau Perchta will come
Frau Perchta will come
Everybody, run!"

It was the same rhyme that John'd told me the night b'fore. The rhyme that his friend said last night just b'fore he was killed. Just like the night b'fore when we went and got Doc Taylor and just like the night b'fore that when we found us the body of Jim Wilson with his belly slit open and blood all over the ground. And just like the night b'fore, we loaded the body in Doc Taylor's wagon so he could examine him.

The next day, there was a meet'n in the tavern with all the big folks who lived in the town. They was gonna talk 'bout the murders from the last couple'a nights. There was a'course Mr. and Mrs. Fossey, Mr. Picklesworth and his wife, Mr. and Mrs. Miller, Doc Taylor, and a lot of other folks who owned businesses and farms in town. Ever-body done heard 'bout the murders and ever-body was real concerned 'bout it. Some folks thought it was coyotes but Doc Taylor 'ardy said the cuts looked like they was from a knife and not tooth or claw. John Wessnell was in the center of the tavern yell'n away, convinced it was the Perchta the Old Hag. "It was Perchta, I tell you!

"Mr. Wessnell," Mr. Fossey interrupted him, "you are telling us tall tales and fantasy stories. There are no evil old hags flying through the air killing men for sport!"

"Maybe it was witches!" Mrs. Fossey said. "Or maybe it was Mr. Wessnell. Perhaps Mr. Wessnell lured these men to their deaths."

"I saw her myself!" John Wessnell snapped back at her.

"Doctor Taylor," Mr. Fossey said, "please tell everyone what you told us about the cuts on the victim's bodies."

Doc Taylor stood up from his chair. "The cuts are from some type of blade. The cut is clean and straight. Like if you were slaughtering a pig. Animal claws or bites look more like grinding meat than slicing the flesh."

There was a rumble'n through the crowd. It seemed like ever-body agreed that the deaths was from a human hand and not no animal.

I nudged Mr. Picklesworth. "Should we say someth'n?" I whispered.

He shook his head. "We need ta'stay out of this," he whispered back.

"We should put him in the jailhouse," Mrs. Fossey said back to John.

"You gotta believe me!" John begged. "I'll show you! Come with me tonight and I can prove it ta'ya."

"And be murdered by you?" Mr. Fossey yelled at him. "I think not!"

"I'll go!" A man's voice said from the crowd. Matthew Hewes was a farmer from the far end of town. He was liv'n in the opposite direction from me. Mr. Hewes only came into town ta'sell his produce and meat from his farm. He never did leave his farm much. "We need ta'prove Mr. Wessnell did it and I'm happy ta'go, but I'll be bring'n my rifle."

"I'll go too!" A second man came outta the crowd. This was Mr. Dunning. He was a farmer too. "Me and Mr. Hewes can keep an eye on Mr. Wessnell. If he's wrong, we arrest him. If he's right, then we have us a hell of a story ta'tell."

None'a this was right. There ain't no way in hell these two men'd go out into the woods if they thought John's story was true. They figured they'd go out there ta'prove John wrong and then hang him for murder when Perchta din't come. This was a bad idea. A real bad idea.

The three men went out to the woods and I went ta'my house. I din't know what ta'do 'bout this whole thing. The only thing I could figure do'n was call up the Devil and Holda. I walked fast as I could out ta'my house. It was dark by the time I got home so, I turnt on the oil lamps and candles and lit up that fireplace. I had me my pitchfork with a candle b'tween the tines on the left side of the fireplace and the broom on the left of that. I lit that candle and I called to the Devil, "I call to you, Horned Master, Witch Father, he of the cloven hoof, Devil. I ask that you bring your power into the vessel. Light the way so that them who serves you may follow you."

I put ma'self into a trance just like b'fore. I felt the power of the stars and the power of the land flow'n through my blood. I focused on the flame in b'tween them tines of the pitchfork. When I focused on that flame, my forehead started ta'burn with power. I could feel the Devil in my heart. I took a breath and breathed him out into the pitchfork. The pitchfork was now his sacred place. A place for him ta'stay dur'n my rite. I could feel the power of the Old Ones flow'n through me. I looked at that there broom and the cook'n pot right next to it. I thought 'bout Holda, the Queen of Elphame. I thought 'bout the well. I thought 'bout the Otherworld, and the power Holda had. I could feel Holda in my heart. I took a breath and then breathed her into the broom. A place for her ta'stay dur'n my rite.

The Old Ones was here. I could see 'em over the broom and the pitchfork if I used my 'magination. Sometimes when I breathed 'em into their tools, I could feel 'em but couldn't see 'em. When that happened,

I would pay ma'self close attention to their virtues, their power, and try ta'imagine what they'd look like from how they felt. I wasn't sure if it was true or not. I mean, I wasn't sure if that was what they really was look'n like, but I din't much care. I 'magined what they looked like for ma'self and that was good 'nuff. I could talk to 'em, too. I would ask 'em things and could hear what they was say'n in my heart. I know that sounds strange, but it works. When I talked to 'em, they'd be talk'n back ta'me in my heart. Sometimes I had a hard time hear'n what they was say'n with my ears, so I paid close attention ta'what they said ta'my heart and tried ta'imagine what they was say'n ta'me. Most times that'd work just fine. Alma told me b'fore that if I practice do'n this ever-day, then I'd be able ta'see 'em and hear 'em just like I see folks who's in the flesh.

Now the Witch Father and Witch Mother was here. I needed ta'know what I should do. "Devil, Holda, I have summoned you here tonight 'cause I need your help."

"Yes," said the Devil, "we are aware that the Goddess Perchta has taken her sacrifices."

"Sacrifices?" So it was true. It wasn't John who killed those men. It was Perchta.

"Yes," Holda said, "during the twelve nights of Christmas, if the work of the year is not put to rest and offerings are not made to her, then she will take the offering of your life."

"I don't understand," I was real confused 'bout this. This was the first time I'd ever heard of Perchta or her tak'n sacrifices in our small little town. "She ain't never been here b'fore. Why now?"

Holda smiled like she had her a dark secret, "Perchta comes every Yuletide. She may not always slice someone's belly, but she always takes her offerings."

"There are many who stop all work at Midwinter," the Devil said. "They prepare for Christmas and honor the old way of leaving offerings for her. But those who do not, she may take an offering of killing an animal, making someone sick until they die, or claiming their blood with her knife."

"I'm 'fraid more folks'll die tonight," I said. "How do I stop her?"
"Ask her yourself," Holda said.

With that, I gave my thanks. I gave 'em offer'ns of herbs burn'n on
hot coals and some food that I had. Then I said goodbye ta'both of
'em and blew out the candle on the pitchfork. Holda said that I should
ask her ma'self. So, I figured I had ta'summon Perchta and her ghostly
nighttime hunt. The Devil said that folks stopped all work at Midwinter
'til Christmas and left offerings for her. I fetched a bowl outta the
cupboard and left it on my front porch with some porridge. I thought
maybe if I'd be givin' her an offer'n and ask'n for her help, she might
come ta'me tonight. Then I went outside and said ma'self the rhyme that
John had learnt from Mr. Gullman:

"If the work of the year
Is left undone
As the sun will set
And the darkness comes
Frau Perchta will ride
With the hunt so wild
She will ride the skies
And search for the child
Whose chores are undone
Frau Perchta will come
Frau Perchta will come
Everybody, run!"

After I said that rhyme, I was wait'n for Perchta ta'come outta the
skies. Then the coyotes started howl'n just like b'fore. The howls was
louder than the nights b'fore. I watched the skies for Perchta. Noth'n
yet. I said the rhyme again and the coyote howl'n got louder and louder.
Then I said the rhyme a third and final time. The howls stopped. I
looked up in the sky again and there she was, the ghastly hag Perchta,
lead'n her train of spirits and ghouls. She circled my house and then

swooped down into my chimney and into the house. I ran fast as I could into the house. I had no idea what was go'n ta'happen next.

I opened the front door ta'my house and there she was. Perchta, the winter hag Goddess, was sit'n in a chair, us'n spin'n flax on a spin'n wheel. I walked in real slow like. I din't know what was gonna happen. She could'a come after me as a sacrifice, so I had ta'be ready for anyth'n. I stopped and just looked at her. It was the strangest sight. A terrible hag Goddess, sit'n in front of the fireplace spin'n flax like she was up in her own house.

She din't look up from her spin'n and said ta'me, "Come closer boy, let me rest my eyes upon you."

Alma told me once ta'never be disrespectful ta'spirits. Never ever. She said that even if you din't like 'em or you thought they was the most evilest thing on earth, always show spirits respect. The more you showed 'em respect, the easier it was ta'talk to the spirits and ask 'em ta'do what you need 'em ta'do. I was real cautious but I walked closer ta'Perchta.

"Why did you summon me here, boy?" Perchta said, still spinning.

"The Devil and Frau Holda told me ta'ask you ma'self why you're kill'n innocent men," I answered her.

Perchta smiled, still spinning. "Innocent men, you say..."

"They din't deserve ta'die."

Perchta lifted her eyes from her spin'n ta'look at me, "And what authority do you have to decide who deserves to die and who does not deserve to die?"

I din't say a word.

"Humans think that they know everything that happens on earth," Perchta said more sternly. "They do not. There is a balance to the earth that must be held. Do you not hunt deer in those woods for food. Why do animals deserve to die by your hands and humans don't deserve to die by mine?"

"We kill for food," I said. "We hunt ta'keep us fed."

"And I hunt to keep all things in balance," Perchta said. "We Gods give humans many blessings for their survival. We only ask for what is rightfully ours."

My whole life I was taught that God gave us animals for food, clothes, and anyth'n we needed for ourselfs. It never occurred ta'me that the Gods might do the same thing ta'us.

"All things in nature must die," Perchta said. "Either by old age, sickness, or by the hand of the Gods; all things must return to the spirit world where they came."

Perchta kept spin'n and spin'n on her spin'n wheel. Spin'n and spin'n and spin'n She guided the flax into the wheel. She looked up at me again and said, "I see that you have the mark of Cain on your spirit. The Old Ones have claimed you for themselves. I have been watching you for a long time, boy."

"You been watch'n me?" I asked. I din't like the sound of that at all. It's comfort'n ta'know that the Devil and Holda was watch'n over me, but Perchta was a frightn'n Goddess.

"I watch over all of the Children of Cain," she said.

"Cain?" The only Cain I knew was the son of Adam in the Bible.

"Tubal Cain," Perchta said, "Some say that the Devil is Tubal Cain, but what you call the Devil is a God who is older than time. He walks this earth in many forms and in many cultures, teaching humanity to fight against oppression and teaches them how to have free Will."

I learnt later what Perchta was say'n was that the Witch Father, the Horned One, Lucifer, the Devil, and his many other names is a great spirit or God, if you will, who teaches us ta'go 'gainst what common folk be tell'n you. He teaches how ta'face your own darkness so you can kindle your own light. He teaches that we gotta face the consequences of our actions. Only then can we grow spiritually. He tests us. He tricks us. He pushes us to the ground so we can learn ta'pick our own selves up without need'n no one else ta'do it.

"Come," Perchta said, still spin'n. "Let me show you the mystery of Fate."

I walked over and stood right next ta'her, watch'n her spin that flax.

"To spin the flax into threads is to be the master of Fate," Perchta said. "I have the power to weave the threads of Fate into the tapestry of all life. All life upon the earth has a thread. Each human, animal, and plant have a thread that I create with my spinning wheel. Once I create the thread of each being's life, I weave it into the great tapestry of all things. Even your thread is here. Come and see."

Perchta took a thread from her distaff and began ta'spin it on the wheel and showed it ta'me. "Look with your heart. Imagine seeing your life as it was, as it is, and as it will come to pass."

I looked at the thread and put ma'self into a light trance. I opened up my heart and my mind and cleared my thoughts of anyth'n that'd distract me. When I looked at the thread ta'see my Fate, I wasn't just look'n at the thread. I was look'n into the thread. You might even say I was look'n through the thread. It was kinda like when I was look'n in that cauldron. It was like I was look'n into a deep well or into a winda' of time and space. That's when I saw it. I saw ma'self with my family; Momma, Daddy, and my two brothers, I saw ma'self as a child. Then I saw the Devil give me the powers of the witch. I saw Mr. Picklesworth give me a job at the store. I saw ma'self use the rowan cross ta'control the corpse ghosts. Then I saw what's ta'come in the future. I saw ma'self perform'n powerful acts of witchcraft. I saw ma'self teach'n the magic ta'young witches, too.

After a while, I came outta the trance vision. There was so much ta'see I could'a spent a lot more time in the trance. But time was short. Perchta had more ta'show me.

"You can see the Fate of others, too," Perchta said. "All you need to do is take a thread of any kind and connect your heart with the heart and spirit of the person you seek. You do not need to spin the thread. Any sewing thread will do. You must be firm in the knowledge that you are seeing their Fate."

Perchta pulled 'nother thread from her distaff and began spinn'n it. "The answer to your questions are here."

As Perchta was spin'n that flax into a thread with the spin'n wheel, I went again into a trance. This time it wasn't a Fate strand of my own, it was a Fate strand of someone else. I looked deep into the thread, and I saw the terrible truth. The terrible, terrible truth. It was more dreadful than I could'a thought! I had ta'act fast! "Thank you, Perchta, for your wisdom and your help tonight. I gotta go and take care of this here horror. Farewell."

With that, I grabbed me my rifle and ran into the woods where John and the other two men was at. I ran fast as I could. The coyotes started howl'n again. Louder and louder they was howl'n. I ran and ran and ran, carry'n my rifle. Perchta would be come'n again. I saw it in the Fate strand. She'd be take'n her sacrifice. I heard a voice in the distance. I stopped and hid ma'self in the trees. I wanted ta'stop this horrible thing, but I froze. I think I froze 'cause part'a me wanted ta'see if it was true, and the other part'a me couldn't believe it was really gonna happen.

John Wessnell, Matthew Hewes, and Steven Dunning was walk'n through the forest. They was all carry'n their rifles. Mr. Dunning and Mr. Hewes din't believe that John was tell'n the truth. They thought that ever-thing that John'd said was a lie and that he hisself had murdered those two men. They was wait'n it out 'til they had 'nuff and was gonna take John to the jailhouse for murder.

I stood there for a minute, watch'n the three men walk through the woods, look'n for Perchta. I was just 'bout ta'say someth'n, ta'call out to 'em, when I heard a familiar voice. John Wessnell stopped where he was and said him in a loud voice:

"If the work of the year
Is left undone
As the sun will set
And the darkness comes
Frau Perchta will ride
With the hunt so wild
She will ride the skies
And search for the child
Whose chores are undone
Frau Perchta will come
Frau Perchta will come
Everybody, run!"

Then the coyotes started howl'n. Louder and louder, they howled. Mr. Hewes and Mr. Dunning aimed their rifles at the darkness of the woods, wait'n for someth'n ta'jump out at 'em. They was wait'n for a bear, a coyote, or someth'n ta'jump out and attack.

Then the coyotes was silent again and in the black of the night sky, the 'ole hag Perchta led her ghostly train through the darkness.

"Lady Perchta! Come! Take your sacrifices on this Yuletide!" John Wessnell screamed to the sky. "For this offer'n I give you, I ask in return the power of magic!"

Perchta flew through the air and then landed her down to the ground. She walked toward them three men. Mr. Hewes and Mr. Dunning pointed their rifles at her. *BAM! BAM! BAM!* The bullets din't hurt her none. They must have went right through her. I never seen men who looked s'scared in my life. The men was froze in fear. Perchta walked closer and closer to 'em. They reloaded their rifles. I could see the men shake'n. Their death was approach'n. I shoulda done someth'n. I shoulda helped those poor men, but I was scared ma'self. What if Perchta came after me? What if she'd kill me too? I stayed hidden in them trees. I held my breath without even realize'n what I was do'n. I shoulda helped those men. I still regret that I was too scared ta'do noth'n. Perchta slowly walked towards the men.

John Wessnell was stand'n next to Mr. Hewes and Mr. Dunning. Perchta came s'close ta'those men and she put her face right close to Mr. Hewes' face. Her nose was touch'n his nose. He could feel her breathe'n on his face. Mr. Hewes was s'scared he couldn't even speak.

Mr. Hewes was stabbed in the belly.

Not by Perchta. It was John Wessnell who done sliced open Mr. Hewes stomach and his bowels came out. Mr. Dunning was watch'n the whole thing happen in disbelief. B'fore he could come ta'his senses and shoot John Wenssel, John stabbed Mr. Dunning in the belly, too. He looked at Perchta and said, "Your sacrifice on this Yuletide eve, Perchta."

Perchta looked at the men bleed'n on the ground. She watched as their lives gone faded away. She said noth'n to John Wessel. She turnt and walked away. As she walked away, the ghosts of Mr. Dunning and

Mr. Hewes followed her back ta'her ghostly train of specters. They was now a part'a Perchta's wild hunt...forever.

John Wessnell turnt 'round and looked right at me. He must have known I was in the woods scared ta'death, watch'n the whole thing. He smiled like he'd lost his damn mind. He turnt away from me and he walked into them dark woods. He was gone.

The next day, I told ever-one in town that it was indeed Mr. Wessnell who'd done murdered them men. A'course, I din't tell no one 'bout Perchta take'n the spirits of those men. They'd have thought I was crazy if I did. I told 'em how scared I was and how I shoulda helped 'em but I din't want him ta'kill me too. I told 'em how I froze in horror as those poor men was gutted. Now that Mr. Wessnell's secret was out, he prolly wasn't never gonna return ta'this town. But we couldn't be sure. Mr. Wessnell followed the old lore, so I figured we all should leave out a bowl of porridge for Perchta. You never know when a murderer'd be knock'n on your front door 'cause you din't leave no offer'n for the old ones.

10

The Spirit Doctor

꩜꩜꩜

THE WINTER WAS RELATIVELY MILD. It got cold a few times, but live'n here in the South it never got too cold. Not like it does in the North. Hell, in the North you even might get you snow that stays on the ground all winter. Not here. Here it might freeze overnight on a real cold day, but it never stays that way none. If it snows, it's only a light dust'n and it goes away by midday. This pa'ticular winter was milder than ones I'd seen b'fore. I got me plenty of wood stacked up in the barn ta'fill the fireplace, so I din't have ta'worry 'bout heat much. Momma always had plenty of blankets in the house so I could wrap ma'self in them, too. The thing 'bout winter here where I live is that when the leaves be fall'n off the trees, ever-thing just looks brown. Brown and dead. Like the cold hardness of death be come'n over the land and stays that way 'til spring.

I keep work'n at the general store with Mr. Picklesworth dur'n the day, and at night I mostly be go'n home and read'n my books. Ever once in a while, I'll go over to the tavern and have me a whiskey and listen to the old folks tell their stories. Or listen to the drunk'n men sing'n their songs. It'd been a few weeks since all that business with

Mr. Wenssel. I ain't never seen him or Perchta since. I guess we won't be see'n her 'til next Christmas. There wasn't much ta'do on the farm but feed the animals and make sure they was fine dur'n cold nights. Not many folks came to the general store in the winter. The ones who did come bought basic necessity things and that was it. I think Mr. Picklesworth liked have'n me work in the store, even though we din't get much business. We kept each other comp'ny. I wanted ta'ask him more questions 'bout witchcraft and what all he knew. He never brought it up none and ever-time I tried ta'talk 'bout it, he gave me a list of chores that I needed ta'be do'n. So, I guess that was that.

It was the end of Janur'y, and little by little it was get'n brighter ever-day. It was still cold as hell outside, but at least it wasn't as dark as it was dur'n Christmas time. Early dark nights always'd bothered me. Never felt like you got a whole day's work done b'fore it was 'ardy dark. Not much needed ta'be done anyhow, but still. It was a welcome sight ta'have a few minutes extra of daylight. That winter, there was a influenza outbreak in the nearby towns. I was hear'n that many children was die'n. It's a right shame when children gotta be die'n. They don't deserve the suffer'n. Their families don't be deserv'n the sadness and despair after they die. 'Specially their Mommas. I ain't never had no children of my own, but I can tell you, there ain't no heartbreak like a Momma's heartbreak when lose'n one'a her children. It got s'bad that a lot of folks was keep'n their children inside and not let'n 'em outside other than ta'use the outhouse.

Mr. and Mrs. Curtis had a daughter named Betsy Curtis. Betsy started have'n the chills and a mighty fever one day. We dunno where she got it from 'cause her Momma was real strict 'bout Betsy be'n 'round other children with the flu go'n 'round like that. "Straight to the outhouse and straight back." her Momma'd say. Far as I can tell, Betsy wasn't 'round no other kids. No one but her brothers and sisters, but her Momma was strict with 'em too. But you know how it is. You're fine one day and the next day you're sick as a dog. Betsy had that fever and those chills for a few days. Doc Taylor did the best he could by give'n her medicines here and there, but in them days, the flu wasn't someth'n you could treat s'easy. Dur'n church that Sund'y the whole town prayed real hard for Betsy. I think I prayed harder than I ever did pray b'fore. It broke my heart ta'know little Betsy was suffer'n so. A few days later, Betsy died. Her little grave is on the Curtis property a few miles from town. The whole town gone went ta'her funeral. I can't 'member much 'bout what the pastor was say'n. Prob'ly someth'n 'bout God and salvation. Mrs. Curtis din't say a word dur'n the funeral. She kept her pain ta'herself and never spoke ta'nobody 'bout it. I wonder whatever happen to Mrs. Curtis. I ain't never seen her again. Mr. Curtis comes into the store from time ta'time. He ain't never been the same either. Can't blame 'em.

After that, there was a few more folks who got sick. Most of 'em got better. Some din't though. The ones who never got better was mostly children. Ever Sund'y we was pray'n 'bout someone who had the flu. It was real bad this year, and nobody knew what we as gonna do 'bout it. Doc Taylor did what he could, but it wasn't 'nuff.

One Saturd'y, there was a knock on my door. I opened the door and there was Mrs. Fairfax look'n all kinds of distraught and anxious. Without me even say'n ta'come in, she done shoved me over ta'get inside. She was pace'n back and forth like a wild dog trapped in a cage.

"Johnathan, I need your help," Mrs. Fairfax said.

"I'm happy ta'help if I can," I said. "What's the matter?"

Mrs. Fairfax looked s'upset and outta sorts. "It's my daughter, Emma. She's got the flu. She's real sick."

"I'm s'sorry ta'hear that," I said. "I'll be pray'n for her."

"Thank you, Johnathan," She said, "but I need more than prayers. I need your magic."

I wasn't sure quite what ta'say. There was rumors 'bout me be'n a witch thanks to Mrs. Fossey, but it was always best ta'keep things a rumor and not prove such things ta'be true. "I'm not sure I'm know'n what you mean."

"I was in town on Halloween," Mrs. Fairfax said. "I was run'n through town on Halloween night try'n to find someone to help with those ghosts when I saw you use your magic and banish 'em to the grave."

I stood there not know'n what ta'say. "Well, I mean...I din't..."

"Johnathan, almost every single child who caught the flu has died," Mrs. Fairfax looked s'sad and s'desperate. "Please do something and don't let Emma die."

"But Doc Taylor..."

Mrs. Fairfax shooked her head in frustration and partly in disgust, "Doc Taylor is a good man, but he's not know'n how ta'save folks from this flu. Maybe no doctor is. That's why she needs you, Johnathan."

"Ever-body will be pray'n for her," I said. I wanted her ta'think of some other way ta'help Emma and not have me be do'n it. "You could have the pastor come by and have him pray over Emma. That might help."

"Folks' been praying this whole time for everybody who's sick," Mrs. Fairfax said. "Those prayers din't work for those children. They all died."

See'n Mrs. Fairfax like this just broke my heart. I wish I knew how ta'help her, but I din't. The spells I knew was ta'get things you needed. Not ta'heal someone. "Even if I did have magic, I wouldn't be know'n how ta'help Emma. That's noth'n I know how ta'do."

Mrs. Fairfax was a Momma bear take'n care of her baby. She wasn't 'bout ta'let someone say they won't be help'n her child. "You're a witch, Johnathan, figure out a way."

"You're a woman of faith," I said. I was try'n ta'appeal ta'her Christian senses. I figured if I did help her then ever-body would know I was a witch and things could get real bad for me. "God doesn't want you ta'use magic for Emma."

"God let those other children die," Mrs. Fairfax was speak'n sternly now. "I figure I can save Emma and then pray for forgiveness later."

I stood there look'n at her brown eyes look'n back at me s'desperate like. She knew I was a witch, and she knew that witches was have'n the power ta'heal. I've seen s'much these last few months. I've seen things I never'd think was possible. Things that I thought was only told in stories. There had ta'be a way ta'use magic ta'heal her daughter. Otherwise, what good was be'n a witch if you couldn't help someone who done need it?

"Give me a day or so ta'figure this all out," I said, "Maybe I can figure out someth'n."

"I'll have my husband come with the wagon tomorrow morn'n to take you to our house," Mrs. Fairfax said. "She's terribly sick and I don't know how much time she has."

Mrs. Fairfax left, and I stood there think'n what I should do. I din't know noth'n 'bout no heal'n. Alma and the three witches was clear in the next town, and it'd take me a few hours ta'walk there and then more ta'walk back. I don't even know if she'd be able ta'help me. Mr. Picklesworth could maybe help me, but he wasn't the kind ta'be talk'n 'bout no witchcraft. I'm not even sure he'd know what ta'do. I had ta'think of someth'n. The only thing I knew ta'do was ta'summon forth Old Henry. I took the cat skull that was hidden away on the shelf and lit a candle. "Old Henry, Old Henry, I summon thee, Old Henry, Old Henry, I conjure thee." I said that little rhyme three times just like I done b'fore.

"I'm here, Johnathan," Old Henry appeared b'fore me. "What may I do for you?"

"Mrs. Fairfax's daughter, Emma is sick someth'n terrible with the flu and she's ask'n me ta'use my magic ta'heal her. I ain't never done that b'fore and I dunno know what ta'do."

Old Henry paced 'round the room look'n like he was in deep thought. He had ta'know what ta'do. He was a witch's familiar, after all. He must know how ta'help. "Johnathan, you seem to have a way with spirits and ghosts. Perhaps this is the kind of witchcraft you are called to do."

"Ok, what d'you mean?" I asked.

"You see, all witches have magic, but there are different types of magic and different things you can do with your magic," Henry said. "All witches should have a basic understanding of magic in general, but there are some witches who excel in certain types of magic. Some witches are good with herbs and healing while others are good with fascination and mind control. You, my dear Johnathan, are good with the spirits."

"You mean the ghosts?" I asked. Maybe he was talk'n 'bout how I helped Samuel Toberson escape the ghost road or how I helped Mr.

Picklesworth with the ghost corpses. "That wasn't no special talent or skill, Henry, that was me just do'n the best I could ta'help folks in need."

Old Henry cracked a smile, "Oh, my dear boy, you were able to help those people because you have that skill. Otherwise, the outcome of each experience may have been different."

I wasn't sure I believed what Henry was say'n. Maybe he was right. Maybe the reason I was able ta'help those folks was 'cause I'm good at call'n the spirits. Or maybe I was just s'scared shitless that I was try'n ta'survive the best I could with what magic I was know'n. But Henry often knew what he was talk'n 'bout. He was my familiar sent ta'me by the Devil hisself. My spirit friend and teacher. I guess I best be listen'n. "So how do I use the spirits ta'help Emma Fairfax?"

"Why, summon the spirit of a healer, of course!" Henry was real excited 'bout this.

When night fell, that's when me and Old Henry started. We gathered the things we would be need'n ta'find the spirit of a healer. A single white candle was put on the center of the table. The fireplace was put out so the only light in the room'd be from that candle. The only warmth, besides the clothes I had on, was from one'a my blankets that I could wrap 'round me. I got me a piece of coal and put it in a dish. Henry done said ta'put the herb mullein on top of that coal. The spirits was drawn to it. Henry told me ta'pour some whiskey in a shot glass and leave it out as an offer'n for when the spirit come. He also had me sit in Momma's rock'n chair.

The white candle was lit. The fireplace was put out. I poured the whiskey. I put mullein on the coal. I wrapped ma'self in a blanket and sat in that rock'n chair. I started rock'n back and forth in that 'ole chair. Back and forth. Back and forth. Back and forth. I started go'n in a trance. I din't stop ta'think that this 'ole rock'n chair could be used ta'go into a trance. Let me tell you what, that 'ole rock'n chair did the job real good. I took a breath and breathed down the power of the stars into my heart. I breathed up the power of the earth into my belly. I took 'nother breath and mixed 'em all together. I rocked back and forth. Back and forth. Back and forth. I went deeper and deeper into trance. Back and forth. Back and forth. Deeper and deeper into trance. Back and forth. Back and forth.

"Imagine yourself in the spirit world," Old Henry said. "Imagine that you are standing up from the rocking chair. See yourself standing in front of your front door. In the spirit world, the door is a gateway from your world into the world of the spirits."

I did just like Old Henry was say'n, and in my mind, I 'magined stand'n up from the rock'n chair and walk'n up ta'my front door. I could still feel my physical body rock'n in that chair, but my spirit was up and move'n 'round. It was an odd feel'n. I could feel my physical body rock'n and in trance, and at the same time I could feel my spirit body get'n up and go'n to the front door.

"Open the door, Johnathan. Imagine you see the spirit world and walk through."

In my mind when I opened that there door I din't see the outside. I din't see the ground and the trees and the barn next to the 'ole house. I saw me a hallway that was all white and gold like. I walked down the hall, and I could see many doors.

"Call out to the spirits," Henry said. "Tell them you need to speak with a healer. Tell them why you have come."

As I walked down the bright hallway I said, "My name is Johnathan Knotbristle, I'm here ta'speak with a healer. Someone I know is right sick with the flu and I need someone ta'help me heal her. Her name is Emma Fairfax, and she is a little girl 'bout six years old."

I got the feel'n in my gut that I should stop in front of a certain door. The door was gold and bright, just like the other doors in the long hallway. There wasn't noth'n more special 'bout this door, but I just got a feel'n. Stop. Just stop. I knocked on that there door and the door slowly opened. When I stepped through, I wasn't no longer in the bright white and gold place. I was in what I thought to be an 'ole doctor's office. The room was filled with dried herbs hang'n from the ceil'n and there was all kinds of books ever-where. There was a pitchur hang'n on the wall that looked like it had someth'n ta'do with astrology 'cause it had pitchur of the zodiac drawn all 'round a draw'n of a naked man. There were a man wear'n a blue coat and he was do'n someth'n on a big wooden table. He din't seem ta'notice that I'd walked into the room. He either din't notice or din't care. I got closer to the man. I was curious ta'see what he was do'n. When I got closer to the table I saw what he was do'n. He was cut'n open a man who was lay'n on that big wood table.

"Jesus Christ!" I was startled 'cause the man in the blue coat was just slice'n open some poor man on the table. The man on the table din't bleed none. He was just cut all open and I could be see'n all his guts.

The man in the blue coat was wear'n a white wig and had glasses. "Dear sir, please do not scream while I'm performing a delicate operation."

I just stood there not know'n what ta'do. "I'm sorry, sir, I just...I..."

"You just interrupted me," said the man in the blue coat, "that's what you did." He reached down and grabbed a pile of herbs that was sit'n on the table and stuffed 'em inside the man on the table. He then started ta'sew him up.

I looked over at the face of the man lay'n on the table and he was alive. He was alive, awake, and look'n right at me. "Oh, the doctor will be with you in a moment," the man on the table said. "He's almost done. Once the doctor's finished, I'll be good as new."

"You're a doctor?" I asked the man in the blue coat.

The man in the blue coat did not look up at me. He was bent over the man on the table still sew'n them herbs in nice and tight. "Yes, my name is Doctor Hale."

"Then maybe you can help me," I said. "I'm look'n for..."

"*Shhhhh!*" Doctor Hale shushed me. "My boy, this operation needs all of my attention. Once I am done, I will be right with you."

I stood there try'n ta'be as quiet as I could. I din't know what was happen'n but I was in the spirit world, and I guess it wasn't up ta'me ta'always know what was go'n on with spirits. Spirits be do'n their own thing. What is normal in the physical world don't have much ta'do with the spirit world and what's go'n on there. When we're in the world of spirits, we best be keep'n our manners 'cause one thing I've learnt is it's no good ta'piss off no spirits.

Doc Hale finished stuff'n those herbs inside that man on the table and then looked over ta'me. "Now, how can I help you?"

"I guess I'm 'sposed ta'be ask'n you for help," I said.

"My boy," Doc Hale said, "what is it you are here to ask me?"

"I dunno how ta'heal a sick girl named Emma Fairfax and I need your help," I said.

"Hmmm," Doc Hale looked at me up and down. He looked like he was examine'n me for someth'n. "And you want me to heal her?"

"Yes."

"I see," Doc Hale said. "You will need to summon me in your world and allow me to use your body."

It seemed ta'me that spirits really like ta'use the bodies of the live'n. Makes sense though. They ain't got a physical body, so they need ta'jump in your body ta'do what they need ta'be do'n. Yes, they can influence things in our world. They can put thoughts in someone's head and make it seem like it was their thought. They can do all kinds of magic. They can even influence the weather if you get the right spirit who knows what they're do'n. But most times when you need 'em ta'influence the physical world and influence it fast, they like ta'use your body ta'do it. Alma and the four witches'd told me b'fore that you never work with a spirit that you dunno what's what. You need ta'know their name and you need ta'be tell'n the spirit your name. Yout gotta get ta'know 'em and have a relationship with them. Like be'n friends, or at least a professional relationship. You can't take no chances of have'n some crazy spirit mess'n things up for you even worse than they 'ardy are. "Ok. I can do that. Can you tell me more 'bout yourself?"

"Of course," Doc Hale said. "My name is Doctor Theodore Hale. I lived in Pennsylvania from 1727-1791. Which of course is the year I died. I was a renowned doctor when I was alive. I treated everyone I could. I turned no one away, no matter what they could pay or who they were. When I died, I continued to watch over humanity the best I could. There are many spirit teachers here in the spirit world. They have taught me things that I could have never learned in the physical world. I have learned to use magic and healing side by side for the best outcome."

"Who was that person you was help'n on the table?" I asked. The man on the table was gone. He had dis'ppeared while Doc Hale was tell'n me his story.

"Oh, that was a living human man," Doc Hale said. "You see, many folks who are of the living come to see me in their dreams when they are sick. That's when I do my best work. People fall asleep and when they are asleep, they come here to me. Or rather, they are guided here by spirits to me. It's so much easier to heal the sick in the spirit world. I can cut them and they don't bleed; I can put healing medicines inside their bodies without them swallowing. I can even cut them wide open, take out the infection, and then sew them up again without them screaming in pain. The best thing that could have ever happened to me as a doctor was dying."

"Amazing," I said. "You can do all that as a spirit?"

"Indeed, I can," Doc Hale said. "Now, when you are ready for me to heal the young girl, you must open your mind, your heart, and your body and then call me into you. Then allow me control of your body so that I can do my work."

I gave Doc Hale my thanks and then said goodbye ta'him. I took ma'self a deep breath and found ma'self still rock'n back and forth in that rock'n chair. I opened up my eyes and I saw Old Henry sit'n at the table, wait'n for my return from the spirit world. "I found a spirit who's a doctor named Doc Hale."

"Yes, yes. I was able to see into the spirit world," Henry said. "You are ready to heal that young girl."

I gave my thanks to Old Henry and 'magined him go'n back into his home, the cat skull. I blew out the candle and then put ma'self ta'bed. Tomorrow was gonna be a long day.

The next morning, Mr. Fairfax done showed up with his wagon as promised. I got in and sat next ta'him. The whole way ta'his house he din't say a word. I wasn't sure if he was just worried for his daughter, or he wasn't s'happy that his wife was have'n him take a witch ta'do witchcraft over his daughter. Either way, the way there was silent. It was a'right for me though, 'cause it gave me time ta'my thoughts and to figur'n out what I was gonna do. I din't need no kinda magical tools or anyth'n. I just needed ta'contact the spirit of Doc Hale and he'd do the rest. We got there a little while later. Mrs. Fairfax was happy ta'see me, but still looked as desperate like as she did yesterday. She invited me into her house and poured me a cup of coffee. I could tell she was anxious ta'have me start the heal'n.

"What do you need us ta'do?" Mrs. Fairfax asked. She wanted ta'get the heal'n started. She had sat up most of the night with Emma who was still have'n a bad fever. It was get'n worse and worse. Emma hadn't eat'n anyth'n in a few days and it was hard for Mrs. Fairfax ta'get her ta'drink no kinda water. She was just wait'n for me ta'start.

"Just keep pray'n and ask'n God ta'help her," I said. I walked into the Emma's room where she was sleep'n. She was wrapped in blankets. Her face was red and sweaty like and looked like she'd had her a hard night last night. I put a small wooden chair next to Emma's bed and I took ma'self a few deep breaths. I sat there in that chair, hope'n that I could summon the spirit of Doc Hale and that all this'd work. I really wanted it ta'work. Mr. and Mrs. Fairfax looked like they'd come to their last chance. Truth be told, I find that when Christians start ask'n for witches ta'do magic for 'em, then they'd tried ever-thing else first. Noth'n else was work'n and that's why they was call'n a witch to their house.

It was time ta'start. I put ma'self into a trance. I 'magined the stars and breathed the power of the stars into my heart. I 'magined the powers of the earth and breathed the power of the earth into my belly. I took 'nother breath and mixed those energies real good in my body. Once I did that, I 'magined ma'self open'n up my mind and my heart to the spirit world. I 'magined what Doc Hale was look'n like, his blue coat and his white wig. I brought ta'mind what he felt like, too. There was a certain feel'n I had when I seen him. He had a certain presence 'bout him that he had that was his own. I brought ta'mind that feel'n. The feel'n of his presence. I whispered his name, *"Doc Hale. Doc Hale. Doc Hale."*

I waited for a bit, and whispered his name again, *"Doc Hale. Doc Hale."*

I 'magined ma'self open'n up my whole self and called again, *"Doc Hale."* Then I felt him. I felt the presence of the odd doctor wear'n a blue coat and white wig. I could feel him real strong like. His presence felt gentle and strong at the same time. The feel'n in the room felt safe. Like we was in the safest place on earth. I took a breath and opened up my mind, my heart, and my body to Doc Hale. I felt him step'n into my body. He was wear'n my flesh like clothes. I had ta'relax my mind more and more so he could have control over my body and be do'n his work. I released my mind just 'nuff ta'give him full control, but I held onto ma'self 'nuff ta'where I could see what he saw and could hear his thoughts in my mind.

Doc Hale saw through my eyes. He could hear through my ears. When he spoke, he was speak'n through my voice. "Dearest Emma. I will help you as much as I can."

Mrs. Fairfax was watch'n the whole thing. She could hear that the tone and inflection in my voice had done changed. She could be hear'n that Doc Hale was now in my body. She was excited and right scared at the same time. If she doubted her decision ta'bring a witch into her home, it was too late now.

Doc Hale, use'n my body, placed his hands on her head. I could see him look'n at the energy of her body, her life force. It was weak and we din't have s'much time. He stood hisself up for a minute and walked toward her stomach. He could see dark power swirl'n inside her belly. I was hear'n his thoughts as he looked at her through the eyes of spirit, *"There is a dark spirit inside her,"* he said ta'my thoughts.

"A spirit?" I spoke ta'his thoughts as well. *"What is it? How'd it get there?"*

"My dear boy," Doc Hale thought, *"most diseases are a spirit of one form or another. They look like a disease to the human eye, but in spirit, they are dark spirits who are parasites. Only using the patient as a food source. Once they dry up, then they move to another."*

"You mean, once they die?" I thought.

"Unfortunately, yes." Doc Hale thought.

"What do we do?" I asked him.

"We remove it." He thought.

Doc Hale done placed my physical hand over Emma's stomach where the spirit was attached ta'her. As my hand hovered over her, Doc Hale reached out with his spirit hand and grabbed holt of the dark spirit. He grabbed it real hard and wasn't 'bout ta'let go. The spirit felt Doc Hale pull'n it out and it resisted. It resisted hard. It coiled real tight 'round her organs. It wasn't budge'n.

"Johnathan," Doc Hale thought ta'me. *"Join your mind to my mind more powerfully. With our combined psychic strength, we can summon light that will force the spirit to release Emma."*

I did what Doc Hale said and I done joined my mind ta'his mind in a strong way. We connect ta'each other. We connected s'strong that at one time I couldn't right tell who I was or who he was. We was one mind. One soul. One spirit. Then together, we focused on the stars and the heavens. We brought a powerful light from the sky, and it done shot the dark spirit like a ray of sunlight hit'n a shadow. The dark spirit must have been shocked or weakened or someth'n 'cause it released its holt on Emma.

Doc Hale grabbed the dark spirit through my arms as hard as we could. He wouldn't be let'n it escape, none. *"Johnathan, call to your familiar,"* Doc Hale thought.

"Call ta'him?" I thought, *"I ain't never called ta'him without his cat skull and his candle. I dunno how ta'do call him without it."*

"We don't have time for doubts! Call him now!" Doc Hale demanded.

Without hesitate'n, I went deep into my own soul. With all the excitement, I din't think too much 'bout it. I brought my thoughts into that place behind your heart. The place where some say your soul is be'n. I brought my thoughts into my soul and called to Old Henry. "Old Henry, Old Henry, I summon thee, Old Henry, Old Henry, I conjure thee!"

"I am here, Johnathan," Old Henry appeared in the room with us.

Doc Hale held out the dark spirit to Henry. *"Take this to its rightful home away from this place."*

Old Henry grabbed holt of the dark spirit and then vanished. I dunno where he went, but I 'spose he went and got that dark spirit that was make'n Emma sick outta here. I could feel Doc Hale's relief when

Old Henry took the dark spirit away. He told me in his thoughts that get'n that spirit away was only half the heal'n. He said that it was like cut'n away the infected tissue. The old sick part had ta'be taken away, but then the body needed ta'be healed with medicines. There was always two parts to heal'ns. Take away the dark sickly part, which is almost always a spirit cause'n the sickness, then heal the wound with medicines. In Emma's case, we wasn't gonna give her no herbs or teas or noth'n. She needed life force. She needed power so's she could heal right quick. Doc Hale walked over to the head of Emma's bed and done placed both hands on her head again. He closed his eyes and done called upon power from the stars and the heavens ta'pour down into my body, and he directed the power through my arms and into Emma. I could see her body fill'n up with the medicine of the white light. Doc Hale kept his hands on her head for quite a long time, it seemed like.

After a while, Doc Hale took his hands off her head. *"She will be fine. Her fever will start going down now and she will be good as new by tomorrow morning."*

"Thank you, Doc Hale." I thought.

"Of course, my boy," Doc Hale thought ta'me. *"Whenever you have need for me to heal again, please call upon me. You may release me now."*

I 'magined Doc Hale be'n released from my mind, my heart, and my body. I could feel him separate'n from me and go'n back to the spirit world. I took ma'self a deep breath and found ma'self alone in my own body as it oughta be.

Emma opened her eyes.

"She'll be just fine," I said to Mr. and Mrs. Fairfax. "Her fever'll go down by tonight and she'll be right healed by tomorrow morn'n."

11

The Witch's Bottle

THE WINTER WAS OVER and warmer days was come'n soon. We had us a few cold days here and there, but ain't noth'n like we've had in previous years. I can 'member one winter where it snowed pretty good. I thought Momma was gonna lose her mind 'cause she said she ain't never seen s'much snow in her life. Ever-thing was s'white and pretty. Ever-thing looked clean and brand new. Noth'n like that this year. Just a few cold days. Noth'n real special 'bout it. Spring comes 'round here in early March. It warms up pretty good and the town comes ta'life again. Some of them farmers has their own seed that they saved from the last harvest, but some folks get their seed from Mr. Picklesworth's general store. It made me happy ta'see farmers plant'n again. That means warmer days and summer ain't too far away. Once spring comes, I knew there'd be lots of work ta'be done at the store.

Mr. Picklesworth planned a trip to the next couple'a towns nearby. There was folks on farms way out where who'd mailed him a few weeks back, ask'n if he could deliver some seed, feed, tools, and other supplies they might be need'n. I asked Mr. Picklesworth why he wanted ta'deliver things hisself. It made more sense ta'me if he'd mail some of them things ta'folks. He said the folks who mailed him was customers he hadn't been see'n for a long time. Old friends of his who he'd known for many years. Truth be told, I think he liked the chance ta'take a trip outta town. He once told me it does a marriage good if once in a while a man goes travel'n here and there. Him and his wife been together twenty years, and I'm sure he likes a chance ta'get gone for a bit.

He told me he needed my help deliver'n ever-thing. He said he's get'n old in years and his back ain't as strong as it used ta'be and he was need'n my help. I figured I'd go with him. Hell, why not? I ain't been outta this town for a while, and it might give me a opportunity ta'ask Mr. Picklesworth 'bout what he knows 'bout witchcraft and things of that nature.

When the day come for us ta'pack up for our journey, I done helped him put all the supplies in his wagon. I helped him hitch them horses and we made sure we had ever-thing we needed. He kissed his wife and daughters goodbye and we was on our way. The ride on the trail was mostly quiet. Mr. Picklesworth was hisself mostly a quiet man. He's the type of man you could tell who was hav'n lots of thoughts but din't say much ta'folks unless he thought he was need'n to. After couple hours, I thought it might be time ta'ask him 'bout witchcraft.

"Mr. Picklesworth, how d'you know 'bout witchcraft?" I asked him, hope'n he'd finally tell me after all these months.

"It's a long story, Johnathan," Mr. Picklesworth said.

"I think we got time," I said.

Mr. Picklesworth din't say noth'n for a little bit. I could see he was in his thoughts, and I gathered he was think'n 'bout what he was gonna tell me.

"The magic we do," Mr. Picklesworth said, "we don't call it witchcraft."

"No?" I thought that was a strange thing ta'say. I figured all magic was witchcraft. Anytime someone says anyth'n 'bout magic I always heard 'em call it witchcraft.

"Witchcraft has a bad reputation, " he said. "When folks hear witchcraft, they think of curses and stealing babies for Satanic rituals, blighting crops, and hurting folks."

"I don't think that's what witchcraft is," I said.

"Of course not!" Mr. Picklesworth said. "Witchcraft is simply the craft of the witches. Most times that craft is magic. But not always. Sometimes it's healing. Sometimes it's helping folks find lost things. Other times it's protecting folks from those who wish to hurt them."

"You don't do no witchcraft?" I asked. "So, you ain't a witch?"

Mr. Picklesworth smiled. "I prefer 'charmer' over 'witch'."

Charmer. I 'membered that word. I all a sudden 'membered when the corpse ghosts was go'n after those boys on Halloween. That's when someth'n came over me and I was filled with power. I felt s'strong and s'powerful that I called ma'self, *Johnathan Knotbristle the Charmer.* I thought I just made that up. I had no idea why I'd thought of the word 'charmer'. It just came ta'my mind when I felt that power flow'n through my veins.

"Charmer," I said. "I know that word. I once called ma'self 'charmer'. I dunno why. It just came ta'me."

"Truth be told, Johnathan, 'charmer' and 'witch' are pretty close in nature." Mr. Picklesworth said. "Some might say they're the same thing. You see, folks have all kinds of fears of witches. But a charmer. That doesn't sound so bad. Doesn't bring up all the fear that 'witch' does. In fact, some might say charmers help folks when they need it most. Folks have been coming to magical folk for thousands of years. Usually only when they have exhausted all other means. They come to magical folks like us 'cause they know we have the power to help them. But they won't come to a witch unless as a last resort. But they will come to a charmer."

It was start'n ta'make sense. Some folks changed the word 'witch' to someth'n else like 'charmer' or other words so that folks wouldn't fear 'em. Fear could be a powerful thing. Folks kill folks over fear. Fear makes folks do real bad things ta'one 'nother. "How long've you been a 'charmer'?"

"Oh, many, many years," Mr. Picklesworth said.

I was wonder'n why Mr. Picklesworth never said noth'n 'bout witches, charmers, or magic. Why we worked together ever-single day and he never once said noth'n. I knew he knew I was a witch, so why din't he help me none? Why din't he teach me things he's know'n? "Why haven't we talked 'bout magic b'fore? 'Specially after Halloween."

"It's said that a witch comes to know things when the time is right for them," Mr. Picklesworth said. "I've been watching you, Johnathan. You have been learning well."

"But if you been watch'n me, then why din't you teach me more magic?"

"The witch must learn on their own," Mr. Picklesworth said. "You must have an experience that teaches you the way of magic. Yes, there are those of us who can teach you spells and things of that nature, but the truest learning happens when you need magic the most."

"What d'you mean?"

"Magic is created when you need something the most. It's more than a simple desire," Mr. Picklesworth said. "The most powerful magic comes from deep in your soul. When the need of something outweighs all other things. When you need something so much that you must have it, or else."

"Is that why I found ma'self my power when them corpse ghosts came?" I asked.

"Precisely," Mr. Picklesworth said. "The power of the witch is not necessarily about someone teaching you magic. It's about learning to feel the virtues and powers of the land, the stars, and the dead. When you learn the virtues, the essence of power that is, then you can connect to those virtues and use their powers to help you achieve your means."

Mr. Picklesworth and I talked us for a long time 'bout magic and witchcraft. He told me stories 'bout how he learnt spells and other magical rituals. We had the whole day ta'travel in that wagon of his so we had plenty of time for talk'n. We din't talk the whole time though. Mr. Picklesworth said that one'a the best ways ta'learn magic was ta'shut up and just listen to the land. He said sometimes if you stop your mouth from flap'n and you quieted your thoughts you could listen ta'what the land was say'n. He said that the spirits of the land, the trees, the rocks, and the sky had things ta'teach us and all we had ta'do was listen with our heart. Sometimes spirits be talk'n ta'ya with a feel'n. Mr. Picklesworth said that spirits of the land don't always be talk'n with words. He said sometimes they be talk'n with feel'ns. We spent us a long time listen'n to the land. I dunno how much the land was say'n, but I got me the feel'n that the spirits knew we was there and maybe they had stuff ta'say.

That night, we finally gone made it to the next town. It was too late ta'be deliver'n no packages, so we stayed us in a room at the town's inn. We had our supper and went right ta'sleep. Mr. Picklesworth said that we had ta'get up at the cock's crow early the next morn'n. That was fine with me. I was tired from travel'n the whole day and I knew we had our work cut out for us in the morn'n. The next morn'n, we got ourselves up at sunrise and got stuff ready for our day. We rode the wagon all the way to the other side of town ta'make our delivery.

Out on the other side of town there was a little house on a little farm. It wasn't much bigger than mine. It was just big 'nuff ta'feed a family and that was 'bout it. There was chickens and geese run'n 'round the yard and a little barn out back. I figured there was goats and cows back there, too. We pulled up the wagon close to the front door and there was a dog just bark'n away. Three women look'n ta'be in their 30's came out the house with big 'ole smiles on their faces. They was pretty 'nuff, but no men came out with 'em. That was an odd thing ta'see. Women never was liv'n out on their own unless they was old and their husband died or someth'n.

Me and Mr. Picklesworth got outta the wagon and them three women eagerly surrounded him. Then he gave each of the three of 'em a kiss on the lips. It wasn't just no kiss. It was the kinda kiss you give your wife behind closed doors. I din't say a word. My heart fell down ta'my stomach and I tried not ta'look surprised but I'm sure the three women knew I was think'n someth'n.

The women smiled with big smiles and one'a them said, "Mr. Picklesworth, who might this pretty young man be?"

"This is Johnathan Knotbristle," Mr. Picklesworth said. "Johnathan, this is Elizabeth."

"How d'you do?" I said politely. I could feel my cheeks turn'n red.

"Very well, my pretty thing," Elizabeth said.

Then Mr. Picklesworth introduced the other two women, "Johnathan, this is Margaret and Helen."

"How d'you do?" I said.

Margaret and Helen extended their hands ta'me and I shook it like any other person I'd meet. Mr. Picklesworth made a gesture with his hand and lips like I was 'sposed ta'take their hand and kiss it. That was strange ta'me. Why would I be kiss'n their hands? A good handshake is how you can tell the measure of someone. Sure, women had them a lighter handshake than men, but it was still as good a way as any ta'meet someone. I kissed all three of their hands. I felt stupid do'n it, but maybe Mr. Picklesworth had a reason. Or maybe he was be'n formal. Either way, I felt real dumb do'n it.

"Come in, Mr. Picklesworth," Margaret said.

"Yes, do come in," Helen said as she giggled like she was up ta'no good. Elizabeth opened the front door to their house, "It's been a long winter since we have seen you."

"Johnathan," Mr. Picklesworth said, "take the supplies for these lovely ladies and put it in the barn." He then went into the house with the three ladies and shut the door.

I took out some seed and a few odd items and put 'em in the barn like Mr. Picklesworth done said. It din't take me too long and I went back over to the house. I was 'bout ta'knock on the door ta'see what he wanted me ta'do next and I heard some noises come'n from the house. I stopped for a minute ta'listen. And sure 'nuff, Mr. Picklesworth was have'n sex with all three of those ladies. I din't know what ta'think! He has a wife and children back home. Well, I figured it wasn't none'a my business. I went back to the wagon and sat there 'til the door opened and Mr. Picklesworth came back outside.

"Johnathan," Mr. Picklesworth said, "come inside and let's get us some food."

Helen, Margaret, and Elizabeth cooked us some eggs, toast, and some bacon. They also had them some biscuits and some jarred fruit that they must've had since last summer or fall. I was grateful ta'have a good meal.

As I sat there eat'n my breakfast, Helen eyed me up and down for a bit. "Mr. Picklesworth, is this your new witch?"

I stopped eat'n for a moment and waited ta'hear what Mr. Picklesworth was gonna say.

"The Devil gave me strict instructions on this one," Mr. Picklesworth said. "He's to be on his own until the time is right."

"Oh, we hope the time is near," Margaret said. She placed her hand on my shoulder, "His power is strong. He could be an asset to us."

"Not yet," Mr. Picklesworth said.

I kept eat'n my breakfast, not know'n what ta'say or what ta'think 'bout all this.

"Johnathan," Mr. Picklesworth said, "these ladies are part of my coven out here in this town. They are witches who I've taught the mysteries of magic."

"He's our magister," Elizabeth said, "Our leader. We are one coven of several."

"I created three covens," Mr. Picklesworth said.

"You have three covens in this town?" I asked.

Mr. Picklesworth chuckled. "Heavens, no. I have three covens in three towns. You see Johnathan, with my deliveries through various small towns around here, I have met both women and men who wish to become witches or charmers and learn the ways of magic. I teach them what they need to know and let them lead their covens the way they see fit."

Helen placed her hand on Mr. Picklesworth's shoulder. "We govern ourselves, but he is still our leader and teacher."

I been work'n for Mr. Picklesworth for several months now. I considered him a friend and now maybe someone I can be look'n up to ta'teach me magic. I din't know how much experience he had with witchcraft, but through the looks of things, he knew a lot more than I thought he did. Three covens. I sat there wonder'n how many witches he was teach'n. Was he have'n sex with all of 'em? Well, that was none'a my business and I figured that I'd best be mind'n my own. "Don't we have other deliveries ta'make today?"

"We can wait on that," Mr. Picklesworth said. "I came here also to help these women."

"Help 'em with what?" I asked.

"Magic," Margaret said. "Someone is cursing us. Sending dark magic to destroy our little farm and make us sick."

"Yes," Elizabeth said. "Poor Helen was very sick a few weeks prior. She almost died because of the sickness. It took all of our magic to heal her."

"How d'you know it was a curse?" I asked.

"You can feel it," Mr. Picklesworth said. "When dark witchcraft is used, there's a feeling of darkness that you can't help but to feel."

"Why would someone want ta'harm you, Miss Helen?" I asked.

Elizabeth was silent for a bit. She looked over at Mr. Picklesworth who gave her a nod of approval. "When witches curse one another, it could be because they feel it's justice for something you may have done wrong, or they are cursing you to show you their power."

"And she's not the only who was cursed," Margaret said. "I was cursed too. Not but a few weeks back. I fell sick and couldn't get out of bed for a week."

Mr. Picklesworth was silent for a bit. I could tell he was deep in his thoughts, think'n 'bout what ta'do next. "We need to find out who is do'n this and why."

We finished our breakfast and Mr. Picklesworth knew just the thing ta'send back the curse and draw out the witch who was curse'n them ladies. He told Margaret ta'fetch a bottle, three candles, pins, and nails. Margaret gone gathered the things that Mr. Picklesworth'd asked and placed 'em on the table. Mr. Picklesworth made a triangle with the three candles with the apex point'n towards the front door. He said that if we were want'n ta'send the dark magic back and draw out the witch, the apex of the triangle of candles would be need'n ta'point to the door which led into the house. He told us that the front door, and windas, too, but mostly the front door, was a way for magic and other power ta'come into the house. Doorways and windas was gateways to the spirit world 'cause they was in "between." Doors and windas was not fully outside or fully inside. They was magical. But Mr. Picklesworth done told us, if we can use doorways and windas ta'send magic outside, dark witches can use 'em ta'send magic inside if they ain't protected with magic.

"Elizabeth," Mr. Picklesworth said, "I need a few strands of your hair and some nail clippings."

Elizabeth did what he done asked and pulled a few strands of hair from her blond head and handed 'em to Mr. Picklesworth. She took her a small knife and cut a few of her fingernails off and handed 'em ta'him. Mr. Picklesworth put the hair, nails, and fingernails in the bottle. He handed the bottle to Elizabeth. "Take this bottle outside and pee in it. Fill it almost all the way up."

Without question, Elizabeth did what he was ask'n. I could see the trust that them three ladies had for Mr. Picklesworth. They trusted him with their magic and their lives. After a few minutes, she came back in the house with the full bottle. Mr. Picklesworth took the bottle and placed a cork in it ta'seal up what was inside. He put the magic bottle in the center of the three candles. "Everyone, gather around the table. Place your hands over the bottle."

We all did what we was told and went over to the table and put our hands 'round the candles with our palms face'n the bottle.

"Now, concentrate on ridding Elizabeth of this dark magic and on forcing the witch to reveal themselves," Mr. Picklesworth said. "See in your mind the dark power leaving Elizabeth and going into the bottle. See in your mind that the power is going back to the witch. All that was given, so shall be received."

Hold'n my palms towards the bottle, I 'magined that the dark power was a cloud of blackness that was leav'n Elizabeth and go'n inside the bottle. I then 'magined that the dark magic was go'n out the door back to the witch who done sent the magic.

Mr. Picklesworth started speak'n in spirit tongue, "Koya dee-nay-mi-ya-to-no quee-ya-ka."

We was all connect'n our powers ta'each other. I could feel the power of Mr. Picklesworth, Elizabeth, Margaret, and Helen flow'n through me. In my mind, I 'magined a whirlwind of power circl'n 'round us.

The power became stronger and stronger. We was all connected. We could all be feel'n Mr. Picklesworth's words of power as he spoke the spirit tongue. Without no hesitation we all said the magic words that he received from the spirits, *"Koya dee-nay-mi-ya-to-no quee-ya-ka."*

The energy b'tween us got more and more powerful. We said them spirit words again, *"Koya dee-nay-mi-ya-to-no quee-ya-ka."* As the power b'tween us all grew, I couldn't feel my power or Mr. Picklesworth's power, I felt ever-one's power at the same time. We done said the spirit words a third and final time, *"Koya dee-nay-mi-ya-to-no quee-ya-ka."*

Then we felt the power fade. The bottle gathered all the power that it was need'n from us. Mr. Picklesworth took the bottle and put it in the fireplace.

"What do we do now?" I asked.

"We wait for the magic to work," Mr. Picklesworth answered. "Everyone, stay back from the fire."

We was all in a trance as we gazed into the fireplace ta'watch the bottle get hot. None'a us said a word as the bottle got hotter and hotter from the flames of the fireplace. I could still feel the magic connection b'tween the five of us. I could feel the magic work'n. After what seemed like a long while, the bottle exploded in the fireplace, leav'n hot piss and nails all over. The piss was sizzlin' in the flames, and at that moment in time, I was feel'n our magic work'n. I still had me in a trance, and I looked at Elizabeth and I could'a swore I saw black power leave'n her body and go'n out the door.

"I felt it," Elizabeth said. "The curse is gone."

"What 'bout the witch who done sent it?" I asked. I was real curious how all this was gonna happen. How would the witch be found? Was she just gonna confess, or was someth'n more sinister gonna happen?

Later that day, Mr. Picklesworth and me helped the ladies 'round their little farm. We helped 'em get their ground ready for plant'n and we made sure them animals was good and fed. We opened up a wooden crate that had three brand new dresses. One for each of the ladies. The dresses was a gift from him. I was wonder'n if we was gonna do more deliveries that day, but Mr. Picklesworth said that we had more magic we needed ta'be do'n and it needed ta'be at night. In fact, he said that it needed ta'be in the darkest part'a the night when most folks be sleep'n and dream'n. He said that the best time ta'do magic, 'specially dark magic, was when normal folk are sleep'n. He said that when ever-body is 'wake, there's too much psychic power come'n and go'n from ever-body and sometimes it gets in the way of magic. It makes the magic muddy and sometimes it don't come out the way you be want'n it to. He said it is easier ta'do magic when folks was asleep. When the night air was quiet, it was better ta'do magic.

B'fore it got dark, Mr. Picklesworth and me done hitched up the wagon and went into town. We wasn't go'n for no delivery. We was go'n ta'see if we could figure out who was the witch that sent the dark magic to the ladies. We went to the local tavern and Mr. Picklesworth ordered us both a whiskey. I ain't never seen Mr. Picklesworth at a tavern b'fore. Usually when he closed up his store he went straight away home 'cause Mrs. Picklesworth woulda had supper ready and he din't want ta'keep her wait'n. He was the type of man who din't need ta'be away from his family at the tavern, drink'n his life away. From what I know 'bout him, he's quite happy with his life and his family.

We wasn't at the tavern but a few minutes when some man sit'n up at one'a the tables started talk'n ta'his friend 'bout the "damndest thing that happened." Mr. Picklesworth started a conversation with the man ta'get more information. "What happened today?"

"The damndest thing..." the man said, "Old Mrs. Knowles' house just caught fire!"

"Caught fire?" Mr. Picklesworth said. "Oh, no! That's terrible."

"Damndest thing. She said she was in her house cook'n and clean'n and the fireplace exploded and caught fire ta'her house."

"Is she alright?" Mr. Picklesworth asked.

"She's fine," the man said. Her neighbors got some water out the nearby creek and put it out. It din't burn much. They was able ta'get it out b'fore it got too bad."

"Did Mrs. Knowles live here for a long time?" Mr. Picklesworth asked.

"Her and her family've lived here for more than 20 years," the man answered.

"So, an old strong family line?"

"I'd reckon so. They been here long as I can 'member. Her husband's family too, the Knowles family."

"What does the Knowles family do?" Mr. Picklesworth asked.

"I know they has a family farm, just like most families in this town," the man said. "Other than that, I dunno what they do. They don't come up to the town and spend much time with other folks. They pretty much spend most their time by themselfs."

Mr. Picklesworth got all the information he needed. We finished our whiskeys and headed back out. On the way back to the ladies' house, Mr. Picklesworth told me the fireplace explosion was a sure sign our spell'd worked and it was her that sent the dark magic to the ladies. He said that most country witches don't like ta'spend time with ordin'ry folk for no kinda reason unless they was really try'n ta'hide the fact that they's witches. Some witches are clever like that. Most, he said, minded their own business and stayed outta ever-body's way. He trusted his gut and his gut said that that 'ole witch wasn't done the ladies yet. We had ta'stay ta'help the ladies defend themselfs. I din't mind much. They was real good at be'n hospitable and nice and I was learn'n more magic.

When we got back to the ladies' small farm, Mr. Picklesworth told 'em what he found out. They was real happy that he was stay'n 'round that night ta'help 'em keep away any magical attacks that might be happen'n. That night after supper, we sat 'round the table play'n cards, tell'n stories, and talk'n 'bout magic. We had ta'wait 'til well after midnight, so we best be keep'n ourselfs busy and not fall'n asleep. Mr. Picklesworth said that we was gonna send 'em a good curse right back. The kinda curse that keeps witches from send'n anymore dark magic. I was excited ta'do this. It turns out there was more witches than I thought there was. Hell, when the Devil gave me the powers of the witch, I thought I was the only one. I din't know there was more of us witches all over the place and that sometimes they send curses and shit ta'each other.

The clock said it was approach'n midnight. Soon, we'd be do'n magic ta'keep the ladies safe. Elizabeth, Margaret, and Helen all looked a bit nervous. They kept look'n at the clock and then ta'each other. The night was real dark. No moon tonight. The dark moon. Good for do'n dark magic, the ladies said. We was sit'n 'round the fireplace, talk'n 'bout magic and things like that, then the air changed. It felt like there was a void in the room. Like all the life got sucked outta the room.

Scratch scratch scratch scratch scratch scratch.

Scratch scratch scratch scratch scratch scratch.

"Something is scratching at the door," Margaret said.

We all heard them scratch'n sounds and looked at the door. Margaret looked out the winda' and saw a dog scratch'n at the door. "That's the strangest thing, why is there a dog out on the front porch?"

Margaret was open'n the front door when Mr. Picklesworth screamed, "Don't open the door!"

It was too late. Margaret opened the door and that dog gone jumped inside and started growl'n at ever-body. We all backed up away from the door. It was growl'n someth'n fierce. That dog had a crazy look in his eyes. Like he had rabies or someth'n. We slowly backed away and the dog was eye'n Margaret.

"Slowly walk to the door and shut it," Mr. Picklesworth said.

As the dog was growl'n, Margaret slowly backed to the front door. She was gonna shut it but then she saw six more dogs. Each of 'em growl'n, too.

"These are fetch dogs," Mr. Picklesworth said. "These are the spirits of witches that took the shape of dogs to attack us."

The other six dogs was slowly come'n into the house and they was growl'n away. We all was real nervous and, might I say, we was 'fraid. Mr. Picklesworth looked 'round the house for a weapon but din't see noth'n off hand. "Do you have a gun?"

"Yes," Elizabeth said, "but it's in the bedroom."

The bedroom was down a little hallway on the other side of the house. There was seven dogs in the way, though. Mr. Picklesworth took him a deep breath. He looked like he knew what we should do but was hesitant ta'do it. "We need to out power them. We need to shapeshift and become inhumanly stronger than we are."

I never heard of shapeshift'n 'cept for in storybooks and things like that. Was that really someth'n we could do as witches? "What d'you mean 'shapeshift'?"

"Johnathan," Mr. Picklesworth said, "I know you haven't had the training, but you are gonna have to shapeshift into your animal form if we are to get out of this. The ladies already know what to do. Johnathan, we are gonna shapeshift at the same time. As we change into our animal form, I'll walk you through it step-by-step."

Me, Margaret, Elizabeth, and Helen was wait'n for Mr. Picklesworth ta'give us instructions. The dogs was walk'n closer and closer ta'us. Their growls was get'n louder, too. It looked like they was ready ta'attack and jump on us.

"Go into a trance," Mr. Picklesworth said. His voice was slow and calm. He din't want ta'make no sudden moves or sounds ta'aggravate them dogs. "Take a few deep breaths and summon the power of the stars and the earth. Connect to the power of the earth with your feet. Breathe the energy of the earth into your pelvis and your belly. Keep breathing in the energy of the earth. Build the power more and more with each breath. Now, close your eyes for a moment and go within yourself and connect with your animal self that we all have naturally."

I did what Mr. Picklesworth done said. I was in a trance, and I breathed me in the power of the earth. I could feel it build'n up in my pelvis and belly. I felt like I was connected ta'ever single animal on earth. Like we was one big animal spirit. My adrenaline was just a go'n. My heart was race'n and my blood was pump'n real hard through my veins. I closed my eyes just like Mr. Picklesworth'd said and tried real hard ta'connect ta'my animal spirit. I never heard that we all had an animal spirit, but we din't have no time ta'ask questions. The dogs was 'bout ta'get us and we had ta'do this fast! I 'magined that in my body, in my spirit, somewhere, there was an animal wait'n for the chance ta'get out. An animal that was s'strong and s'powerful that noth'n could defeat it. When I was do'n all this, I kept breathe'n the earth power up through the ground and into my belly.

Mr. Picklesworth saw that I was connect'n with the animal inside my spirit. The ladies was, too. "Johnathan, take a deep breath in your lower belly. This is the place of our animal urges. The place of our powers of survival. Keep your connection to your inner animal. Now...growl!"

Growl? I opened my eyes and looked at Mr. Picklesworth. Did he mean ta'say growl? We was 'sposed ta'growl?

"Growl! Johnathan, do it now! Growl!" Mr. Picklesworth started growl'n like a pissed off animal. Like an animal who was 'bout ta'get into a big fight!

The ladies all started growl'n too! I took 'nother deep breath and when I exhaled, I let out the deepest, strongest growl I could. My heart was pump'n s'hard and I was s'scared of them dogs that I used that fear ta'make me real mad. Real mad! I growled like I was 'bout ta'attack them dogs with my teeth! The earth energy swirled and pulsated in my belly and my pelvis. We was all growl'n like rabid animals. That's when I saw 'em. I could see ever-one's animal spirit. We growled and growled and growled. Our bodies din't change, but our animal spirits was come'n out. Maybe it was 'cause I was scared and growl'n s'hard or maybe it was 'cause I was deep in trance, but I stopped see'n ever-one's body and only saw their animals.

The growl'n helped me bring out the animal in my spirit. I dunno if what I seen was just all in my head, but it helped me go deeper into ma'self and bring out the animal power that I had. With each growl and each breath of earth energy, I felt more like an animal and less ma'self. Johnathan Knotbristle was go'n away and the animal inside was take'n over. I felt powerful. I felt the rage of power take'n control over me. I ain't never felt s'strong and so alive ever b'fore. Each of us was shapeshift'n into an animal in spirit. The power of the animal was give'n us strength; the power of the earth itself. The power of our inner spirit animal was take'n over our bodies. I could feel the power of the animal in my belly. I could feel the power of the animal in my arms and legs. I could feel the power of the animal in my head and heart. I was no longer Johnathan Knotbristle. I was the rage of a wild animal.

One'a the dogs leaped at Helen and b'fore it could bite her face, she used her animal strength and caught it in mid-air. The dog growled and tried ta'bite her, but Helen threw the dog back on the ground. 'Nother dog bit Elizabeth's ankle. She kicked the shit outta it. She kicked it s'hard that it flew 'cross the room and hit wall. A dog jumped on Mr. Picklesworth, but he was the most powerful animal of all of us. Without s'much as a flinch, he grabbed that dog with one hand and swung it 'round and threw it 'cross the room. Elizabeth grabbed 'nother one'a the dogs and threw it outside. Margaret let out a howl that shook the house itself. She looked mad with animal rage. She ran towards a couple'a the dogs and they backed themselfs away in fear. One'a the dogs gone bit my leg, and it only made me growl with more animal rage. The dogs was not give'n up. The more we threw or kicked them dogs, the more they came after us.

One'a the dogs leaped up and tried ta'bite my neck. I threw my hands in the air ta'protect ma'self and pushed the dog back again. There was a knife on the table, and I was close 'nuff to it that I grabbed it and stabbed that dog in the back. Then, it just dis'ppeared. Use'n my animal strength, I took that knife and stabbed ever-single dog there. Each of 'em dis'ppeared like they wasn't even there in the first place.

When the last dog dis'ppeared, Mr. Picklesworth, Helen, Elizabeth, and Margaret stopped growl'n and took some deep breaths ta'calm their animal spirit. With each breath they became more and more like themselfs again. But me...I was still in animal rage. I was ready ta'fight anyth'n and ever-one. I turnt to Mr. Pickclesworth and ladies and growled. One bad move and I was gonna leap on 'em and tear 'em ta'shreds. I saw red. I saw only that I needed ta'defend ma'self.

Mr. Picklesworth put hisself in front of the ladies. "Johnathan!" He yelled at me.

I recognized my name for a moment, but then that animal rage returnt. Attack! Bite!

Mr. Picklesworth called my name again, "Johnathan! Come back to yourself!"

He put his index finger over my heart and sent his power ta'my heart, ta'my spirit. I stopped where I was and thought for a second. I'm Johnathan. I'm ma'self again.

"Remember you are Johnathan Knotbristle," His voice was calm but firm. He never stopped send'n power ta'my spirit. "Take a deep breath

Johnathan. Breathe the power back into the earth. Focus on your heart. Focus on your spirit. Take another deep breath and find now that you are Johnathan Knotbristle."

I took deep breaths, and with ever-breath, I was return'n ta'my normal self. My animal spirit was los'n control over my body and I could feel his animal power go'n back into the shadows of ma'self somewhere in my spirit. "I'm a'right now."

Ever-one was relieved that I was me again. Hell, I was relieved I was me again. Now'd I could think normal again, I realized I din't know how I made them dogs dis'ppear. "What happened to them dogs? Why'd they dis'ppear?

"Those were not real dogs. They were the spirits of witches who shapeshifted into dogs to attack us," Mr. Picklesworth said. "Metal destroys them. Good work stabbing them, Johnathan."

"I was just try'n ta'get the dog off me," I said. "I din't know they was gonna dis'ppear."

"Well," Mr. Picklesworth said. "Let's get you bandaged up from that bite."

"I'll get some cloth to make a bandage," Helen said.

I was real confused 'bout the witches who used their spirit fetch ta'shapeshift into dogs ta'attack us. "If I stabbed the dogs and they dis'ppeared, what happened to the witches? Did I kill 'em?"

"No, Johnathan," Mr. Picklesworth said. "The witches are not dead. But they sure will have a few slices taken out of their flesh when they come back to their bodies."

All of us stood there real quiet. What the hell was go'n on? Why was witches attack'n us?

Mr. Picklesworth had a real concerned look on his face. "Ladies, make sure your protective wards and charms are up. Especially at night. This was a powerful magical attack and whoever these witches are, I don't think we've seen the last of them."

12

The Faeries in the Woods

ME AND MR. PICKLESWORTH made a few deliveries here and there in the surround'n towns throughout the spring. Some the deliveries was to them witch covens that he was the leader of. Three of 'em was his. He started 'em. He's what is called the magister. He's kinda like a pastor, but for witches. There was a little 'ole lady who was a witch who lived far out. We went ta'deliver some stuff ta'her and it took us near three days ta'get there. Her name was Mrs. Plunket and she looked ta'me like she was 100 years old. She prob'ly wasn't that old, but she sure was close to it. Mr. Picklesworth said that she was the nicest lady and best witch he ever did see. He'd been know'n her his whole life. He told me a story that her husband died when they was newlyweds and she never got over it. She had no one ta'help her and ain't got no family. She was start'n ta'lose her mind and was gonna hang herself in her own house when the Devil showed up and told her not ta'do it. The Devil said that in exchange for not kill'n herself that he'd give her the powers of the witch. Ever since then, she gave her life to help'n the sick. She helped anyone who needed it. When she got ta'be too old for heal'n, Mr.

Picklesworth'd travel ta'her house a few times a year ta'give her supplies and things she might need. He said there was others in the surround'n towns who watched over her, too. She helped folks her whole life and now it was time for others ta'watch over her.

It was get'n real close to May and the general store was busier than ever. Dur'n the day, Mr. Picklesworth and me worked the store like we usually done and sometimes at night we'd talk us 'bout magic and witchcraft. Mr. Picklesworth said he'd only show me magic and spells when I was need'n it. I asked him why and he said that when it comes ta'magic, that if you don't be need'n someth'n real bad, then it won't be come'n true. He said that do'n spells for no reason at all was a waste of the spirits and your own power. But he said not ta'worry 'cause we always be need'n someth'n in our life and that I'd learn soon 'nuff.

Mr. Picklesworth done said that most of the times we learn magic and witchcraft by pay'n attention ta'our dreams, the land, and our feel'ns. He said to never stop pay'n attention ta'how you feel. Sometimes when we don't have no words for stuff or are confused, our feel'ns know what is really go'n on. He gave me a book called *The Three Books of Occult Philosophy* by Cornelius Agrippa. He said there was other books on magic I could be order'n from the post. I spent ma'self a lot of time read'n that book. He also said that he had him a book of formulas and recipes that I could copy from when he done thought I was ready.

Mr. Picklesworth said that the best way ta'learn witchcraft was ta'sit with the land and the stars. He said that at differ'nt times of the day and night, I needed to be go'n outside and just be sit'n. I needed to be listen'n to the powers of the land, the trees, the water, and the animals. He said that I oughta sit on the ground, take ma'self a few deep breaths, go into a light trance, and feel ever-thing with my heart. The more I be connect'n to the virtues and the powers of the land and trees, the more I'd understand 'em and what magic they got. He said that the powers of the land be change'n throughout the day and night and throughout the seasons. Trees in the summer feel differ'nt than they do dur'n the fall and winter. He said when I was feel'n the power of them trees with these differ'nt times, I'd learn ma'self the true properties of magic.

The closer we got us to May, the hotter it got, and my house wasn't cool 'nuff in the summertime. May wasn't s'bad, but I knew it was only gonna be get'n hotter as them days went by. I din't mind sit'n outside on the ground at night none 'cause the night was cool and was refresh'n after a long hot day of work'n at the store. One night I was sit'n on the ground, and I could hear ma'self the cicadas and toads and nighttime songs of them critters who lived in them woods. I took ma'self some deep breaths and listened ta'those woods with my heart. I did that night after night. At first, I couldn't feel much at all. I often wondered if the stuff I was feel'n was just my 'magination. Mr. Picklesworth said that what I was feel'n *was* in my 'magination, but that was a'right, 'cause all magic and psychic power come from our 'maginations anyhow, so who was ta'say what was magic and what was just me think'n I was feel'n someth'n?

Night after night I listened ta'those woods. Each night I was think'n I was feel'n a little bit more than I did the night b'fore. I felt this presence in my heart. Like them trees was talk'n ta'me. This strangely made sense ta'me 'cause trees don't be talk'n like ever-body else. They don't speak like us and say howdy. They speak with feel'ns and that's what I was listen'n for...feel'ns. On one'a those nights, I was listen'n ta'those trees and I could'a swore I heard some sing'n way deep in them woods. I couldn't tell what song it was, but it did sure sound like sing'n ta'me. I din't think much of it, s'after a while I went inside and went ta'bed.

The next night, I went out ta'listen ta'those trees and I heard that sing'n again. This time I went walk'n in them woods. I took a lantern with me, 'cause those woods be get'n real dark sometimes. I walked a while in them woods and the sing'n got louder and louder. I walked 'round ta'where I thought the song was come'n from but I din't see noth'n. I stood there for a while, listen'n ta'that song. It was some language I ain't never heard b'fore. From what I could hear, it sure was a pretty song. Strange thing, though, is that I couldn't be tell'n if it were a man's voice or a woman's voice, one voice or several voices. I still din't see noth'n, s'after a while I went ta'bed.

On the third night I decided ta'go out and see if I could hear that song again. I went out to them woods with my lantern and waited ta'hear the song, but noth'n was happen'n. Noth'n. So, I decided that since I was out there in those woods anyhow, I might as well keep practice'n listen'n to them trees. As soon as I sat down on the ground and started listen'n to the trees with my heart, someone started sing'n that song. This time it was differ'nt though. The song sounded the same, but my heart was be'n filled with thoughts of magic, trees, and them stars above. I closed my eyes ta'listen to the beauty of the music. I was s'overjoyed with the song that I cried. I was s'moved I cried my eyes out.

When I opened my eyes, I could see ma'self a light in the distance. I thought maybe someone was carry'n a lantern or someth'n ta'light their way through the woods. I got up off the ground and walked towards 'em. The closer I got to the light, the louder the song got. When I got closer, I could see someone wear'n a cloak, carry'n a lantern just like I was think'n. I wanted ta'say someth'n, but their song was s'beautiful I din't want 'em ta'stop sing'n. I dunno why, but I decided ta'keep my distance and follow 'em. I followed 'em deeper and deeper into them woods. The whole time they was sing'n away at their song. It felt like we was walk'n for hours. The woods 'round here wasn't that big, s'maybe we was walk'n in circles.

The person in the cloak with the lantern stopped. They kept sing'n though. All a sudden, the fog started roll'n in. It was strange that fog would be come'n in dur'n the night like this. Usually when fog came in it was early in the morn'n 'round these parts. I wasn't sure 'zactly where I was or where I was go'n, so I thought it might be best if I made my way home. I turnt 'round ta'try ta'find my way back home when I heard a woman's voice behind me.

"I know you are following me," the woman said.

I was caught. I slowly turnt back 'round, feel'n kinda dumb for sneak'n 'round, follow'n her. "My name is Johnathan Knotbristle, what's yours?"

"Kothria," she answered.

"It's nice ta'meet you, Kothria," I said. "It's real foggy out here tonight. We should get outta the woods b'fore the fog gets us lost."

"Follow me, Johnathan Knotbristle," Kothria held her lantern in front of her ta'light the way and started walk'n her deeper into that fog.

"I don't think that's a good idea," I said. "We don't want ta'get lost."

Kothria was silent as she walked deeper into the foggy woods. Part of me wanted ta'go back home but I din't want to be leav'n her in these woods all by herself. She started sing'n her song as she walked on. I wasn't quite sure 'bout this. Then, all a sudden, the fog cleared and we was in 'nother town. We must have walked for miles and miles. Mr. Picklesworth and me'd traveled all over the area and went to the towns 'round here, and this town din't look noth'n I'd 'membered. Where inna hell was we? There was a lot of folks walk'n 'round the town and all of 'em was dressed real fancy like. Everyone was beautiful and wore them fancy trousers and shirts and them women was wear'n beautiful dresses. They was s'fancy they seemed like they shoulda been heavy but they wasn't. They lightly blew in the wind. I followed Kothria into the town and the thing I noticed most was that the whole town was smell'n like pine trees and flowers.

Kothria led me down a path that led past that little town and into 'nother patch of woods. These woods was differ'nt from the woods that was by my farm. The trees here seemed ta'be real ancient. They had a wisdom and a power that I couldn't 'splain none. The trees had the secrets of magic. I could feel the trees speak'n their language ta'my heart. Them trees had a language that was older than time, maybe even older than the earth itself. I followed Kothria down the path. This was both a long and yet a short journey at the same time. Normally I have ma'self a good sense of time, but not here. Here, I couldn't none tell how long time passed or even where I was. I kept follow'n Kothria down that path which eventually led to a castle in the middle of these here woods. The castle was made'a white stone, and at each corner of the castle there were a tower.

When we got to the castle, the gates was opened for us and Kothria led me inside. As she done walked through the halls of the castle, ever-one inside bowed they head ta'her. She walked with mighty grace and beauty 'til we got us to the throne room. It was here she put down her lantern and took off her cloak.

Sit'n on one'a the thrones was what looked ta'be a king. He was tall and looked real strong. He was the most handsomest man I had ever done seen. His hair was dark as midnight and his eyes was equally dark. "My dear," the king said to Kothria, "you have brought a guest."

"Yes," Kothria said and sat her down on the throne next to the king, "this is Johnathan Knotbristle the Charmer."

The king done looked at me and gave a smile, "Welcome, Johnathan Knotbristle the Charmer. I am Mithrolo, King of the Faery people."

"It is nice ta'meet you, King Mithrolo," I said. I couldn't take my eyes off'a that couple. They was the most beautiful things I'd ever done saw. They was both dark, mysterious, and there was someth'n 'bout 'em both that I wanted. Like someth'n in my gut that said that I ain't never wanted ta'leave 'em or this mysterious place.

"And I am Queen Kothria," Kothria said, "I am Queen of Faery People and the Lady of the Woods."

I bowed my head ta'her. I din't know she was a queen when I followed her into the woods. There weren't a castle or noth'n like this where I live. This had ta'be the Otherworld. The world of faeries that Alma and Mr. Picklesworth done told me 'bout. This world was like be'n 'wake inside a dream. Or be'n lost and yet found at the same time. I never wanted ta'leave this place. The white stones of the castle had a song of thems own. I din't hear the song with my ears none. I heard the song inside my heart.

"Come," King Mithrolo summoned his men, "take young Johnathan Knotbristle to his bedchamber."

Three men came from what seemed like nowhere, and I 'spose they was men of his court. They was dressed in fine clothes too, but not near s'pretty as the king and queen. They had them dark hair, too. They stayed quiet like as they took me to a room up the stairs. The room they took me to had the biggest bed I ever did see. It was the softest bed, too. There was a big winda' that looked over them woods, too. In the center of this here room was a bathtub made entirely of silver.

"You may take a bath and redress before dinner," one'a the king's men said. "The water is warm and there are fresh clothes on the bed."

When them three men left the room, I done took off my clothes and got into the tub. The water was the perfect temp'ature. So warm. So sooth'n. That bath healed my soul in a way that made me be forget'n my troubles. It were like drink'n the finest wine on a warm night. After my bath, I put on them fine clothes that was left out for me. They fit me perfect and was a beautiful crimson color. When I was dressed, I opened up the bed chamber door ta'find the three king's men wait'n for me. They done led me back downstairs and into a big dine'n hall. There was a long gold table. The only ones sit'n at that table was the king and queen. I found it bit odd that this big table was there, and it was only gonna have three folks.

Them three king's men led me to the third chair that was at the big, long golden table. The faery king sat at the head of the table and Queen Kothria sat ta'his left. I sat 'cross from her on the king's right. The table was filled with all differ'nt kinds of food. There was wild boar, chicken, venison, fruits and vegetables, and cakes. Ever-thing looked delicious. At that moment, I couldn't 'member the last time I had eat'n. Maybe it was an hour or maybe it was day. Things always did be blur'n in together whenever I was in the faery Otherworld.

King Mithrolo took him a glass container that was hav'n wine in it and poured some into a glass that was sit'n in front of me. "The wine is especially good today. The food as well."

I was sit'n with faery royalty. I figured I had ta'be extra kind and choose my words real careful like. "Forgive me, I was instructed ta'politely decline food or drink in the Otherworld."

Queen Kothria softly laughed. "Why would you have to decline the gifts of the faery kingdom?"

"I was told that once a mortal done eats the food from the faeries, then they is forever bound to the Otherworld," I said. "And sometimes what looks ta'be like a glorious meal is actually a glamour that turnt out ta'be sticks and rocks."

King Mithrolo started laugh'n. I'm sure he was laugh'n at me and my silliness. He poured a cup of wine for the queen and then hisself. "My handsome boy. These tales are often told to scare mortals who are not ready for the great mysteries of the Otherworld."

Queen Kothria took her glass of wine and took a sip. "Even if those stories were true, you are a witch, are you not?"

"I am," I answered the queen.

"As a witch, you are forever bound to the Otherworld once the Devil gives you his power," the queen said. "Witches always have one foot in the mortal world and one foot in the faery world. They are always between the worlds, are they not?"

"And further," King Mithrolo said, "it's simply rude not to accept gifts from faeries."

I sat there for a little bit think'n 'bout what they said. It made sense ta'me. Us witches, one way or 'nother, had us our hearts and minds in the spirit world or faery world, whatever you want ta'call it. We was always call'n up spirits, ghosts, and devils of one sort or 'nother. Even when we ain't do'n magic and spells, we still is attached to the faery world. Our hearts is always know'n what's happen'n with the faeries and other otherworldly spirits. I wonder if some of them stories came from folks who was 'fraid of faeries. You know, them folks who thought a long time ago that faeries was fallen angels or some horseshit like that. Even if it was true, would it be s'terrible if we was forever live'n with faeries anyhow? If you say you wouldn't wanna stay in the faery world, then you ain't been here then.

I figured I ain't had noth'n ta'lose, so I drank faery wine and had ma'self a good faery supper. The king and queen spent the whole night ask'n me questions, get'n ta'know me, and they told me I could ask 'em anyth'n I wanted. So I asked 'em what kinda magic tools they might be have'n. They told me they had them a magic cauldron that always had food in it and could be call'n of the spirits of the dead. They said they done had them a magic sword that never missed no target and could make a door to the faery world by cut'n thin air. They said they had them a spear that always'd be strike'n their enemies and could stab your fate and bring it ta'you. They said they had them a magic stone that'd keep the dead in the spirit world or call 'em up whenever you wanted to. I told 'em I was envious of magic like that, and I'd do anyth'n ta'have faery magic tools.

They said that any witch could turn them tools into faery tools. What they said was you needed to be decide'n which of your tools you wanted ta'turn into a faery tool. When you was ready, put that tool down in front of you on a table. Then you had ta'go into a trance and have your spirit leav'n your body and go'n into the faery world. Just close your eyes and 'magine you was leave'n your body and fly'n to the faery world. Sometimes I just close my eyes and 'magine I'm there. Simple as 1, 2, 3. Then they said you have ta'get in good relations with the faeries. Once you do that, you can be ask'n 'em for a faery tool and ask 'em ta'put faery magic in that tool you got on your table. Then when they give you the faery tool, you take it back in spirit ta'your physical tool. B'fore you get back in your body, be make'n sure to put that faery tool inside the physical tool in front of you. After you do that, you can jump back in your reg'lar body and open your eyes. Once that is done, you gotta seal the faery tool inside'a the physical tool by consecrate'n it to the faeries, the nature spirits, and the Gods.

We ate and drank wine all night long. I can't tell you how late it was, 'cause time is differ'nt in the faery world than it is in the real world. You ever be have'n s'much fun that you can't tell if it's been 10 minutes or 10 hours? It's just like that in the faery world. The king decided it was time for us ta'go ta'bed, 'cause in the morn'n he wanted the three of us ta'go hunt'n. Hunt'n boar. He said hunt'n boar was real fun, and that I hadn't lived 'til I hunted wild boar in the faery woods.

So the king and queen went off ta'bed and I walked up them white stone stairs up to the room I was stay'n in. I opened the door and it turnt out it wasn't my room, it was the king and queen's bedchamber. I was s'embarrassed I got the wrong room and politely excused ma'self. I turnt 'round and walked down the stone hallway and tried 'nother door, think'n it was my bedchamber, and when I opened this here door, it was the king and queen's bedchamber again. That was the oddest thing.

Again, I politely excused ma'self and shut their door. I walked down the hall and wasn't know'n which room I was in. So I walked ma'self a little ways down the hallway and tried 'nother door. Damn it! Again, it was the king and queen's bedchamber!

"Johnathan," the king called out ta'me, "please come in."

I stood there in that doorway not know'n what ta'say. This was the king and queen's bedroom. I was think'n it wouldn't be right none ta'come in their bedroom like that. I also was know'n that you ain't 'sposed ta'refuse the king of the faeries. I was try'n ta'think of someth'n polite ta'say, but I couldn't think of noth'n right then.

Queen Kothria was in the great big bed under them covers. I couldn't see her body none, but she was naked. "Johnathan, it's impolite to keep the king waiting."

I figured there wasn't no way I could think ta'get outta this, so I best be do'n what the king says. I slowly walked into the bedroom. King Mithrolo was sit'n up in the bed, shirtless. I walked over to that there bed and stood a couple'a feet away.

"Join us," King Mithrolo said, and he patted him the bed.

I sat ma'self down on the bed and din't move, not one bit. I was shy and embarrassed and I din't know what ta'do. Queen Kothria sat up in bed and her covers fell down, show'n her breasts. She leaned over ta'me and kissed me. King Mithrolo was take'n off my shirt and the queen undid my britches. I ain't never done noth'n like this b'fore. Never. I din't say a single thing. I figured anyth'n I said was gonna come out wrong or I'd sound stupid or someth'n like that. The queen kissed me again and I closed my eyes and let ma'self enjoy her lips. I could feel the king kiss'n the back of my neck. He put his arm 'round my chest from behind and the queen was grab'n my waist. B'fore I knew it, we was all three naked together. We was kiss'n each other and after a while, I done lost sight of who I was kiss'n and where.

We started have'n sex with each other. I felt s'strong and powerful with the king and queen, and at the same time I also was feel'n like I was their servant. I felt like anyth'n they wanted me ta'do, I had ta'do it. It's funny how do'n anyth'n someone else wanted made you feel more powerful. In the physical world, I don't think I could ever be hav'n sex with a woman and a man, but in the world of faery, it felt like that's I was 'sposed ta'be do'n. Have'n sex with the king and queen was like be'n lost in a fever dream. I was lost in both of their eyes, and yet I was feel'n both of their bodies 'round me. I could feel ma'self inside of 'em and I could feel both of 'em inside of me. Our bodies blended into each other. Our breath was becom'n the same breath. Our hearts was becom'n one heart. Our powers became one power. We was connected in such a way that I couldn't right tell what thoughts was mine and what thoughts was theirs.

When we ended, I reclaimed my body for my own. Not 'cause I wanted to, but 'cause I had to. I couldn't keep up the energies needed ta'stay within the minds and hearts of the faery king and queen. I needed ta'breathe on my own. I layed there next to 'em and I was look'n up at the ceil'n and saw right through it. I looked passed that ceil'n and I saw them stars. I saw stars and all of the celestial creation. We fell us asleep, each know'n each other's secret names. The part of ourselfs we kept hidden from ever-one else, even from ourselfs.

The next morn'n I woke up ta'find ma'self alone in the bed. King Mithrolo and Queen Kothria must have woke up early and got the day started. I got outta bed and found me my clothes. I found a basin of water and warshed my face and fixed my hair. I wanted ta'look somewhat presentable for 'em. I walked downstairs and again found 'em at the large dine'n table. I sat ma'self down at the table next to the king and queen.

"Johnathan, how did you sleep?" Queen Kothria asked me.

"Good," I said. "I slept like I was in the deepest of sleeps."

"Good!" King Mithrolo said. "I'm glad you got some rest. For today is the hunt, and we must be at our best!"

After our breakfast, the faery king's three faery men done escorted us to them stables and me, the king, and the queen each got us up on a horse. The king's faery men each got themselfs on a horse, too. They was carry'n spears, swords, and food and drink for the hunt. Once we got ourselfs settled on our horses, the king led the little party into the faery woods. The queen was ride'n beside me and the three king's faery men was ride'n behind us.

We walked us our horses on a dirt path that was lead'n into the forest. As soon as we got inside them trees, it became a lot darker than it was. It wasn't real dark, but dark 'nuff ta'where there was a little chill in the air, and I started ta'hear the songs of them trees in my heart again. I took ma'self a deep breath, and I could smell them trees and them flowers that was nearby. Walk'n our horses deep in the woods, I started ta'go into a trance a little bit. Listen'n to the horse's hooves hit the earth was sound'n like a drum beat set to the pulse of the earth.

Flop flop flop flop, the hooves went.

Flop flop flop flop.

Flop flop flop flop.

The queen saw my eyes get'n heavy. "These old woods can cast a spell on you."

"What d'you mean?" I asked.

"These trees are ancient," Queen Kothria said. "They are older than the oldest tree on the physical earth. They have a deep magic that is very old and very powerful."

Slowly ride'n into the woods, I was feel'n the powers of the trees. It was sooth'n and gentle like, yet I was feel'n they had the power of the Old Ones. "What is the faery world? Why ain't you just liv'n in my world, the physical world?"

"The world of faery is found between your world of the physical and the spirit world," Queen Kothria said. "Some say it was created by an ancient faery race. Others say that the Source that created all things created the spirit world first, then the faery world, then the physical world. We are not spirit and we are not physical. We truly are between the worlds."

"Why ain't you liv'n in my world? The physical world." I asked.

"Some of my faery folks do live in your world." Queen Kothria said. "But they cannot live forever in the physical unless they are wed to a mortal. Only with the joining of the magic of faery and the life force of humans can a faery live forever in the world of mortals."

"Why'd you pick me?" I asked. "Why'd you pick me and lead me to the Otherworld?"

"Because Johnathan Knotbristle the Charmer, you called out to us. Each night when you came to your woods, we heard you calling to us."

"I see him!" Shouted King Mithrolo. "I see that beautiful, powerful boar!" And then the king and his faery men raced off after the boar. I thought it might be best if I stayed with the queen. I hunted all the time with my rifle but I ain't never been hunt'n with a spear and a sword. I'm guess'n that takes some kinda skill that I ain't be have'n. Me and the queen watched the king and his faery men run off. It din't take 'em long to dis'ppear in the shadows of them ancient trees.

Me and Queen Kothria kept walk'n our horses at a nice slow pace. I never wanted ta'leave these faery woods, but I felt it in my gut that I had ta'go home sometime, 'cause if I din't, I might be trapped up in here and never make my way back home. It seemed like the more questions I done asked her, the more questions I had. "Queen Kothria, what kinda magic can I learn from this place?"

"There is ancient magic in all woods and all lands," the queen said. "The earth has life force and power that flows from its center to the surface above. This life force creates, births, and nurtures all life on earth. As we breathe air into the world, so too does the earth breathe life force into us. The trees have roots that are connected deep into the earth. They use the earth's life force to grow and to give life to other life forms. The trees take the life force of the earth and give life to the birds, the animals, plants, and to us. If we can learn to harness this power, this magic, then we can change the world to fit our desire and we can heal our wounds."

"Are trees in the faery world more powerful than them trees in the physical world?" I asked.

"The trees of faery are placed between Spirit and the human world," Queen Kothria said. "They harness the pure life force of the Spirit world and the physical world yet are part of neither."

From way in the distance, me and the queen thought we done heard a man scream. The scream done echoed through them ancient woods, or perhaps the trees themselfs carried the voice ta'us. My heart dropped into my stomach. It was King Mithrolo. I could feel it in my bones. Queen Kothria held her breath and waited. The whole wood'd gone silent. Even the birds held their breaths, wait'n for news of the faery king. A short while later, the king's three faery men come race'n back ta'us on their horses.

"My lady!" one'a them faery men called out to Queen Kothria. "It is King Mithrolo! He has been gored badly by the boar! You must come!"

Queen Kothria right quick leaned down towards her horse's ear and whispered, "Go!" and she and her horse gone dashed through them woods, follow'n them faery men. I right quick followed fast as I could, but the queen's faery magic made her go s'fast she was almost outta sight. I followed her best I could. After a short while, I was finally able ta'catch up ta'her. She was 'ardy off her horse, sit'n beside King Mithrolo. When I got near 'em, I could see how bad the king was gored. His lower stomach was tore up someth'n awful. He was bleed'n a lot. I tried ta'hold a steady face. I din't want either the king or queen ta'know I was panick'n and din't know what ta'do.

I could see that Queen Kothria was hold'n a brave face for her king. She was hold'n him in her arms then looked up at me. "Johnathan, we must use faery healing magic to heal his wounds."

"I dunno how ta'do that," I said. "What do I do?"

"We must use the power of the faery world and the power of the physical world together," she said. "The king needs the life force of the human world and faery magic. He needs the magic of both worlds to heal him. I cannot do it alone."

I kneeled down next ta'her and looked at her, wait'n for her ta'tell me what ta'do.

"You cannot be afraid," she said. "You must release your fear for now and connect to the magic of the faery world."

"How do I do that?" I asked. I looked down at the king and I was see'n that he was lose'n too much blood and we was lose'n him.

Queen Kothria took holt of my hand and placed it above the king's wound. "Close your eyes. Bring to mind the magic of the faery world. Imagine its power and its beauty. Know that the life force of the earth and the stars flows through the faery world. Know that this magic has the power to heal and transform. Take a deep breath. As you breathe in, imagine breathing in the healing light of the faery world. Know with all of your being that this light has the power to regenerate the bones, organs, blood, and flesh of the king. This is the healing light found in all things. The heat of the stars. The beauty of the trees. The connection of all things in the web of life. The healing light *is* what the web of life is made from. It has no limits. Only magic. Only healing."

I listened carefully ta'ever word the queen done said. I put away any doubts and fears I had. Just for now. Just 'til the magic was done. I did 'zactly what she said. I 'magined all the heal'n light of the faery world. I 'magined that this here light was the connection of all life in all the worlds.

"Breathe this faery light in," Queen Kothria said. "Breathe in the faery light into your heart. Now, connect with me. Let us breathe our breath together and become one breath. Breathe with me, Johnathan. Connect with me. Connect with the faery light through me and allow me to connect with the human life force through you."

Me and Queen Kothria started breathe'n together. I connected ma'self to the faery world and breathed in the faery heal'n light. I connected with the queen and her power flowed into my hands, too. I could feel her connect'n with me. We was one life. One breath. We was one.

"Johnathan, take a breath," the queen said, "and exhale the faery healing power through your arms and hands and direct it over the king's wounds."

The faery heal'n power that flowed through me done felt like the sun, the moon, the stars, and the trees wrapped up into one. I had my eyes closed and in my mind, I saw the power go'n into the king and fix'n his body. I could see his flesh regenerate'n and go'n back ta'normal. In my mind, I could see the faery heal'n light go into ever-single part'a his flesh and give that flesh power. Like it was give'n him fuel ta'heal. Like how the sun gives a flower life, the faery heal'n light was give'n the king life.

Me and the queen sent the king faery heal'n light for what felt like a mighty long time. While the light was flow'n through me, I felt connected ta'ever-thing. The world, the stars, the plants, trees, and the earth. Ever-thing. After a while, we was see'n that the king was get'n better. The bleed'n had stopped and he opened his eyes. The queen released my hand and then grabbed the king and hugged him real tight.

The queen was s'happy the king was better. I got the feel'n though that she done knew the king'd be fine. I felt in my gut that she was know'n the whole time that I'd help her heal the king. "Johnathan, the faery healing magic you learned today, you may use in your world as well. Call upon me. Connect with me, and through me, you may harness the powers of the faery world and heal those who need you."

The king rested as the faery men raced back to the castle ta'fetch them a wagon. King Mithrolo weren't in no shape ta'be ride'n his horse back to the castle. When the wagon came, we helped the king into the wagon and them faery men drove him back home. The king done rested in his bed for three days as his wounds was heal'n. I guess in the faery world, you be heal'n lot faster than you do in the physical world. While King Mithrolo rested, the queen gone took me out into the faery woods ever-day ta'teach me 'bout the spirits of the trees, the plants, and the rocks. She reminded me that all live'n things had a spirit, just like animals and folks do. She said that I needed ta'remember that humans ain't more important than a tree or a stone. Ever-thing was alive and had a spiritual purpose on earth. She told me that I needed ta'learn from all live'n things. The trees had things ta'teach me. The rocks had things ta'teach me. And the animals had things ta'teach me. She also said that the best way ta'learn from all these things was ta'talk to 'em with my heart. To close my eyes and 'magine ma'self talk'n to the spirit of these things. Oh, and ta'give offer'ns of water or someth'n. The queen said never forget your offer'ns.

On the third day, King Mithrolo was feel'n right good and healthy again. He went 'bout his daily duties and none'a the kings faery men blinked an eye at his remarkable fast heal'n. Queen Kothria said that that the faery world has its own way of do'n things and that three days heal'n for the king was plenty. I was glad ta'see the king up and 'round. On that third day, now'd I knew the king was well, I got a strong feel'n in my belly that I needed ta'be home. I wasn't sure how long I was gone, but my farm needed tend'n and I would be need'n ta'expain to Mr. Picklesworth why I was gone from work s'long.

When I told the king and queen I was ready ta'go home, they din't look surprised one bit. In my time here, I learnt that them faeries has a lot of magic and they be know'n things like witches be know'n things. It was time for me ta'go.

"Before you go," Queen Kothria said, "let us share bread and wine to connect the magic of fellowship between the world of faery and the human world."

Queen Kothria, King Mithrolo, and me walked us back through them woods that led back to the physical world, my home. I was glad that the king and queen took me down the path, 'cause if I had ta'go by ma'self, I woulda never found it none. We walked and walked 'til we came to a foggy part'a the woods. I figured this was the same fog that'd led me here, so it must be that same fog ta'get me out. We took hands and made us a small circle of three. The queen done closed her eyes and took her a deep breath. "Let us connect to one another."

All three of us took a breath and connected our hearts ta'each other. The queen let go of my hand and she held herself a horn full'a honey wine. I dunno where the horn came from. I 'spose that was just part'a her faery magic. Queen Kothria lifted the horn to the sky and said, "Holda, Queen of Elphame, Goddess of the Otherworld. Send your powers into this vessel so we may connect to your deep magic."

The queen took 'nother breath and all three of us 'magined the power of Holda fill'n the honey wine with her power. "Devil, Witch Father, Horned One, send your powers into this vessel so we may connect to your deep magic."

We did just like b'fore and 'magined the power of the Devil fill'n the honey wine with power. The queen lowered the horn s'we could see the wine inside the horn. "Imagine that the powers of Holda and the Devil are combining to form an elixir of magic and healing."

King Mithrolo presented a bowl filled with bread with his faery magic. "Johnathan, now that your heart is open to the world of faery and the magical beings who live here, know that all bread in your magical rites is a gift from the world of faery. For it is the magic of the faery Otherworld that gives life to the grain. Know, too, that the grain is a gift from the land spirits themselves. For we owe our very lives to the spirits of the land."

I din't say noth'n 'cause I was think'n 'bout the things that the king and queen taught me in the faery world. I was think'n 'bout how we is all connected and how all liv'n things, and even the stones, has life force and a spirit. I was think'n how the faery world and the physical world is connected through life force and magic. I was think'n how it was the Otheworld that helped ta'give the physical world life.

Queen Kothria done poured some of that honey wine on top of the bread and said, "We combine the powers of the Gods, the faeries, and the land, for this is the sacred meal. Shared in fellowship with the Gods, faeries, humans, and the land."

Each of us took a piece of bread and ate it. When I was eat'n the bread, I could feel a connection b'tween me and the spirit of the land. We drank the wine and the power of the Gods gone flowed through my veins. We passed the horn 'round the three of us 'til it was gone. Then we gave the enchanted bread back to the earth as our sacred offer'n to the land spirits.

It was time ta'say goodbye to the king and queen of the faery world. They both hugged and kissed me goodbye, and I knew I was go'n ta'miss 'em. I walked through the fog just like b'fore and then I ended up back in the woods at nighttime. I wasn't sure how long I was gone, but it had ta'have been several days.

The next morn'n, I hurried to the general store. I figured I was gonna get a tongue lash'n from Mr. Picklesworth. When I got to the store Mr. Picklesworth din't say a word and was work'n just like normal. "Mr. Picklesworth, I'm sorry I've been gone s'long."

"What are you speaking of, Jonathan?" Mr. Picklesworth said. "You were just here yesterday."

"Yesterday?" That couldn't be right. I've been gone for several days. I stood there try'n ta'understand what happened. I guess time is differ'nt in the world of faery. It's a mysterious, wonderful, magical place. I must go back there again one day.

13

The Spirit Box

SPRING 'ROUND HERE always comes and goes way too fast. We start ta'warm up a little from winter and then we jump straight away ta'summer. I'd say we only get a month or so of nice weather b'fore the Southern heat scorches 'ya almost dead. Work'n outside is tough, but you get yourself used to it a little bit. But there is lots of days in the summer, used to it or not, that're hot as hell and it feels like you ain't never gonna cool down. Nighttime in the summer's nice though. You got the cicadas just a sing'n away. It's a funny sound'n thing, but hear'n those cicadas at night, I never feel alone. I feel like they's a welcomed friend that watches over me at night. They's always there when I go outside. Hell, they're s'loud sometimes that you think they're in the house with 'ya.

With the Gods and spirits I been know'n since I became ma'self a witch, I know I'm never alone, but it still ain't the same as be'n with physical folks. I go to the tavern now and again after a day of work'n at the general store with Mr. Picklesworth, but drink'n with the men is only so much for entertain'n. It gets tire'n play'n cards or listen'n to the newest tall tale that one'a those men has ta'tell. They're entertain'n though. Most nights if I don't have a whiskey with the boys, I'll come home and talk to Holda and the Devil. It's comfort'n ta'do that most times, but sometimes I still get lonely. I do my best and try not ta'complain.

Over the last year, most town folk have gotten ta'know me better. Most folks forgot the stories 'bout my family be'n trouble. Maybe they just moved on 'cause I don't act like that. Seems ta'me that you should always try ta'be a good person no matter what folks is say'n. There's gonna be folks who'll always think the worst of you no matter what you do and then there's folks who don't make no judgment 'til they see how you act. If you're act'n right, folks won't be believe'n no stories. So I try ta'act right as much as I can. That don't mean I don't do dumb shit and get folks mad at me now and again. But I try my best, and I think that's someth'n.

This pa'ticular summer was a hot one. I dunno what happened. Maybe it was too much rain in the winter and early spring, but it din't rain a lick that summer. I was worried that the well would dry up. If it did, I'd have ta'be take'n my ass down to the stream aways and fill me up a bucket of water here and there. The stream was dry'n up, too. When I was work'n at the store, I heard lots of the farmers complain'n that without no rain, their crops was gonna dry up. If that happened, I wasn't sure what folks was gonna do. Their best as always, I 'spose.

One hot day, Mrs.Tracy was work'n on their farm with Mr. Tracy and the summer sun got a holt of her and she done passt out. Like she fainted or someth'n. Mr. Tracy was in a frantic, look'n for Doc Taylor ta'help her. He wasn't find'n him at his house, and he came to the general store ta'ask Mr. Picklesworth if he'd seen him. Mr. Picklesworth told him that Doc Taylor was 'ardy tend'n ta'someone else on the other side of town. Mr. Tracy was real upset. He said Ms. Tracy was in bad way. He done saw me in the store that day and told me he'd heard how I doctored up Emma Fairfax. Mrs. Fairfax was tell'n folks that I'd done healed her daughter. Now, as I was hear'n, she din't use the term "witchcraft" but ever-body knew that I was use'n magic ta'do the heal'n. Mr. Tracy was look'n worrisome and asked me if I'd go over there to his farm and see if I could be doctor'n Mrs. Tracy. I looked at Mr. Picklesworth and he gave me a nod. He was mean'n that I oughta go over there and see what I could do.

Me and Mr. Tracy went down to their farmhouse and I found Mrs. Tracy lay'n on the bed with cold cloths on her head. Her face was real red and puffy but ain't had no sweat. I called the spirit of Doc Hale and let him take over my body again so he could be use'n his heal'n powers ta'heal her. After while, Mrs. Tracy looked like she was feel'n better and opened her eyes. Mr. Tracy was grateful ta'me for do'n my magic, but he never done spoke of it like that. He called it my "doctor'n'" and that was that. I guess good Christian folk think that if they ain't call'n it "witchcraft" then it ain't "witchcraft," it was some special doctor'n. Either way, he was mighty grateful. He gave me 15 cents and said he wished he could give me more, but that's all he could be afford'n. I turnt the money down, but Mr. Tracy was firm and said I needed ta'take the money for the doctor'n I was do'n that day. I took the money, but I din't do it for that. Sometimes you do things 'cause they right, not 'cause you're get'n someth'n outta it.

The drought and the heat hurt a lot of folks' crop that year. Folks was struggle'n and do'n the best they could. Some of the farmers was able ta'save their crops with a little plan'n and a lot of extra work. I wasn't s'much of a farmer like Daddy was, so my little crop died with all that heat. I tried carry'n some water from the stream a bit away, but it needed more water than I could carry in them buckets I had. The well was get'n low and I figured I'd best save the water in the well for drink'n. I wasn't sure what I was gonna do. Mr. Picklesworth was good ta'me and I don't think he'd ever let me starve, but I din't like owe'n nobody and I din't like folks think'n I couldn't take care of ma'self none. I needed ta'figure how ta'make more money ta'buy food and things I needed. Mr. Picklesworth 'ardy paid me a fair amount and I din't want ta'ask him for no handouts.

On one hot night, I took the rock'n chair and put it out on the front porch. It was too damn hot ta'be sit'n inside. There was a little breeze, and the cicadas was sing'n like they do ever-night. I was try'n ta'think on what ta'do ta'make more money. I was rock'n in that chair, back and forth, and I got ma'self to think'n that what was the good in be'n a witch if it couldn't help me make a little bit of money. Mr. Tracy gave me money ta'doctor his wife with the help of a spirit, so why couldn't I be do'n that all the time? I was figure'n I could work at Mr. Picklesworth's store dur'n the daytime and do magic for folks who needed it at night. I was think'n too that I couldn't just go 'round tell'n folks I was gonna do magic for money. On the other hand, most town folk knew I was a witch anyhow, just ain't no one ever talked 'bout it.

After rock'n back and forth in that chair for a while, I had an idea come ta'me. I needed ta'conjure the spirits and have 'em bring me folks who needed me ta'do magic for 'em. But what should I do? What kinda spell or magic should I do? I kept rock'n on that chair, back and forth, back and forth, and put ma'self into a trance. I breathed in the power of the earth and the stars and kept rock'n, back and forth, back and forth. I let my mind be released from my worries and opened my heart and connected to the spirit word.

Back and forth, back and forth, back and forth, back and forth.

Then it came ta'me. I could make me a spirit box. I sat on that chair connect'n to the spirit world, let'n the power of them spirits flow into my heart and mind. They was the ones who was tell'n me ta'make a spirit box. A spirit box, they was say'n, is a box you put magical things in that attracts a certain kinda spirit for someth'n. Then you tell the spirit what you be want'n ta'happen. Once you get what you be want'n, you give the spirit an offer'n of someth'n like whiskey or tobacca. That was it. I had ta'make a spirit box. I needed money. I needed folks ta'come ta'me and pay for me ta'do magic for 'em.

I knew I had a little wooden box inside the house somewhere. I went inside and looked high and low for a box. I 'member Momma had a small box that she kept little things in, but I couldn't 'member where it was none. Momma's trunk. Momma kept all kinds of things in that trunk, and I'd be guess'n there'd be a little box in there too. I went into the bedroom where the trunk was, opened the lid, and dug through that trunk. Tucked under in the bottom of that trunk 'neath some blankets was that little box. I took that box out and put it on the table. I had been save'n some dried herbs in some jars, so I went into the cupboard ta'see what I had that might work ta'call a spirit of money. I looked through the dried herbs and I found juniper berry, cedar, and vervain. I put my hand over each of them herbs ta'see how they felt ta'me. My gut said that they was the right herbs ta'use ta'call a spirit of money. I saved that 15 cents Mr. Tracy paid me, and I figured that'd be perfect ta'put in the box 'cause it was money I needed, and this money came from payment for witchcraft. The last thing I needed was some dirt. I went outside and pulled me up some dirt with my hands and put it on a dish. I took that dish inside, sett'n it on the table next to them other things I had collected.

It was time ta'summon a spirit that'd help make me some money. I lit the candle that was in b'tween them two tines of the pitchfork and called the Devil, the Old One. I thought for a bit 'bout what the Devil meant ta'me. What he done looked like and what he done felt like when he was in the room. As I called ta'him, I could feel his presence. I no longer saw the pitchfork. I saw the Devil stand'n next to the fireplace. Then, I focused on the broom. I had me a small candle next to the broom on the floor. I lit that there candle and called out to Holda, Queen of Elphame. I thought 'bout what she looked like ta'me, then 'bout how her presence felt. I no longer could be see'n the 'ole broom, I saw Holda stand'n next to the fireplace.

Now'd the Old Ones was here, I could do my magic. I took the candle that was sit'n on the table and held it in my hand. I opened up my mind and my heart and went into a trance. I breathed in the power of the stars and the power of the earth. Hold'n that candle, I 'magined a spirit come'n ta'me and help'n me get the money I needed. I 'magined that spirit fly'n all through town and the nearby farms, whisper'n into folks' ears, tell'n 'em ta'come see me for magic and heal'n. I held that candle and 'magined have'n plenty of money ta'help me get by. When I felt like that was 'nuff power sent to the candle, I sat it back on the table and lit it.

After that, I opened up that little box. I held that box in b'tween my hands and 'magined that this box was the perfect house for a spirit that'd help me get my money. I 'magined that the spirit who was gonna live there was real happy with that box as a house. Then I put that dirt in the box. I done scooped out the dirt with my bare hands and I said, "This is the dirt that comes from my land. The land of Johnathan Knotbristle the Charmer. This is the land that the spirit will call ta'folks who will pay me for my help with magic and heal'n."

Once there was a nice bed of dirt in the box, I grabbed me a handful of juniper berries. While in my hand, I 'magined these berries attract'n a spirit of money. These juniper berries made'a nice magical home for the spirit. The spirit would love live'n in this box. I put the juniper berries in the box on top the bed of dirt. After that, I took me a handful of the vervain and 'magined that the spirit used its power ta'call out ta'folks who needed my help and would bring 'em ta'my land. Anyone who needed help would know ta'come and see Johnathan Knotbristle the Charmer. I put the vervain on top of the juniper berries. Then I took the cedar in my hand and 'magined all the money folks was glad ta'give me for do'n magic for 'em. I put the cedar on the vervain. Last, I took the 15 cents in my hand and 'magined always have'n 'nuff money ta'live and be happy. Them coins would attract more coins. The spirit who lived in this here box would make sure I always had coins. To entice a money spirit further, I put a pinch of tobacca inside the box as a little offer'n.

I closed up the box and put it on the table next to the candle. I put both hands on the box on either side. Again, I opened up my heart and my mind and went into a trance. I 'magined that my mind was connect'n to the spirit world. I 'magined that my voice was be'n heard by the spirits, no matter how far away they was. "I call out into the spirit world. Spirit of money, spirit of wealth, I summon, I stir, I conjure you forth. Come ta'me and live in this spirit box I have made for you. I summon, I stir, I conjure you forth. Go out to the town folk near and far. Whisper into their ears that when they need magic or heal'n, ta'come see Johnathan Knotbristle the Charmer. I summon, I stir, I conjure you forth. Come, be here now, by the power of the Devil and of Holda. Come be here now!"

I let my heart feel my surround'ns. I could feel ma'self a spirit's presence in the room. I could feel the spirit go'n into the box and settl'n into its new home. I opened my heart to the spirit in the box and let it feel my power, my presence. I wanted the spirit in the box ta'get ta'know me. We would be work'n ta'gether for a long time. When I was done, I hid the spirit box away s'anyone who might come here wouldn't see it. It was done.

Not too long after that, I had folks knock'n on my door, ask'n me ta'do all kinds of things for 'em. Some folks was ask'n me ta'find things they lost or what they thought might be stolen. Other folks came want'n me ta'do some heal'n on 'em when they was sick. That year there was a mighty drought just like I said b'fore, and some of them farmers asked me ta'make it rain. Now, there was plenty of spells ta'make it rain, but this pa'ticular summer the rain just wasn't come'n. I told them farmers that kinda magic wasn't work'n, and it was true. It kinda felt like someth'n was make'n us a drought. Maybe it was the spirits or the Gods. Who knows. I wouldn't even consider do'n magic ta'make it rain 'cause it wasn't work'n. Even Mr. Picklesworth was stumped with that one. Most folks knock'n on my door was look'n for simple things. Some wanted money, others health, then a'course there was the love spells.

Love spells was pa'ticularly tricky. You never know what's lurk'n in someone's heart. Sometimes it's true love. Sometimes it's a big mess. You never can tell how a love spell is gonna effect someone. One day, in the middle of July, Sarah Williams come knock'n on my door. She was cry'n and upset that her lover'd been seen kiss'n 'nother girl in town. Miss Williams was the daughter of Mr. Williams, 'nother farmer who lived just outside of town. Now, I happen ta'know that Mr. Williams was a faithful Christian and him and his family'd be seen in church ever-Sund'y. So I was think'n that he had no idea his daughter was at my house, ask'n for witchcraft ta'bring back a wayward lover. Even so, I wasn't try'n ta'judge why someone was over here ask'n for witchcraft. Sarah was 15 and her Momma and Daddy thought of her as a woman, and it was time for her ta'get herself married.

Sarah came into my house look'n like she was at her wits end, "Mr. Knotbristle, I need your help. George Clay promised me he'd marry me, but now he's been seen with Annie Doyle."

I wasn't real keen on the idea of do'n no kinda love spell. I knew that's what she'd be want'n me ta'do. "Maybe, he'll come back ta'ya. Boys can be swayed back and forth sometimes."

Sarah was in tears and ta'her, this was the worst thing in the world that could'a happened ta'her. "No, he's been kiss'n on Annie Doyle. He's in love with her and I want him ta'forget 'bout her and come back ta'me."

"Love spells can be hard and complicated," I was warn'n her. "Love is a mysterious thing and it's hard ta'control with magic."

"I want you ta'do it," Sarah was determined ta'get her way. "I know you can, Mr. Knotbristle. I've heard that you can work miracles."

"How well d'you know this man?" I asked her. "What d'you know 'bout him? How d'you know he's the one for you?"

"I know enough that I love him, and we should get married," Sarah said. "I'm 15 and it's time for me ta'get married. I can't grow old alone and be a spinster."

"Sarah," I said, "If you cast a spell on him the responsibility of it will be yours and only yours. If I cast the spell what happens will be your responsibility alone."

Sarah had her a small purse. She reached in that there little bag and took out several coins. "This is 50 cents; this is double what folks are pay'n you."

I was hesitant ta'take Sarah's money. My gut was tell'n me this may not go the way Sarah'd be want'n it ta'go. "Sarah, I don't think..."

"70 cents!" She interrupted. "Take the money, Johnathan."

I decided ta'take the money. Most folks payed b'tween 15 and 25 cents for my services. 70 cents was a lot of money. I got the feel'n though that this was gonna be a lesson for both of us. "If we do this spell, we're gonna be do'n it together. Then the magic belongs to you."

"Of course," Sarah was relieved that she was get'n me ta'do the magic for her.

In the kitchen cupboards of my house, I had collected quite a few herbs, threads, pins, feathers, candles, stones I found in the woods, differ'nt animal bones, furs and pelts, sticks, and many other things that I might be use'n for my witchcraft. I took out a large candle, pins, red thread, and the feathers from a dove.

I had ma'self a special iron fry'n pan that I used for magic. I put the candle in that pan and melted it over the stove. Once it'd melted, I let it cool for a bit then, b'fore it got too hard again, I fashioned it into a small doll ta'resemble a man. That din't take too long 'cause s'long as the wax was soft, it could be made into a doll real easy like. Then I took that doll to the table and put it on a plate. I told Sarah that I'd be need'n a bit of her blood. I took a pin and done pricked her finger, place'n a drop of blood over the head, the heart, them private parts, and the feet of the doll. I took out more pins from a little box I had and some of them dove feathers. I told Sarah ta'think of her lover, George Clay, and ta'pin a dove feather to that there spot of blood on the doll's head and say, "George Clay, you will only think of me."

Sarah pinned the feather to that doll and repeated what I done said.

I told Sarah ta'pin the feather to the blood spot that be over the heart and say, "George Clay, you will only love me."

Sarah pinned the feather to the doll's heart and repeated what I said.

I told Sarah ta'pin the feather to the blood spot over the private parts of the doll and say, "George Clay, you will only have sex with me."

Sarah pinned the feather to the doll's private parts and repeated what I done said.

I told Sarah ta'pin one feather ta'each of the doll's feet and say, "George Clay, you will come back ta'me."

Sarah pinned a feather ta'each of the doll's feet and repeated what I done said.

Then, I handed her the red thread. "Wrap this here doll completely from the head to its feet with this here red thread. As you is do'n so, think of him love'n only you. This red thread'll bind George Clay ta'ya with feelings of love."

Sarah began ta'wrap the red thread 'round the doll, start'n with the head. She closed her eyes and poured out ever-ounce of love she had for George Clay. She wrapped up that doll with the thread faster and faster. She started ta'wrap the doll s'fast she was in a frenzy. She kept wrap'n faster and even faster. She was move'n back and forth, back and forth. She went into a trance. All she could see was her and George Clay together. When the thread done ran out, the doll had turnt into a little man that was clothed in noth'n but string.

Sarah calmed herself and came outta her little frenzy. "What do I do now?"

"Take you that doll home and hide it away somewhere ain't no one'll ever find it," I told her.

Sarah took the doll, set down 70 cents on the table, and went home with her doll.

Not s'long after that, George Clay came back to Sarah just like she'd wanted. They was seen in church and she seemed real happy like. They got engaged right quick and Sarah was plan'n the wed'n. One night, I was at the tavern with some of them boys, and George Clay was there, drunk as hell. He picked a fight with one'a the men and ended up get'n mighty beat up. Well, I guess George din't like get'n licked and he came back the next night, drank his fill of whiskey, and started 'nother fight. This time it was a big ruckus. He did that the follow'n night too, so the tavern owner told him ta'stay the hell out 'til he learnt ta'act right. Him be'n drunk and all, he was threat'n ta'burn the tavern down to the ground. Sarah's Daddy got wind of George act'n all crazy and told him that he shouldn't be marry'n his daughter. As you can 'magine, George din't take this too kindly and threatened her Daddy. They got them in a fight, and he beat up Sarah's Daddy real bad.

Sarah was scared as hell of him and done ended the engagement right quick then and there. George left for a while and went back ta'his house and got hisself drunk again. He done come back to Sarah's Daddy's house and you know what he done? He set the damn thing on fire. They was both inside, too. Luckily, both Sarah and her Daddy got outta the house. B'fore she did though, she went right quick and got her that doll that we'd made and took it with her. She was think'n she needed ta'stop the spell from go'n no further.

The next day, Sarah came back ta'my house and told me ever-thing that happened. She wanted me ta'do one more thing ta'help her, 'cause she said b'fore George left the house after start'n that fire, he done swore ta'come back and kill Sarah if she din't marry him. When she told me what all'd happened, I sat for a while, connect'n with the spirits. I was ask'n the best way ta'handle all this. Then they told me what ta'do.

I had 'nother small box I took outta the cupboard. This box was big 'nuff ta'fit the doll. I told Sarah ta'unwrap the red thread and as she did so ta'imagine that the love b'tween her and George was over and done. She did like I told her, then we went into town that night together. While folks slept, oh, it must have been right at midnight, we quietly walked us over to the graveyard next to the church. I had brought me a small shovel and we dug us a hole in the graveyard. We was make'n a small grave. I put the doll in that little box and wrapped the whole box with that red thread. As I wrapped the box with that red thread, I 'magined that George Clay wouldn't never hurt Sarah or her Daddy ever again. Then I put the wrapped box in the hole in the graveyard and covered it back up with the graveyard dirt. As I did that I said, "I ask the spirits of the grave ta'bind George Clay into this spirit box. Never shall he hurt Sarah or her Daddy again."

Once we buried the doll and the box, we walked outta the graveyard and ain't never spoke of it again.

14

The Witch's Tree

HARVEST TIME. As the summer gone went on, ever-one in the town'd hoped the crops would produce someth'n but the crops was die'n off. The summer droughts was too much for many of the farms. Some folks' crops done failed all together, while some of the farmers was able to irrigate 'em a little from the stream down yonder. The farmers who done lived close to the stream was able ta'get some water and do the best they could. For the farmers who lived on the other side of town away from the stream, there wasn't no water ta'be had. Ever-farm had a well, but wells dry up if they're overused and they couldn't chance use'n up the only drink'n water they had. Folks was say'n that there was a bad drought that year in the whole country. Many folks'd be suffer'n if the rains don't come. Ever Sund'y, we was pray'n for rain. Day after day, the summer sun was s'hot you could barely stand be'n outside.

As the summer days passed, I was notice'n that not many folks was come'n into the general store, and if they did come, they only got what they needed. Folks was save'n their money 'cause if the drought went 'til late summer, then the chance of have'n any kinda harvest was low. I was also notice'n that folks din't come ta'my house as much ask'n for magic. Ever-so often I'd get folks knock'n on my door, ask'n if I could make it rain, but that wasn't no magic I'd be know'n 'bout. The last time someone came ta'my house ask'n for magic, Old Mrs. Bridget Griffin was want'n me ta'do my witchcraft ta'find her iron cook'n pot. She said one day when she wasn't look'n, someone came into her house and done took it. She said they must've been do'n witchcraft 'cause she was home all that day and she din't see no one come in. She said she was there in her kitchen, turnt 'round, and then it was gone!

Now, the thing you need ta'know 'bout Mrs. Griffin is that she was an old kindly lady who never did noth'n ta'nobody, but the thing was, well, she was old as hell. Folks be say'n she done lost her mind. I'd say it's less 'bout her be'n crazy and more 'bout sometimes old folk don't be 'member'n things like they once did. I asked her if she look'd 'round her house for her cook'n pot, and she done said she looked high and low and couldn't find a thing. So she said that means a witch stole it, so 'nother witch can find it. My gut said that ain't no witch took her pot, but maybe I could help Old Mrs. Griffin find her pot anyhow.

I took out some dried bones I had in a jar on my cupboard and threw 'em on the table. I lit a candle that was sit'n on the table and waved my hands over them bones like I was cast'n a spell. Now I knew Mrs. Griffin din't need no magic, 'cause I was bet'n she done forgot where she put that 'ole cook'n pot. I din't need ta'cast a spell ta'go over and help her find it, but sometimes folks be need'n some hope, so I pretended ta'cast a spell ta'find her pot. She was real excited when I threw down them bones and pretended ta'chant a spell, 'cause she really wanted her pot back. When we was done with our "spell," she tried ta'hand me 10 cents and I said I din't need her money, that maybe instead she have me over for supper one night. I told her part'a the spell was I needed ta'go ta'her house with her and find the pot for her. That's the only way the spell would really work.

We walked a few miles back ta'her little house. On the way home, Mrs. Griffin told me how her husband had died recently, and she was s'lonely without him. Her son had moved away for work to the big city, and she was only see'n him once or so a month. She was say'n that she tried ta'make herself busy with chores and such, but at night she got to miss'n how things was. Soon as we went inside her house, we found the iron cook'n pot in her kitchen where she left it. She was happy ta'see that the magic worked and that the witch had returnt her pot. That night, she made me supper and we talked 'bout her life, her husband, and what it was like in this town b'fore I was born. B'fore I left that night, I told her anytime her pot was lost ta'come find me and I'd cast my spell and she could make me supper again. Then she can tell me more 'bout how it was back when.

One night, it was pa'ticularly hot, so I sat on my front porch, sit'n in my rock'n chair, stare'n off into those woods listen'n ta'those cicadas. I rocked back and forth in that 'ole chair and had ma'self a glass of whiskey. Sometimes when I'm rock'n back and forth in that chair, I gaze into the darkness of them woods. I don't think 'bout anyth'n much. I just look deep into the darkness and try ta'connect with them trees. Once in a while, it feels like there's someone gaze'n back at me. I wonder what they're think'n 'bout when they stare back at me when I stare at those trees.

That night I was stare'n into the dark of the trees when someth'n move'n caught my eye.

Hop hop hop hop hop hop hop hop hop hop.

Be'n half in trance and half 'wake, I saw a little hare hop'n right up ta'my front porch. I sat there watch'n that hare stand perfectly still, eye'n me, try'n ta'see what I was gonna do. "You're a'right," I said. "I ain't gonna bother you."

The little hare sat there all quiet like for a time, then hopped towards me. It stopped again, wait'n ta'see what I was gonna do.

"You're a brave little fella," I said ta'that little hare.

The hare hopped closer ta'me. Then stopped again.

"Whatcha want'n me ta'do, little fella?" I asked him.

The little hare turnt away and started hop'n towards them woods. I figured that was that, but he stopped and was wait'n for me.

My gut was tell'n me that little hare was try'n ta'tell me someth'n.

The little hare hopped a bit more and stopped again, look'n at me dead in the eye.

"Are you try'n ta'get me ta'follow you?" I said. This time, my gut was tell'n me that I was 'sposed ta'follow the little hare into the woods. "A'right, a'right. I'm come'n."

I followed that little hare towards the woods. It hopped deeper and deeper into the woods. If he got too far ahead of me, he'd stop and wait 'til I caught up. The deeper we got us into the woods, I could be feel'n the presence of old, ancient magic. I dunno how I knew it was ancient magic, I just knew. I've learnt this past year that when you're feel'n someth'n in your gut, ta'trust it. Your gut always knew what was go'n on.

After a while, the hare led me to a twisted 'ole tree in the middle of the woods. It was dark as hell in them woods, but I could still see that the bark on this tree was black, and branches twisted back and forth into the sky. The tree wasn't nearly as tall as the grand 'ole trees that surrounded it. Look'n 'round, it seemed ta'me that the other taller trees was protect'n this twisted tree from outsiders who wasn't 'sposed ta'stumble on this 'ole tree. I could feel the ancient magic that was inside. It looked ta'me ta'be as old as the earth itself, maybe even older. It sure looked ta'me like a witch's tree.

The little hare hopped away, and then outta the shadows of the woods stepped out folks who was hidden by black cloaks. I couldn't see anyone's face 'cause of the hoods and the dark of the woods. The cloaked folks surrounded me in a small circle. I wasn't scared or noth'n. I was just wonder'n who these hidden folks was and what they was want'n with me. Still surround'n me, they stepped closer and closer. One'a the cloaked folks was taller than the others. They took off their hood and revealed themselfs ta'me. Mr. Picklesworth said, "Johnathan, I'm glad you were able to find us."

"I had a ma'self little help," I said, refer'n to the little hare.

Once Mr. Picklesworth showed hisself, the rest of the cloaked folks did too. Alma, Harriet, Clara, and Viola was all there. I din't know they knew Mr. Picklesworth, but think'n 'bout it now, it makes sense that they did. Then there was a'course Helen, Margaret, and Elizabeth. They all looked real happy ta'see me and I was glad ta'see them. It had been a long summer and it was mighty good ta'see them witches who taught me s'much this past year.

Alma came up ta'me and gave me a kiss on the cheek. "I can feel that your power has grown since we saw you last."

"I been do'n my best," I said ta'her, smile'n.

Elizabeth smiled at me. She looked happy ta'see me too, "Hello, Johnathan."

I smiled back at her, "It's good ta'see you, Elizabeth. It's good ta'see you all."

Mr. Picklesworth looked like he had some thoughts on his mind, "We have business to attend to, Johnathan. I feel it's too soon to include you, but we're in desperate times."

S'long as I've known Mr. Picklesworth, I ain't never seen him look so concerned. Someth'n bad was happen'n. It din't take no magic ta'know whatever it was, it was real bad. You could see it on his face. "What's happen'n?"

"Johnathan," Mr. Picklesworth said, "before we allow a new witch to join the circle, we train them for a year or more. You are almost at that year, but you have much training to learn. But time is running short. We can't wait until you're ready. We need you now. Times are dire."

Alma put her hand on Mr. Picklesworth's shoulder ta'show support. "The drought this summer is causing many people to suffer. We believe that the drought is caused by dark magic."

"Witches?" I asked. That din't make no sense ta'me. If witches hurt the crops, that'd only hurt them too. "Why would witches want ta'make a drought ta'destroy food that we all need?"

"Power," Mr. Picklesworth answered. "Desperate folks are easier to control. Starv'n folks, even better."

"You see," Clara spoke up, "we believe that there is a coven of dark witches seeking to control the town. Once that happens, they can banish us and control everyone, including their businesses, farms, and whatever money they have."

"If we're defeated," Mr. Picklesworth said, "then no one will be able to protect the people of this town and all will be lost."

"What do we do?" I asked. "Curse 'em? Send a spirit ta'stop 'em?"

"A spirit or a curse won't stop them," Helen said. "A coven will be expecting that and will know how to stop it."

"We must defeat them in the spirit world," Mr. Picklesworth said. "We must defeat them in the astral world, the world of dreams and spirits."

This din't make no kinda sense ta'me. Not one bit. "You mean like a battle? A war?"

"Not my choice of words," Mr. Picklesworth said, "but yes. We must destroy them in our spirit bodies."

Someth'n took Margaret's attention. She was look'n up in the branches of that 'ole witch tree. All of us watched her as she slowly was creep'n ta'that tree. She stopped for a bit, took a deep breath, and snatched a spider that was hang'n on one single web it'd cast from its belly. She squeezed it with her hands and when she opened 'em up we 'spected ta'see a squished spider, but instead there wasn't noth'n. It had vanished.

"There are spies everywhere," Mr. Picklesworth said, "witches can use animals and bugs to spy on us. We can't say any more tonight."

"What do we do now?" I asked.

"Go home to your bed tonight," Mr. Picklesworth said, "You'll know when the battle has begun."

The next days was unbearably hot. Doc Taylor told folks that if they could ta'stay outta the sun. There was a few folks who had done fainted 'cause of that heat. Dur'n the day, nobody went outside unless they had to. Many of the crops that was planted in spring was die'n. I made sure my cow, goats, and chickens had plenty of water ta'drink. I din't want 'em ta'go die'n on me. A couple'a the nights was s'warm that I slept with a cool cloth 'round my neck. If the drought was be'n caused by dark magic, then they was powerful as hell. I din't even know if we could do anyth'n 'bout it when the time came.

One night, the wind done picked up and brought a cool breeze into the house. I went outside and just sat ma'self out there on the front porch. I left the front door open ta'cool off the house. It was feel'n real good ta'finally cool down. The moon was dark that night. When I looked up in the sky, I could see s'many stars. But I could also see the clouds roll'n in. These dark clouds din't look right. Normally, I'd say these was storm clouds bring'n in some rain, but when I looked up at these clouds, they wasn't right. Noth'n 'bout these clouds was right.

CRACK!

Heat lightn'n. If you ain't never seen heat lightn'n, it happens in the summer when there's humidity in the air and dark clouds. The lightn'n is orange and yellow. It don't look like no normal lightn'n. It don't look right at all. The wind picked up even more and my gut told me I best be get'n inside. Trouble was come'n. I latched the front door just ta'be safe. If this past year's taught me anyth'n, it's that the further you are from town, the more the witches and spirits come a knock'n. B'fore I went ta'sleep that night, I had me a glass of whiskey and calmed my nerves. Mr. Picklesworth said when the battle began, I'd know. I figure he'd come knock'n on my door, or at least send a hare like he did the last time.

I drifted off ta'sleep. It was uneasy sleep, but it was still sleep. I was think'n I may not be able ta'sleep that night 'cause my gut was tell'n me someth'n bad might be happen'n. But there I was, sound asleep.

Thump...thump...thump...

Someth'n was on the rooftop of my house. I opened my eyes. Maybe I was hear'n things.

Thump...thump...thump...

There it was again! I got up outta bed right quick and looked out the winda'. Only the night's darkness and the occasional crack of light'n. Somebody was up on my roof. I turnt 'round and saw my body still sleep'n in my bed. It wasn't my 'magination. It was clear as day. I was in my spirit body, stand'n in my house, while my physical body was still sleep'n in my bed. I touched my spirit body with both hands ta'see if I was "real." My spirit body felt just as real as if I was wide 'wake on a Sund'y. I stood there in the middle of my house silently. *What do I do?* I thought to ma'self. *Do I go outside? Do I call Mr. Picklesworth with my thoughts? Maybe I should...*

"Johnathan..." I heard a faint voice whisper.

I held my breath and waited ta'see if someone was in my house.

"Johnathan..."

I walked real slow like through my house, look'n 'round in case someone was hide'n, ready ta'come get me.

"I can see you, Johnathan," the voice whispered. "Can you see me?"

Fuck. Fuck. What do I do? Listen ta'my heart, I told ma'self. My heart knows things I don't know. My heart and my mind will know. I closed my eyes and was gonna put ma'self in a trance when someth'n magical done stopped me. Someone else's magic wouldn't let me focus 'nuff ta'do my own magic.

"Dickery, dickery, dare," the voice said. "The pig flew up in the air, the man in brown soon brought him down, dickery, dickery, dare."

Hear'n that Mother Goose rhyme gave me right chills down my spine. I could feel the dark magic be'n cast. I quickly spun 'round and there he was, the murderer John Wessnell who'd done killed his own friends ta'give a blood sacrifice to the Winter Goddess, Perchta. As soon as I realized it was him, he done grabbed my arms and threw me right hard into the air. I hit the ceil'n of my house real hard and then slammed on the ground. He done lifted me back up and punched me square in the face. I fell back and tried ta'regain my senses. I reached for my pitchfork by the fireplace and I swung it real hard, hit'n him on his side. I think the pitchfork has it some extra power in the world of spirit 'cause it threw him 'gainst the wall and he looked like he done lost his senses. When he done found his balance again, he leaped towards the fireplace and flew up the chimney. It was clear as day that John Wessnell was one'a them dark witches that Mr. Picklesworth was talk'n 'bout.

I held tight ta'my pitchfork. I dunno what's gonna happen this night, but if the pitchfork has power in the spirit world, then I was sure's hell gonna use it. Carry'n my pitchfork, I flew up the chimney after John Wessnell and landed on my roof. I looked 'round for him, but I din't see him nowhere. I could hear him laugh'n out in the darkness somewhere far away.

Thud!

Someone landed on my roof right next ta'me. It was Mr. Picklesworth. He stood right there next ta'me, hold'n a pitchfork too. Looks like I made the right choice keep'n this thing as a weapon. "Johnathan, I see you're alright. It's time. We have to stop those dark witches from causing the drought and destroying any chance we got for any harvest this year."

"What do we do?" I asked him.

"Follow me," he said "We have to fly into town. That's where the battle will be."

Mr. Picklesworth jumped up into the air in his spirit form and flew hisself towards town. I jumped up too ta'follow him. In just a few minutes, we both was fly'n above the town. Mr. Picklesworth flew to one'a them houses near the center of town and I done followed him. "Stay on the roofs. We'll be able to see the witches better as they fly through town."

Both of us stood on that roof, look'n 'round for the witches. I could feel the madness in the air like it was be'n carried on the spirit wind. It was quiet, but that din't mean noth'n. Someth'n was happen'n. Then we both saw it. 'Cross the way we saw us George Clay, Sarah William's crazy lover, land'n on one'a them roofs. He was carry'n him an old gnarly look'n staff. Then next ta'him landed Helen, hold'n her broom. She swung her broom hard as she could, but he blocked the swing with his gnarled staff. He then swung the staff low, knock'n Helen off her feet.

Me and Mr. Picklesworth saw Helen fall. "Johnathan, stay here and keep looking for those witches. I'm gonna help Helen." He jumped in the air and flew over ta'that rooftop. George and Helen was fight'n someth'n fierce, and Mr. Picklesworth landed on the roof next to 'em and started swing'n his pitchfork.

"Aaaaaaahhhhhh!"

I heard a woman's scream come'n from down the road. I jumped in the air and started fly'n in that direction. Down below me I saw Mr.

Jones, the man from the Halloween party, hit'n Clara real hard with another large, gnarled staff. She was on the rooftop, try'n ta'cover her face from get'n hit. As I flew, I dashed down to the rooftop and readied my pitchfork. B'fore I even landed on the roof, I swung it as hard I could, knock'n Mr. Jones off the roof and onto the ground. When I landed on the roof, I helped Clara ta'her feet. "Are you a'right?"

"Yes," she answered. "He took me by surprise. I'm fine now."

I peeked over the edge of the roof, and I saw that Mr. Jones was gone. He must'a flew away somewhere.

"They're fly'n too fast!" I said. "How do we stop 'em if we can't catch 'em?"

"Come, Johnathan," Clara said. "We have to help the others!" With that, both Clara and me flew us up into the air again. We could see the witches fight'n on the rooftops in the town. Pitchforks and brooms was battle'n gnarled old magical staffs. From above, I could see Mr. Picklesworth and Helen fight'n George on the rooftop. Clara and me was just 'bout ta'fly down and help 'em when I felt a hard blow ta'my head.

BAM!

I lost my senses and fell down to the ground real hard. I thought 'cause I was in spirit form hit'n the ground wouldn't hurt me none, but it sure as hell did. It hurt bad.

BAM! I was hit again. When I looked up ta'see who'd hit me, it was Doc Taylor. *Fuck!* I thought to ma'self. Was ever-body in this town a witch? He landed right over me while I was on the ground. He lifted his gnarled staff ta'hit me again. That's when Clara hit him with her broom real hard and he flew down the road. Clara must have hit him right good, 'cause he flew real far.

"Are you alright?" Clara said, grab'n my arm ta'pull me up.

"Yup," I said. "Thanks..."

"We need to get off the ground and back on the rooftops," she said. "We aren't safe down here."

Both of us flew up in the air and flew to the roof of the general store. Here, we could see anyth'n that was happen'n on all the homes and other businesses in town. We saw Mr. Picklesworth and Helen was still battle'n George. George was able ta'fend off both Mr. Picklesworth and Helen's blows. He was fast and he was strong. Clara and me landed on the rooftop with 'em. As fast and hard as I could, I swung my pitchfork and hit him clear in the face. He got him a big gash on his cheek. He stumbled off the roof and fell to the earth below. He dis'ppeared.

"Did I kill him?" I asked Mr. Picklesworth.

"No," He answered. "You sent his spirit back to his physical body. He won't be coming back to battle us tonight."

"Now what do we do?" I asked.

"Keep fighting," Alma flew down from the sky next ta'us. "We have to find the place where the dark witches are casting their spells to destroy the crops."

"We might know where they are." Margaret and Elizabeth landed on the roof with us.

"We need to all gather and join our magic," Mr. Picklesworth said. "Alma, can you call the others?

Alma closed her eyes and used her magic ta'call to them others with her heart.

"We're here," Viola said as she and Harriet landed themselfs on the rooftop.

"Everyone join hands," Mr. Picklesworth said, "once we join our magic together, we will be more powerful than..."

CRACK!

A bolt of heat lightn'n tore through the sky.

CRACK! Then 'nother bolt of orange light'n lit up the sky.

We all looked up and that's when we saw 'em. Mrs. Fossey and Mr. Fossey, hover'n above us. These was the folks who was try'n ta'get me run outta town for be'n a witch. These was the ones who was get'n all the town folk ta'turn 'gainst me and ruin me, all 'cause I was a witch. Turnt out it was all a lie. She was try'n ta'turn ever-body 'gainst me ta'take the attention off her and her husband! They was the ones who owned the town bank and they was they was the ones who was try'n ta'ruin the farmers crops so's they could own more of the town! It was all 'bout power. Mrs. Fossey shook her head, "Mr. Picklesworth, you should have listened to me and got rid of Johnathan Knotbristle. But you had to teach him. You just had to make your coven more powerful."

"Mrs. Fossey!" Mr. Picklesworth yelled, "Your time as a tyrant witch is over. This town does not belong to you!"

Right then, she was joined by her band of dark witches. Mr. Jones, John Wessnell, and Doc Taylor flew next to Mr. and Mrs. Fossey. They all held them their weapons of gnarled staffs. Without hesitation, me, Mr. Picklesworth, Alma, Clara, Viola, Hariot, Elizabeth, Margaret, and Helen held tight our weapons of pitchforks and brooms. All of us was ready ta'fly into the air and battle 'em when one more witch joined the dark witches. Old Mrs. Knowles. Old Mrs. Knowles was the witch who sent the curses and fetch dogs to Helen, Margaret, and Elizabeth. She was old, but she was powerful.

"Mrs. Knowles," Mrs. Fossey said with s'much venom in her voice, "I think Mr. Picklesworth's coven could use a little rhyme, don't you think?"

Old Mrs. Knowles, hover'n over all of us, raised her gnarled staff and pointed it to the sky. Her voice echoed with ancient magic taught ta'her by the stars themselfs.

"Ring around the rosie, pocket full of posies, ashes, ashes they all fall down!"

We all looked up over our heads to the dark storm clouds and saw us the buildup of lightn'n. There was a rumble'n noise.

"Ring around the rosie, pocket full of posies, ashes, ashes they all fall down!"

CRACK! A burst of lightn'n hit us all from above, knock'n us off the rooftop. We all hit the ground hard. It took me a minute ta'get ma'self back ta'my senses. I got up as fast I could, and I saw Margaret and Elizabeth dis'ppear'n. They must've been thrown back into their physical bodies.

Old Mrs. Knowles raised her gnarled staff back into the air again ta'hit us with lightn'n one more time. This time, Alma flew into the air, took her broom, and hit her as hard as she could. Old Mrs. Knowles fell to the ground and Mr. Picklesworth, Alma, and me all bashed her with our weapons. She, too, dis'ppeared back ta'her physical body.

Mr. and Mrs. Fossey and her gang of dark witches done flew away into the darkness.

"Follow them!" Mr. Picklesworth yelled.

We all rose up into the air and followed 'em into the dark of night. It was s'dark, we couldn't see us a damned thing. Alma said ta'listen ta'my heart, and I could feel where they was go'n. It was true. I could sense their power. It was dark, greedy, jealous, and full'a hate. It wasn't hard ta'follow 'em. Not hard at all. Hateful power like theirs was easy ta'track. Folks who has them a dark heart was easy ta'track. The dark energy follows 'em ever-where. We followed 'em to the outskirts of town to Mr. Mitchel's farm. Mr. Mitchel had him the biggest farm in town. It was close to the stream and he'd done some irrigation ta'get water ta'his crops so they wouldn't dry up dur'n the drought. He sold some of his produce to Mr. Picklesworth's store, but he also sold a lot of it to the neighbor'n towns. If Mr. Mitchel's farm was destroyed, then a lot of folks'd be suffer'n.

Fly'n over the farm, we saw the dark witches was gathered in a circle. They was in the middle of one'a the fields, chant'n. Be'n in spirit form, I could see the magic they was conjure'n as clear as day. It din't take no psychic skills or magic ability ta'see that they was conjure'n someth'n. We all flew to the farm as fast we could. But it looked like whatever the dark witches was summon'n was 'bout ta'appear. We landed on that field, but we was too late. Someth'n was come'n.

In the middle of the circle of dark witches, a spirit appeared. And there he was. It was The Stranger. The Devil figure who tried ta'take away my friend Samuel Toberson. The Stranger had him his magic fiddle and started play'n his music. The music from the fiddle sounded mighty odd. It was the strangest music I ever did hear. The winds was pick'n up like they was from a storm or someth'n. Normally when winds from a storm start blow'n, they's nice cool winds that bring in the rain. But these winds was differ'nt. These winds was hot. Hot like the middle of a summer's day. The Stranger was play'n his fiddle and summon'n the winds of drought. A drought that'd ruin us all.

Mr. Picklesworth raised his pitchfork. He was ready'n hisself for the final battle with the dark witches. "Destroy them! If they win this battle, the town will be destroyed!"

We all flew into the air again, fly'n faster and faster. We flew s'fast we ran right into the dark witches, chant'n away. We swung us our weapons and they tumbled to the ground. We all started hit'n 'em with our weapons as hard as we could. I was fight'n with Doc Taylor. My pitchfork swung at him, and he deflected the hit with his gnarled staff. When he swung at me, I was able ta'block the attack with my pitchfork. I was fight'n as hard as I could. Doc Taylor was gonna be hard ta'defeat.

The Stranger played his fiddle.

Mrs. Fossey flew into the air once more. Mr. Picklesworth flew up ta'greet her. "Stop this madness before you kill us all!"

"It's over, Mr. Picklesworth," Mrs. Fossey said. "The time of the Picklesworth coven is over." She took her gnarled staff and swung at him, knock'n him to the ground. He got hisself back up and flew up again, swing'n his pitchfork at her, but she blocked it with her gnarled staff.

The Stranger played his fiddle.

Mr. Picklesworth and Mrs. Fossey fought and fought, but neither one'a them was relent'n. They both was equal in their power.

The Stranger played his fiddle.

"*Aaaaaaahhhh!*" Harriet screamed.

Harriet's scream got my attention. I looked over ta'where she was, and she was curled on the ground. Mr. Jones was hit'n her hard with his gnarled staff.

"Harriet!" I screamed at her, "Get up! Fight him!"

WACK! I was hit by Doc Taylor. I hit the ground and closed my eyes for a short while. When I opened 'em, I saw Mr. Jones hit Harriet one more time, send'n her spirit back ta'her physical body. *WACK!* I was hit again. I was mighty dizzy and had a hard time find'n my senses.

Mr. Picklesworth saw me fall down and get the hell beat outta me. For a brief moment, he focused hisself on me 'cause he thought I could be gone. Then he felt it. He felt the seeth'n pain of the gnarled staff of Mrs. Fossey's go'n through his belly. He fell down to the earth. He was lay'n there, bleed'n.

The Stranger played his fiddle.

I saw Mr. Picklesworth fall to the ground. Blood was flow'n outta his belly just like the water flowed in that nearby stream. Rage took holt of me. Rage. Rage. Mr. Picklesworth was the kind soul who took pity on me and gave me a job and a friend when no one else would. He'd taught me magic. He'd taught me that ever-thing was gonna be ok. He was my friend. Rage. My rage gave me the magical power of a hundr'd witches. I grabbed me my pitchfork on the ground and swung at Doc Taylor. I hit him mighty hard in the head and he dis'ppeared. Rage. I flew into the air. I aimed them tines of my pitchfork towards Mrs. Fossey's heart. I was gonna kill that bitch. I aimed, but then...

"Johnathan..." Mr. Picklesworth softly said. "No."

The Stranger played his fiddle.

Mr. Picklesworth is my teacher and friend, and I wasn't gonna be fail'n this last lesson of his. I took me the pitchfork and swung it as hard as I could at Mrs. Fossey. My pitchfork sent her 'cross the fields and crashed into the barn. She dis'ppeared back into her physical body. I flew down ta'where Mr. Picklesworth lay die'n. "Mr. Picklesworth..."

"Johnathan, it's over," Mr. Picklesworth said softly. "Without Mrs. Fossey's power, the dark witches can't sustain The Stranger. We've won."

Mr. Picklesworth died. Spirits appeared and surrounded his body. They was his ancestors. They picked him up and got him ta'his feet. He smiled at me one last time as he and his ancestors gone dis'ppeared and went to the land of the ancestors. Forever.

See'n that Mrs. Fossey was gone, Mr. Fossey and John Wessnell knew that the battle was over. They flew away. Away from the fields and back to them physical bodies, wherever they may be.

But The Stranger still played his fiddle and them winds of drought was still blow'n 'cross the fields.

Alma felt someth'n in her bones. "It's not over. There's one more witch."

"Who?" I asked. "They're all gone. Who could it be?"

Alma raised herself high into the air.

"It's coming from the center of town." Without hesitation, she flew back ta'town for one last battle.

And with that, I flew up in the air ta'follow her. Alma was too fast. She got way ahead of me and I couldn't see her none in that dark of night. I flew to the center of town and closed my eyes. I listened ta'my heart ta'find her. Just then, I got ma'self a bad feel'n in my gut. Real bad. Like someone was 'bout ta'die. I closed my eyes and listened ta'my heart. The church. Someone needed help inside the church. I flew down to the churchyard and walked up them steps. The door was halfway opened. I was think'n, *who woulda left the church doors wide open in the middle of the night?* I got the bad feel'n that someone was want'n me ta'come inside. I walked into that church and it was dark as hell. Be'n in church in the daytime was fine and all, but a church at night was prolly the most frighten'n thing I ever did see. I walked real slow. The feel'n of darkness got stronger and stronger. I was by ma'self, so whatever it was, I had ta'handle it on my own.

"Johnathan Knotbristle," a familiar voice said in the shadows of the church, "so the rumors are true. You are a witch."

I stopped where I was and din't move. Like a little mouse, 'fraid that if he moved the cat might see him. "Who's there?"

"Don't you know?" Pastor Howard stepped outta the darkness behind the altar. "Even us holy folk dabble in magic from time to time."

"Pastor?" I looked him straight in the eye. He had dark power come'n off him someth'n terrible. This wasn't no man of God. "What are you do'n here? What d'you want?"

The Pastor spread his arms out wide and the whole church done lit up with the flames of candles all over the place. Now'd the church was all bright, I could see that he was keep'n Alma tied up in them shadows behind the altar.

"What d'you want with Alma?" I asked. I held my pitchfork real tight. I was gonna have ta'use it and I might have ta'do someth'n terrible.

Alma looked at me with glossy eyes. Somehow the pastor had done overpowered her. He was us'n her ta'draw me and the other witches try'n ta'save our town out. She din't say her a word, but I felt like I could hear her thoughts.

"He's strong, Johnathan. But you are strong, too."

I slowly stepped towards him. Slowly. Step by step.

"You witches are so stupid," Pastor Howard said. "I don't give a damn about power or what witch runs this town. I just want to draw you all out to destroy you."

"So, you learnt witchcraft ta'kill us?" I asked.

"Magic is taught to many priests," the pastor said. "We learn to conjure angels, demons, and even summon the presence of God within us. Magic doesn't belong to just witches, Johnathan. You see, I let Mrs. Fossey think I wanted to run the town just like she did. I let her believe that she was more powerful than me. But I knew if I joined her, I could draw out all of the witches in this town and destroy them."

The odd song of The Stranger filled the town square. I could see The Stranger out the church winda', danc'n ta'his own bizarre music.

"What d'you need with The Stranger?" I asked him.

"The drought, of course," the pastor said. "The church fathers have long since known about the Devil known as "The Stranger." I taught Mrs. Fossey how to conjure him. He served both our needs. He would bring the drought that the witches wanted, and I wanted him to steal the souls of all those drunkards at the tavern. You see, it's really a wonderful situation for everyone."

"It's time ta'return him ta'hell," I said. Then I took swung my pitchfork ta'strike the pastor and he done blocked it with his black thorny cane. I swung the pitchfork again, and again he done blocked the attack. I struck again and again. Each time he blocked the swings with his black cane. He counter attacked me by swing'n towards my legs. I wasn't 'spect'n that, and the cane took me off my feet. The pastor took his cane and hit my head. Again. Again. Again. Again. I was drown'n in my own blood spill'n from my nose. I was gasp'n for what little air I had. It was over, I was gonna die in that church. Then without try'n at all, I was in a trance.

"Johnathan," The King of the Faeries, Mithrolo, appeared ta'me like in a dream. Maybe I was dream'n. Or maybe, somehow, I was in the faery world once again. Was this heaven? Was this the place I'd be spend'n all eternity? It was seem'n like all time'd stopped just for me. King Mithrolo caressed my hair. He wiped away the blood I had on my face with his hand. "As you once saved my life, so too will I save yours."

King Mithrolo kissed me. As he placed his lips on mine and softly kissed me, the faery magic poured from his body into mine. I felt the power of faery heal'n pour'n from his lips into me. I felt the heal'n power overcome me. My body, soul, and spirit became new. I was healed. King Mithrolo faded from my eyes.

I stood up and took holt of my pitchfork once more. I opened my heart and mind and summoned down the power of them stars, and then I summoned forth the power of the earth. I connected with Alma, Elizabeth, Margaret, Harriet, Clara, Viola, and Helen. I connected with their hearts and their spirit. We was one.

The pastor leaped for me with his black cane, and I counter-attacked with my pitchfork, send'n that cane fly'n 'cross the church. With my pitchfork, I stabbed him in both legs. "By the power of the Devil, Holda, and the spirits of witchcraft, I strip you of your word, your voice, and your power. You ain't nuth'n!" Then I took ma'self the hilt and knocked him in the head, and he dis'ppeared back into his physical body.

The Stranger wasn't no longer play'n his fiddle. He faded back into the Hellworlds where he'd came from.

15

The Crooked Path

THE RAINS CAME SOON 'NUFF THAT HARVEST. Most of the crops was dead, but there was still some that survived. The rains was such a relief that I could see folks dance'n outside, get'n them all wet. They was s'happy the rain was here and the drought was finally over. The winter would be hard, but them rains would save some of the farms and we could be plant'n us some crops that might be come'n late in the harvest season. We had to at least try. Ever-body came together that harvest season and we all helped each and ever-farmer with their crops. This was the first time I knew of that we was all help'n each other and ain't no one was left alone.

Mr. Picklesworth had a beautiful funeral. He was buried in that graveyard next to the church. Mrs. Picklesworth took over the general store and had hoped I would keep work'n there, but I was hav'n 'nuff folks pay'n me for magic that it was take'n up my whole day anyhow. The pastor couldn't no longer serve the spiritual needs of our small town. He done became paralyzed in both legs and needed help get'n 'round. He told someone that, "his heart just wasn't in it anymore." He still lived in town, and ever-now and again, you might be see'n him in his wheelchair in town for one thing or 'nother. He rarely spoke, and when he did, ain't nobody would listen.

Mr. and Mrs. Fossey still ran the bank, but I din't hear too much 'bout 'em. They kept to themselfs and I minded my own business. Alma told me that when we start get'n into other folks' business, we start ta'give 'em our power. Well, I guess I won't be get'n into nobody's business, then. I never did hear much 'bout Mr. and Mrs. Fossey.

Alma, Clara, Viola, and Harriet would be stop'n by my house from time ta'time and we would practice magic and celebrate the full moon. Ever-time we seen each other, after we done some magic, Alma would tell stories 'bout Mr. Picklesworth. He was the Witch Master of several covens in the surround'n area, and they was honored ta'know him.

Margaret, Elizabeth, and Helen came by my house one day, ask'n me if I'd join their little coven. I told 'em I had ta'think 'bout it some. I was right used to be'n alone and I wasn't quite sure what ta'do since they lived s'far away. But I 'spose we could always celebrate the sabbats in spirit form.

Word got out 'bout the magic I had done for some of them town folk, and folks was come'n from far and wide for love spells, money spells, heal'n, find'n lost things, protection magic, and anyth'n you can think of, folks was ask'n me for. Folks din't know me as Johnathan Knotbristle, folks knew me as *Johnathan Knotbristle the Charmer.*

When the cool fall winds came, they was as welcomed as a good friend you ain't seen in a long time. One night, I was rock'n on Momma's old rock'n chair. Back and forth, back and forth, back and forth. I took up smoke'n a pipe with tobacca and was have'n ma'self a glass of whiskey. The fireplace was go'n and I had Old Henry sit'n next ta'me. I din't need noth'n, I just got used to Old Henry spend'n time with me like an old friend.

KNOCK. KNOCK. KNOCK.

I went to the door ta'see who was there. When I opened the door, I din't see no one. That's strange, I thought.

"Excuse me," A husky voice said from below.

I looked down, and there stood a short, stocky, grey-skinned troll. Well, I was guess'n it was a troll. It was the first time I was see'n the likes of this creature.

"Are you Johnathan Knotbristle the Charmer?" the troll asked me.

"Yes," I said.

The gray-skinned troll grabbed my hand hard and pulled me outta my house. "Hurry! Hurry! You are needed by the Troll King! Things are dire and you must come with me!"

And with that, I was taken back to the Otherworld...

The Spells of Johnathan Knotbristle the Charmer

To Obtain the Powers of the Witch

On the night of a full moon at midnight (modern witching hour) or 3am (traditional witching hour) you must give yourself to the Devil.

1. Walk backward around a church three times.

2. Once you return to the origin of your circle, say,

    "Devil, I call to you.
    I give myself to you in fear and love."

3. The Devil may appear before you as a man, dog, cat, or any animal, a shadow, or simply as an energy.

4. When he/she/they appear(s) before you say,

    "I renounce my baptism.
    May I be free of the shackles
    that once bound my spirit."

5. Place one hand on your head and the other on your foot and say,

    "I pledge all that lies betweend my hands to the Devil."

6. Stand upright once more and receive the power of the witch. It may be a feeling of power coming forth or it may be received in a dream or a meditation.

TO CREATE THE PITCHFORK OR STANG

Your vessel for the Devil may be either a two tined pitchfork or a wooden stang. This is up to the witch to decide which one is correct for them. A two tined pitchfork may be purchased or given to the witch.

For a wooden stang, follow these instructions:

1. Go out to a wooded area and find a forked stick that is about shoulder length. The stang should be a long stick that forks at the end.

2. You must give an offering to the spirit of the tree. Never saw off a living branch from a tree. The branch must have fallen to the ground.

3. Sand down the bark of the stick so that it is smooth.

TO CREATE THE VESSEL FOR THE DEVIL

1. Once you have your stang or pitchfork, you can place a hook about three to four inches down from the fork or tines. On the hook, you will place a small wreath and decorated it according to the seasons, if you wish. The wreath is used as a magickal tool to visualize your target for the art of bewitchment.

2. On the back of the pitchfork or stang, you can place another hook, much lower than the wreath, so that you may place a working knife. The knife should be hung on the hook with a string or cord. This knife is used to summon energy for the witch to use for magick and bewitchment.

3. Place a candle in between the fork of the stang or the tines of the pitchfork. You can use wax to fasten the candle, or you may drill in a candle holder to hold the candle. This is up to the discretion

of the witch. When lighting the candle, you must call the Devil in a way that comes from your heart and feels correct to the witch.

4. Once the stang or pitchfork is made, it must be presented to the four directions to receive the powers therein. It also must be presented to the stars and the spirits who live beneath the earth.

5. Always call to the Devil in your rites by lighting the sacred candle of the stang or pitchfork. You may also give offerings of water, food, and incense to the Devil when needed.

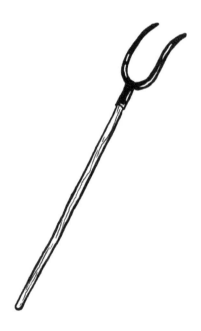

THE WITCH'S TRANCE

The art of witchcraft is practiced more effectively when the witch allows themselves to go into a trance. Some magical formulas require the witch to go into a light trance, while other formulas require the witch to go into a deeper trance. The trance can be controlled by the witch at will. The witch must practice the art of trance in order to maintain control of one's thoughts and powers.

THE WITCH'S ROCKING CHAIR

This formula is one that is used by the old-time witches of Southern Texas and will put the witch into a state of trance for works of witchcraft. The witch must obtain a rocking chair, a tobacco pipe, and a glass of whiskey.

1. Place a rocking chair next to a table where a glass of whiskey and a tobacco pipe sits.

2. Take a drink of the whiskey and begin smoking the pipe. If one does not like tobacco, one may substitute an herb that brings a light trance.

3. Begin rocking back and forth while taking deep breaths.

4. As you rock back and forth, allow the sensation to send you deeper and deeper into the spirit world.

5. Drink the whiskey and smoke the pipe to allow yourself to go even deeper into trance.

6. Continue rocking until the desired trance is achieved.

THE POWER OF THE STARS AND THE LAND

The power of the stars and the land can be summoned into the witch's body for the power needed to work the witch's art of witchcraft. This power will add much magick to spells, healing, and the witch's formula. Summoning the stars and the power of the land will also bring the witch into a deep trance.

1. Close your eyes, bring your thoughts to the skies above and feel your powers connecting to the stars.

2. Inhale and imagine that you are bringing the power of the stars into your belly.

3. Bring your thoughts to the powers of the land.

4. Inhale and imagine that you are bringing the power of the land into your belly.

5. With both the powers of the stars and land in your body, continue to breathe deeply and imagine that the powers are circulating in your body.

6. Continue breathing and know that the powers are bringing you deeper and deeper into trance.

THE WITCH'S CONNECTION TO THE POWERS

The powers of the witch come from the Devil, Holda, the spirits, and the powers of the stars and the land. Without these things, the witch has very little power. The witch depends on the powers for magick and healing. This is the true art of witchcraft. The witch should practice connecting to the power of the stars and land for all the days of their life.

1. Go outside and be with the powers. If the witch is focusing on the stars, go out into the night. If the witch is focusing on the trees and the land, either day or night will do. The witch must remember that the power often changes at different times of the day.

2. The witch should place themselves in a light trance.

3. Then, you must open your heart and mind to the powers of the stars or land.

4. The witch must clear their mind of all things and receive the powers as they will.

5. Each day, practice connecting to the stars and land. Listen to what they have to tell you. Listen to what the spirits say.

6. Remember that not all spirits speak in the English language. Some may speak to you with symbols in your mind or feelings in your heart.

7. Leave an offering of tobacco or whiskey for the spirits each time you connect with them.

TO OBTAIN A SPIRIT FAMILIAR

1. Obtain a vessel (home) for the familiar spirit. This can be an animal skull, resin skull, statue, or clay pot or bowl. Obtain two white candles. Black will do if you prefer. You will also need incense and a bowl of water as an offering to the Devil

2. Light the candle on your pitchfork or stang and call to the Devil with the words coming from your heart.

3. Light your incense. Any incense will do, as long as the scent brings you into a mindset of magick and witchery.

4. Place the two candles on either side of your vessel and light them.

5. Gaze at the flame on your pitchfork or stang and ask the Devil to send you a familiar spirit.

6. Place a few drops of your own blood on the vessel to anchor the spirit to you and to you alone.

7. Place both your hands on either side of the vessel and say,

"Spirit Familiar, I summon thee.
Spirit Familiar, I conjure thee.
Spirit Familiar as I call you,
you are bound to me."

8. Feel the spirit familiar come forth from the pitchfork or stang (the Devil) and visualize them going into the vessel.

9. Name the spirit familiar unless they tell you what their name is.

10. Instruct the familiar to perform acts of magic for you.

11. Be sure to feed your spirit familiar with either tobacco and whiskey, or some other alcohol or herb.

THE MAGICK OF THE CAULDRON (MOMMA'S COOKING POT)

1. Obtain a large cauldron or cooking pot. If a cooking pot is preferred, it must only be used to perform the works of magick.

2. Before you can perform magick, you must present the cauldron to the four directions, the sky, and the spirits below the earth for blessings. You must also ask the Devil and Holda to bless the vessel.

3. Darken the room with only the candle of the stang/pitchfork for light.

4. To see the past, present, or future, place your hands on either side of the cauldron and gaze inside.

5. Bring yourself into a trance.

6. Call upon Holda, the Queen of Elphame, to give you the power to see into the sacred cauldron.

7. Imagine that you are looking deep down into a magical well. You don't see the bottom of the cauldron, you see the blackness of the Otherworld.

8. You may see visions in the black of the cauldron or in your mind's eye. You may only feel the visions in your heart. Either way is fine for the art of seeing.

9. Once you are finished with your visions, thank Holda for her power and give her an offering of whiskey.

10. Practice daily to improve your seeing skills.

TO FLY IN SPIRIT, USING THE WITCH'S BROOM

1. Obtain a broom that you will only use for the art of witchery.

2. Sit in a chair and hold the broom with the bristles on the floor.

3. Place the handle of the broom over your third eye.

4. Place yourself into a trance. Summon the powers of the earth and the skies into your body.

5. Using visualization, imagine that the broom is lifting your spirit up from your physical body.

6. As you hover over your physical body, you may fly wherever you'd like. It is tradition to leave the house through a window or chimney.

The broom may also be used as a vessel for Holda, Queen of Elphame to call into your magical rites. Her candle is placed next to the broom.

TO SPEAK IN SPIRIT TONGUES

This spirit language will be used to summon and speak with the spirits of witchery.

1. Place yourself into a trance.

2. Summon the powers of the earth and stars in your body.

3. Focus your attention on your heart and say any syllables that come to your mind such as:

> "Wa wa wa,
> bo bo bo,
> go de te che,
> may gay fay lay."

4. Once you are comfortable with making up syllables, attempt to make words out of those syllables. Then sentences.

5. Now, focus on your heart again. Bring to mind what you want to say in English, and now bring the words down to your heart, allowing the energies of the land and the stars to change the words into any words you'd like. It will feel like you are making words up as you go.

6. Then, allow whatever words and syllables you imagine to be spoken. Remember to think about what the words may mean.

7. Practice calling the spirits using the spirit words that you "made up."

8. The spirits will always respond better to spirit tongue than to English.

9. You may ask them to perform works of witchery for you with your spirit tongue.

To Summon a Ghost

Items needed:
- One candle.
- Whiskey and/or tobacco.
- Mullein (or another herb that calls spirits).
- Charcoal and vessel for burning incense.
- Lighter.

1. During the darkest part of the night (between 12am and 3am), bring your supplies to the graveyard or cemetery.

2. Place the candle on top of the grave and the vessel with charcoal beside it.

3. Light the candle and place the mullein on the charcoal and say,

> *"I call upon the Queen of Death, Bone Lady,*
> *Lady both Foul and Fair, Lady of Fate.*
> *We ask that you open the gates of the Otherworld*
> *and allow (Name of Spirit) to come to us this night."*

4. Visualize the Bone Queen (Holda or Hella) opening the gates of the Underworld and allowing the spirit you have called to come through.

5. Place more mullein on the charcoal. Imagine that the smoke is summoning the spirit and leading them to the grave. Visualize the spirit following the smoke of the herb to the grave.

6. Say,

> *"(Name of spirit),*
> *come to us from the spirit world.*
> *Join us this night*
> *so that we may speak with you."*

7. Pour whiskey on the grave as an offering. This gives the spirit energy to manifest in the physical plane.

8. Speak with the spirit as you wish.

9. Release the spirit back to the Underworld with the words,

> *"(Spirit), I release you back to the Underworld*
> *where once you came.*
> *Go in peace and be ready to be called back once more*
> *with the art of witchery."*

10. Visualize the spirit returning to the Underworld through the grave.

INVOKING SPIRITS, ANCESTORS, OR GODS

This technique can be used to invoke any spirit you'd like. Word of caution: the witch would be wise to only invoke spirits that the witch is familiar with or has a personal relationship with. Jonathan leaves the responsibility of this spell entirely with the witch and their art.

1. Summon the spirit, ancestor, or God in the way the witch desires.
2. Visualize the spirit behind the witch.
3. Imagine that the spirit is stepping into your legs and putting them on the way one would put on pants.
4. Next, see that the spirit is placing their arms into your arms, their chest and torso into your chest and torso. Allow the spirit to connect with your heart.
5. See the spirit place their head into your head.
6. Now, open your eyes and allow the spirit to see with your eyes, to hear with your ears, and to speak with your mouth.
7. The witch has full control of their mind. You can allow the spirit to have partial or full control of your body. The witch can regain control of their body at any time because the body rightfully belongs to the witch.
8. When finished with the invocation, the technique is then reversed. Visualize the spirit disengaging from your head, then from your heart, then your chest and torso, and finally from your legs.
9. Once the spirit is out of your body, give your thanks and offerings. The spirit may go or stay at the will of the witch.

THE SPELLS OF MOTHER GOOSE

The witch must connect and meditate with each of the Mother Goose rhymes in order to fully understand their mysteries and meanings. Once understood, the witch then says the rhyme while visualizing the desired outcome. The witch may add candles, bones, and herbs to enhance the effects of the rhyme spells. Each rhyme is a doorway for the witch to discover.

"Monday's child is fair of face.
Tuesday's child is full of grace.
Wednesday's child is full of woe.
Thursday's child has far to go.
Friday's child is loving and giving.
Saturday's child works hard for its living.
But the child that's born on the Sabbath day,
Is bonnie and blithe, and good and gay."

"On Saturday night, shall be my care,
to powder my locks, and curl my hair.
On Sunday morning, my love will come in,
when he will marry me with a gold ring?"

"Rain, rain, go away,
come again another day,
Little Johnny wants to play."

THE DEVIL'S FEAST

The Devil's Feast is known as the housel in some traditions of witchcraft. This is a holy sacrament to the Old Ones and the spirits of the land and the witch. It is to be done after each major rite, sabbat, or major working of a witch to show honor and connection to the old powers of witchcraft.

Items needed:
- A drinking vessel. A drinking horn or cup will do.
- Wine, beer, or ale (non-alcoholic works well, too).
- A bowl.
- Bread or some kind of pastry that feels sacred to the spirits.
- A candle, lantern, or sacred fire.

1. This rite is to be performed in a lonely place, away from the eyes of the profane. It is better to be outside with the spirits of the land.

2. This may be done alone or in the company of witches. Gather in a circle and connect to each other, the land spirits, the stars, and the Gods.

3. Pour the wine in the drinking vessel, hold it up to the sky, and say,

"I call to you, Devil,
Witch Father, Old One,
He of the Cloven Hoof, come!
Place your power, your essence into this sacred vessel!"

4. Visualize the power of the Devil coming down from the stars and filling the vessel with power.

5. Then say,

"Dame Holda,
Lady Both Foul and Fair,
Keeper of the Gates of the Underworld, come!
Place your power, your essence, into this sacred vessel!"

6. Visualize the power of Holda coming down from the stars and filling the vessel with power.

7. Pass the vessel counterclockwise to each person in the circle. Each person takes a deep breath and slowly breathes into the cup to share their magick with all present.

8. When the cup returns to you, visualize the energies of the Devil, Holda, and all present changing the wine into a potion of magick. Say,

"By the power of alchemy, of transformation,
do we stir the essence of the Witch Father and the Witch Mother
with the essence of each one of us."

9. Place the vessel aside (have someone else hold it or place it on the ground). Place the bread in the bowl and present it to the spirits of the land. Visualize the land spirits blessing the bread while saying,

"We call to the spirits of the land.
Elves, fey, and land wights.
Place your power, your essence into this sacred bread."

10. Pour a small amount of wine onto the bread while saying,

"We combine the essence of the Gods and ourselves
with the essence of the land to make this sacred meal."

11. Each person should take a small piece of bread and eat of the energies of the land. Then everyone passes the drinking vessel counterclockwise and shares in the sacred potion of the spirits. The drink is passed around the circle until all the wine is consumed.

12. What is left over of the bread is given to the land spirits and faeries as offerings.

TO SUMMON A GHOST FOR A SEANCE

This rite must be performed by the witch during the night. It is set in a dark room with a table that is draped in black cloth. There is one candle at the center of the table, as well as a self-standing mirror that is small- to medium-sized. A black magick mirror may be used in the place of the reflective mirror as the witch wishes it. There must be three or more people who participate in the seance. All lights other than the candle must be turned off.

1. Everyone sitting at the table must hold hands.

2. Everyone should center themselves in the space and open their minds and hearts to the spirit world.

3. The leader of the seance should say,

"Everyone in the room suspend any disbelief. For any disbelief will cause an energy block and the spirits cannot cross over into our world. Ladies and gentlemen. Take a deep breath with me. Now open your minds and your hearts to the spirit world. Imagine that your mind is allowing the spirits to come through for us. Let your heart open. Feel the presence of the spirits. You may see the spirits in your mind, or you may gaze into the mirror. For the mirror is a window into the spirit world."

4. Allow plenty of time for everyone to connect to the spirit world. To connect with the spirits, you may hear them in your mind, your heart, or simply "know" what they are saying to you.

5. If someone sees them in their mind or feels them only in their heart, they may gaze into the mirror to see them more clearly. Mirrors are a portal to the spirit world, and many people find it easier to see the spirits while gazing in a dimly lit mirror.

6. The first person who makes contact with a spirit should say aloud they have made contact.

7. Anyone in the room may ask questions, but for the sake of clarity, perhaps one person is designated as the speaker to the spirits.

8. When all questions are answered or the spirit wishes to leave, the witches should thank all spirits in attendance and wish them farewell.

9. After the seance is over, the room feels heavy with energy or spiritual influence, and it should be cleansed with a technique of the witches' choice.

TO PROTECT AGAINST SPIRITS

Rowan is a wood that is commonly used by witches to protect against ill intending spirits or magick. One way to use rowan is to obtain two small rowan sticks and bind them with red string in an equal-armed cross. The cross acts as a barrier to the spirits, while the red thread shows the power of the witch and as a warning to all spirits. The thread also reminds spirits that witches have power over the fate of spirits and those who perform ill magick. Other woods protect against spirits as well; rowan is but one of many.

TO SUMMON THE DEVIL AND THE DAME FOR MAGIC

With this enchantment, you will use the pitchfork or stang as the vessel for the Devil and the broom as the vessel for Holda.

1. Place yourself into a trance.

2. Summon the power of the stars into your body, then summon the power of the earth into your body.

3. Light the candle on the pitchfork/stang and connect with the sacred flame of wisdom. Think of the Devil and the power he wields. Think of how he is the Master of all Witches and the Keeper of Magick. Call to the Devil and say,

> *"I call to you, Horned Master,*
> *Witch Father, he of the cloven hoof, Devil.*
> *I ask that you bring your power into the vessel.*
> *Light the way so that those*
> *who serve you may follow you."*

4. As you focus on the flame, begin to feel a magical flame burning in your forehead. This is the fire in the head. Visualize the Devil superimposed over the stang/pitchfork.

5. Light the candle next to the broom. Think of Holda, the Queen of Elphame. Think about the well. Think about the Otherworld, and the power Holda has. Feel Holda in your heart. Take a breath and then breathe her into the broom.

> *"I call to you, Frau Holda,*
> *Lady both Foul and Fair, Queen of Elphame.*
> *I bring power into this vessel.*
> *Light the way so that those*
> *who serve you may follow you."*

6. Visualize Holda superimposed over the broom.

7. You may give them devotions, prayers, offerings, or invite them to add power to your witch rites. You may also ask them questions and receive their wisdom.

8. When you are finished with your rites of witchery, leave offerings of food, water, or whiskey for them.

9. Thank them for their attendance and blow out their candles.

PERCHTA'S THREAD: TO SEE THE FATE OF ANOTHER

This spell is to aid the witch in spying on the sacred fate of others. Seeing someone's fate can help them prepare for blessing or bane. Remember, the witch has the power to change all things.

1. Obtain a thick string or cord. Red is better, for it represents the blood of all life. We are born with our mother's blood on us, and we die with our own blood pouring from us. Black will work as well because it is the mystery of all things. White is the next favorite because it shows that the fates of all things are connected to one tapestry.

2. Hold the cord in both hands and place yourself into a trance.

3. Call upon the Goddess Perchta to give you the power to see the fates of others. Summon her energy into your body.

4. Allow your gaze to soften and look into the cord as if the cord were a video screen that showed you all things.

5. Be secure in the knowledge that you are seeing the fate of the one whom you desire to know.

6. Allow images, symbols, and feelings to come to your mind.

7. When finished, thank Perchta for her power and give her an offering of whiskey.

TO HEAL WITH THE POWER OF THE SPIRITS, ANCESTORS, OR GODS

The witch may invoke a spirit, ancestor, or God in order to heal the living. The technique is the same as the previous invocation rite, but the witch must seek the aid of a healing spirit first. You may do this by summoning a ghost who once was a healer, or the witch may invoke a healing God such as Asclepius, Apollo, Thoth, etc. The witch may also wish to summon a familiar spirit who specializes in healing. You may also place yourself in a trance and fly on your broom into the spirit world and call upon a spirit who is a healer. Before working with a healing spirit, the witch must ask the spirit if they are willing to perform acts of healing for you. If yes, then you may proceed. If no, you must call upon another spirit.

Once invoked, the healer spirit may use many different types of healing. Some will banish spirits of disease while others will send the power of the stars to the ill person by way of channeling. It is wise for the witch to remember to trust the healer spirit and allow them to work their craft. Remember to give the spirit whiskey and/or tobacco once the healing is finished.

TO BANISH THE SPIRIT OF DISEASE

Many diseases are caused by spirits who attach to someone and feed on their personal power. This causes the person to lose health and show the symptoms of disease. The witch can use their art to banish the spirits that cause disease in the body. The witch may choose to invoke the spirit of a healer to perform the banishing or may wish to perform the banishing oneself.

1. You may begin by invoking your healing spirit or you may perform the procedure on your own.

2. Have the patient lie on a bed or on the ground. Using your hands, scan the energy of the person while looking for the spirit of disease. You may also wish to place both hands on the head and use the power of witchery to look into the patient's body. This is done in the imagination of the witch.

3. Then the witch must imagine that they are reaching into the patient's spirit body and pulling out the spirit of disease.

4. Spirits of disease are not any more evil than a leech is evil. It is true to its own nature. Therefore, we must take the spirit back to where it belongs. You may do this yourself or ask your spirit familiar to do it for you.

5. Once the spirit is removed, you must send the powers of the land and the stars to heal the patient's spirit body.

6. If you invoked a healing spirit, you must thank them and give them an offering of tobacco or whiskey.

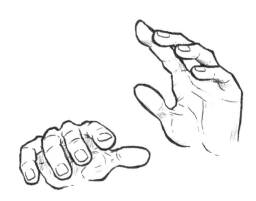

THE WITCH'S BOTTLE

The Witch's bottle can be used for many different purposes such as protection, prosperity, healing, or love. This particular bottle will be used to return a curse that was sent from a dark witch. Once the spell is complete, the sender of the curse will receive every bit of witchcraft that was sent to you.

Items needed:
- A glass or ceramic bottle.
- Nails and pins (rusty are better, but new will work).
- Three black or white candles.
- Hair, nail clippings, and urine from the victim.

1. Create a triangle with the three candles with the apex pointing towards the door.

2. Place all the ingredients (nails, pins, hair, nail clippings, and urine) in the bottle.

3. Place the bottle in the center of the triangle of candles.

4. Place your hands around the triangle of candles and imagine that the curse is leaving the victim.

5. Then, place the bottle in a fireplace or an outdoor fire. The fire must be blazing hot. Use caution when using a fire.

6. Continue to keep the fire blazing until the bottle explodes. Once the bottle explodes, the curse will be broken.

7. Bury the contents of the bottle and the ashes of the fire in the ground.

Shapeshifting into an Animal

The witch has the power to use the art of witchcraft to change one's shape and mind into that of an animal. The witch will change their mental, astral, and etheric bodies into an animal for attack, defense, and communion with the animal world. Some say truly powerful witches can change physically into an animal.

1. Decide on what animal you wish to change into. It may be your spirit animal, or a wolf, mountain lion, bear, etc. The animal must be wild and fierce.

2. The witch must go into a trance and summon the power of the land and stars into the body.

3. Connect to the power currently of the earth itself. Continue to breathe the power of the earth into your belly. Make sure you have a lot of earth power!

4. The witch should attempt to connect with the animal spirits in a near location.

5. Begin growling like an animal, giving a warning to all who trespass on its territory.

6. Continue to breathe in the power of the earth. Keep growling and using this growl to change into an animal.

7. Feel yourself changing shape into an animal.

8. Once you have shapeshifted, you may use your animal power for attack, defense, magic, healing, or speaking with the animal kingdom. Do not growl at another animal. It will attack you in kind. When speaking with a wild animal, use extreme caution. Animals will attack if they feel threatened.

9. When ready to return to normal shape, send the power of the earth back to the ground and regain your center.

Faery Magic

The art of faery healing is an old form of magick. Before the witch can perform faery healing, they must have a connection and a relationship with the faery world. When connecting to the powers of the land, it is helpful for the witch to seek a faery guide or teacher. Do this by connecting to the land daily and expressing your wish to meet a faery teacher. You may go into a deeper trance and journey into the world of faery.

To Slip into the Faery World and Find a Faery Teacher

1. The witch must go into a trance and then connect to the powers of the land.

2. Then, the witch should imagine themselves in the faery world and call out with their heart and ask to meet with a faery teacher.

3. You must imagine meeting a faery teacher, spend time getting to know each other, and make a pact for a student/teacher relationship. The witch must be wary of any request by faeries that may harm themselves or others. Faeries rarely wish to harm the witch, but the witch still must be cautious.

4. Remember, the witch must never lie to a faery teacher. This will sever the relationship.

5. You must meet with the faery teacher as often as you can to learn the ways of faery magic. This is done while always in trance.

6. Create a shrine for the faery teacher and always leave offerings. You may ask the faery teacher what types of offerings they prefer. Only give offerings you are able and willing to give.

FAERY HEALING

Once the witch has learned about faeries and the faery world, then you may perform the art of faery healing. This is done by summoning the power of the earth's life force and the power of the faery world together. The two powers synchronize together to create life on earth. It is this creative force that heals and creates life anew.

1. The witch must bring themselves into a trance.

2. Summon forth your faery teacher.

3. Next, bring to mind the magic of the faery world. Imagine its power and its beauty. Know that the life force of the earth and the stars flow through the faery world. Know that this magic has the power to heal and transform.

4. Take a deep breath. As you breathe in, imagine breathing in the healing light of the faery world. Know with all your being that this light has the power to regenerate the bones, organs, blood, and flesh of the king. This is the healing light found in all things. The heat of the stars. The beauty of the trees. The connection of all things in the web of life. The healing light *is* what the web of life is made from. It has no limits. Only magic. Only healing.

5. Connect with your faery teacher. Imagine that the faery healing magic is flowing through both of you. You are connected. You are sharing your powers with each other. Both of your powers are amplified. You have the life force of the earth, and they have the faery healing power.

6. Imagine the faery healing magic flow from your heart, down your arms and hands, and into the patient. Imagine the faery healing power regenerating the patient.

7. Once you feel the healing is done, thank the faery teacher and give them an offering.

The Spirit Box

The Spirit Box is a form of enchantment that summons a spirit to do the bidding of the witch. This is similar to the familiar spirit but has a singular focus. The spirit who lives in the box will only be able to provide one type of work. The type of work may be prosperity, love, healing, protection, or any other forms of witchcraft the witch may think of.

Items needed:
- A small wooden box.
- One candle.
- Three or nine herbs pertaining to the work of the spirit.
- Stones, bones, coins, trinkets, or any other object that pertains the work of the spirit.
- Dirt from your home if the work pertains to you, dirt from a graveyard if you wish to summon the dead, dirt from the target's home if you wish the spirit to work on someone else.
- A pinch of tobacco as an offering.

1. The witch must go into trance.
2. Light the candle.
3. Next, place all items inside the box.
4. Call out to a spirit and speak of what you need the spirit to do for you. You may say,

"I call out into the spirit world.
Spirit of (type of spirit) I summon, I stir, I conjure you forth.
Come to me and live in this spirit box I have made for you.
I summon, I stir, I conjure you forth.
(Instruct the spirit on what you want them to do for you).
I summon, I stir, I conjure you forth.
Come, be here now, by the power of the Devil and of Holda.
Come be here now!"

5. Visualize a spirit coming from the spirit world and entering the spirit box.

6. Every day, speak with the spirit and tell it what you want it to do for you. Every day, leave a pinch of tobacco and a glass of whiskey next to the box.

7. Do not open the box because it will disturb the spirit's home.

A WITCH'S DOLL OF LOVE

This spell is used to attract the love of someone in specific. You may modify the spell to attract a general lover, but this art of witchery is aimed at a target. Be warned, love spells do not always work how intended. The art of witchcraft is an art for this reason.

Items needed:
- Wax from candles.
- Pins or needles.
- Feathers from a dove (this item may be skipped but will enhance your magic).
- Red cord, string, or yarn.

1. Melt the wax on in a pan, and when it begins to cool, fashion the wax in the likeness of the person you wish to enchant. You may add herbs of love to the wax if you choose.

2. The person wishing to enchant a lover must prick their finger and place a drop of blood on the head, heart, private parts, and feet of the doll.

3. Take the first pin and pin a dove feather (if you have it) to the drop of blood on the head. If you don't have a feather, just place the pin on the drop of blood and say,

   "(Name of target), you will only think of me."

4. Place the second pin and feather on the blood of the heart and say,

   "(Name of target), you will only love me."

5. Place the third pin and feather on the blood of the private parts and say,

   "(Name of target), you will only have sex with me."

6. Place the fourth pin and feather on the blood of the feet and say,

   "(Name of target), you will stay with me."

7. Then wrap the red string around the entire doll and think of the target, imagining that you and your target are in love and happy together. Wrap the doll over and over again until no wax can be seen.

8. Keep the doll in a secret and safe place where it will not be found.

NIGHT BATTLES AND THE HARVEST

In old witchlore, there is a story that baneful witches will try to destroy the harvest so that the people will starve. There are many reasons why witches might want to do this. One reason is that, if the baneful witch is in a position of power, then the people will be subjugated to them. Another reason might be that a witch will profit off the losses of the people. Or simply, the witch is seeking revenge against the people. Harming crops is not the will of the Devil and the Old Ones. This is the will of the baneful witch alone.

The stang/pitchfork and broom can be used as magical weapons in the spirit world against other witches or spirits. The broom or stang is held with both hands parallel to the ground and acts as a magickal barrier against magick. Held upright, it acts as a magical staff that can summon spirits, wind, rain, and other acts of witchcraft. The broom's bristles can be used to sweep away baneful magic and even banish the baneful witch.

About the Author

Chris Allaun has been studying witchcraft, magick, and paganism since 1992. He is one of the founders and an ordained minister with The Fellowship of the Phoenix. He has been an initiate of Traditional Witchcraft since 2002. He also has permission to carry the Lakota Sacred Pipe and walks the path of the Red Road.

He teaches classes and workshops on magick, healing, shamanism, and necromancy. He has been teaching and writing for many years. He is the author of *A Guide to Spirits, Underworld: Shamanism, Myth, and Magick, Deeper Into The Underworld: Death, Ancestors, and Magical Rites*, and *Upperworld: Shamanism and Magick of the Celestial Realms*.

He continues to study and teach the magickal arts to those who seek to balance the three worlds in their own lives.

More by Crossed Crow Books

AVAILABLE TITLES

In the Shadow of Thirteen Moons by Kimberly Sherman-Cook
Merlin: Master of Magick by Gordon Strong
The Way of Four by Deborah Lipp
Celtic Tree Mysteries by Steve Blamires
Star Magic by Sandra Kynes
A Spirit Work Primer by Naag Loki Shivanaath
A Witch's Shadow Magick Compendium by Raven Digitalis
Witchcraft and the Shamanic Journey by Kenneth Johnson
Travels Through Middle Earth by Alaric Albertsson
Craft of the Hedge Witch by Geraldine Smythe
Be Careful What You Wish For: From Cult to Occult by
Laetitia Latham-Jones
The Complete Book of Spiritual Astrology by Per Henrik Gullfoss
Your Star Sign by Per Henrik Gullfoss
Death's Head by Blake Malliway
The Wildwood Way by Cliff Seruntine

FORTHCOMING TITLES

Magic of the Elements by Deborah Lipp
Witches' Sabbats and Esbats by Sandra Kynes
Icelandic Plant Magic by Albert Bjorn
Legends, Tales and Parables by Wycke Malliway
Flight of the Firebird by Kenneth Johnson
Dance of the Sun Goddess by Kenneth Johnson
Witchcraft Unchained by Craig Spencer
Tarot Unveiled by Gordon Strong
Sun God and Moon Maiden by Gordon Strong

Learn more at
www.CrossedCrowBooks.com